Schooling for
Critical Consciousness

Schooling for Critical Consciousness

ENGAGING BLACK AND LATINX YOUTH
IN ANALYZING, NAVIGATING, AND
CHALLENGING RACIAL INJUSTICE

Scott Seider
Daren Graves

HARVARD EDUCATION PRESS
Cambridge, Massachusetts

Paperback ISBN 978-1-68253-429-8
Library Edition ISBN 978-1-68253-430-4

Library of Congress Cataloging-in-Publication Data
Names: Seider, Scott, author. | Graves, Daren, author.
Title: Schooling for critical consciousness : teaching Black and Latinx youth to analyze, navigate, and challenge racial injustice / Scott Seider, Daren Graves.
Description: Cambridge, Massachusetts : Harvard Education Press, 2020. | Includes bibliographical references and index. | Summary: "In Schooling for Critical Consciousness, Seider and Graves draw on a four-year longitudinal study examining how five different mission-driven urban high schools foster critical racial consciousness among their students"-- Provided by publisher.
Identifiers: LCCN 2019028498 | ISBN 9781682534298 (paperback) | ISBN 9781682534304 (library binding)
Subjects: LCSH: Minorities—Education—Social aspects—United States. | African American high school students. | Hispanic American high school students. | Race awareness—United States. | Race discrimination—United States. | Critical pedagogy—United States. | Culturally relevant pedagogy—United States. | Urban high schools—United States.
Classification: LCC LC3731 .S436 2020 | DDC 370.115—dc23
LC record available at https://lccn.loc.gov/2019028498

Published by Harvard Education Press,
an imprint of the Harvard Education Publishing Group

Harvard Education Press
8 Story Street
Cambridge, MA 02138

Cover Design: Ciano Design
Cover Image: Hill Street Studios/DigitalVision/Getty Images

The typefaces used in this book are Adobe Garamond Pro and Monterchi Sans.

CONTENTS

Chapter 1

Learning in Dangerous Times

IN 1963, writer and social critic James Baldwin delivered "A Talk to Teachers" in which he called on educators of Black youth to prepare their students to navigate and challenge racial injustice in the United States. In this powerful address, Baldwin declared to the assembled teachers that if *he* were a teacher of Black youth:

> I would try to teach them—I would try to make them know—that those streets, those houses, those dangers, those agonies by which they are surrounded, are criminal. I would try to make each child know that these things are the result of a criminal conspiracy to destroy him. I would teach him that if he intends to get to be a man, he must at once decide that he is stronger than this conspiracy, and he must never make his peace with it . . . That it is up to him to change these standards for the sake of the life and the health of the country.[1]

In these words, Baldwin argued that teachers have a key role to play—alongside families, churches, community organizations, peers, and numerous other influences—in preparing Black youth to recognize and resist racism. We begin with Baldwin's words for three reasons.

First, without overlooking the meaningful strides toward racial equity that have taken place in the United States over the past fifty years, one might nonetheless have hoped that Baldwin's description of a "criminal conspiracy" against Black youth in the United States would ring less true today. Yet, Black and Latinx children in the United States today are born into systems that produce a multitude of inequities in health care, housing, education, and criminal justice that systematically threaten their opportunities, well-being, and lives.[2] To take the public education system as just one example: Black and Latinx youth in the contemporary United States are 60 percent more likely than their White peers to attend high poverty, under-resourced schools.[3] Black and Latinx youth also have less access to advanced high school coursework, are more likely to be taught by first-year teachers, and are disproportionately suspended and expelled.[4] Related to this last point, the United States Department of Education recently reported that Black *preschoolers* are three and a half times more likely to receive out-of-school suspensions than White preschoolers.[5] Cumulatively, these and many other statistics reveal how race and racism continue to shape opportunity for youth in the United States in ways far too reminiscent of the 1960s about which Baldwin was writing.

The second reason we begin with Baldwin's speech is that, although the term *critical consciousness* would not be coined for several more years, in "A Talk to Teachers" Baldwin was essentially calling for educators and schools to foster Black children's critical consciousness of racial injustice. The term *critical consciousness* comes from Brazilian philosopher-educator Paulo Freire and refers to a person's ability to recognize and analyze oppressive forces shaping society and to take action against these forces.[6] While working as an adult literacy teacher in northern Brazil, Freire realized that the migrant laborers in his classes were motivated to learn to read in order to understand and challenge the social forces impacting their social status and opportunities.[7] From these workers' experiences, Freire concluded that a primary goal of education should be to engage students from oppressed groups in learning to decode and challenge their social conditions—the same goal Baldwin proposed in his talk to teachers. In his 1970 book *Pedagogy of the Oppressed*, Freire invoked the term *conscientização*, or critical consciousness, to refer to this combination of reflection and action on the world in order to transform it.

Finally, we begin with Baldwin's words because *Schooling for Critical Consciousness* is, ultimately, a talk to teachers as well. In the pages ahead, we report on a growing body of research that has found critical consciousness to be an important tool through which youth of color can both resist the negative effects of racial injustice and challenge its root causes. We then share a set of powerful practices for fostering youth critical consciousness that emerged from our four years of research in a diverse group of high schools. Our goal in identifying and sharing these practices is to strengthen the capacity of schools and educators to support their own Black and Latinx students in learning to analyze, navigate, and challenge racial injustice. Like Baldwin, we see such critical consciousness as essential for youth of color to survive and thrive in the contemporary United States as well as to engage in the collective social action necessary "for the sake of the life and health of the country."[8]

WHY CRITICAL CONSCIOUSNESS MATTERS

Paulo Freire described critical consciousness as a powerful tool for societal transformation by motivating individuals to combat oppression, violence, and dehumanization within their communities.[9] Moreover, a growing body of research has found critical consciousness to be an important predictor of positive outcomes for youth marginalized by inequities in race, ethnicity, gender, socioeconomic status, immigration status, and language. Namely, scholars have reported that marginalized youth with high levels of critical consciousness are more likely to demonstrate resilience, mental health, self-esteem, academic achievement, high professional aspirations, and civic and political engagement.[10]

In explaining why critical consciousness might be associated with these positive youth outcomes, scholar Shawn Ginwright has suggested that critical consciousness can replace marginalized adolescents' feelings of isolation and self-blame for challenges they are encountering with a sense of agency and engagement in a broader collective struggle for social justice.[11]

Or as scholar Beverly Daniel Tatum has observed: "We are better able to resist the negative impact of oppressive messages when we see them coming than when they are invisible to us."[12] Accordingly, various scholars have characterized critical consciousness as an "antidote to oppression" and a form of "psychological armor" against oppressive social forces such as racial injustice.[13]

DEVELOPING CRITICAL CONSCIOUSNESS

Scholars often conceptualize critical consciousness as consisting of the development of three distinct yet overlapping qualities: (1) social analysis, (2) political agency, and (3) social action (see figure 1).[14] *Social analysis* refers to the ability to name and analyze the social, political, and economic forces that contribute to inequity and inequality. Paulo Freire theorized that when people from oppressed groups can engage in social analysis, the dominant narratives that hide or perpetuate oppression "lose credibility."[15] *Political agency* is the belief that one has the capacity to effect social or

FIGURE 1.1   Components of critical consciousness

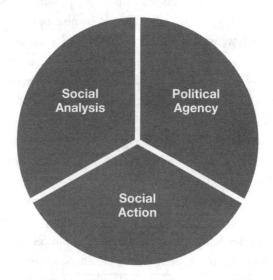

political change.[16] Political agency is a crucial component of critical consciousness because it can transform an individual's recognition of oppression and injustice (social analysis) into a commitment to oppose these forces (social action). Finally, *social action* refers to engaging in events or activities that confront oppressive forces and structures, and the unequal conditions they perpetuate.[17] Social action can be individual or collective, and includes a wide range of forms through which individuals seek to navigate and challenge oppressive forces. Paulo Freire characterized engagement in such social action as the ultimate goal of critical consciousness.

While each component of critical consciousness has a distinct meaning and purpose, they are also interconnected in that development in one component can influence development in others. For example, a young person who engages in social action to protest police violence against African Americans might through that action come to learn additional information about the effects of racism throughout the criminal justice system and thus further develop the ability to engage in social analysis. That same young person could also experience a growing sense of political agency if she comes to see her participation in the protest as having effected social change.

SCHOOLING FOR CRITICAL CONSCIOUSNESS

In his foundational text on critical consciousness, *Pedagogy of the Oppressed*, Paulo Freire described traditional approaches to education as a "banking model" in which the teacher serves as an authority figure who deposits knowledge into students. Freire argued that this banking model is antithetical to critical consciousness development in that students from oppressed groups are taught to adapt to their conditions rather than to challenge the social forces that oppress them. Instead, Freire theorized that critical consciousness is best engendered through a "problem-posing education" in which the educator poses reality as a problem to be investigated by teachers and students in which "both are simultaneously students and teachers."[18] In other words, Freire called for educational settings in which teachers and students work reciprocally to investigate and address real-world issues.

Freire believed that, in such settings, students come to see their community and world as capable of transformation and to see themselves as possessing the agency to bring about such transformation.

This connection that Freire posited between critical consciousness and problem-posing education has served as the foundation for many of the contemporary efforts to foster critical consciousness both inside and outside of traditional school spaces. For example, a number of educators have sought to foster youth critical consciousness through participatory action research projects in which youth identify a problem within their community and then collaborate as equal partners with scholars in constructing research questions, designing the research study, collecting data, and sharing results.[19] Other scholars have reported on the role of ethnic studies courses—programming that focuses on the lived experiences and cultures of particular ethnic or racial groups—in fostering young people's capacity and commitment to challenge oppression and hegemony facing their community.[20] Both of these approaches align with Freire's conception of problem-posing education in that they center the cultural knowledge and identities of the students in their learning, and situate both teachers and students as learners and knowledge-holders.

No Single Approach

Paulo Freire's work on problem-posing education has powerfully informed many of the contemporary efforts by schools and educators to foster youth critical consciousness. Yet, an increasing number of educators today embrace both Baldwin's and Freire's charge to support youth of color in learning to analyze, navigate, and challenge racial injustice but approach this work from a diverse set of pedagogical traditions.[21] These educators are committed to fostering their students' social analysis skills, feelings of political agency, and commitment to social action—the three dimensions of critical consciousness—but via curriculum and programming that are consonant with the respective schooling models from which they come.[22]

The diverse approaches of such educators and schools offer an important opportunity to explore whether different pedagogical approaches might prove adept at fostering different dimensions of youth critical consciousness. For example, have educators coming out of experiential schooling traditions such as expeditionary learning and action civics developed programming particularly suited to fostering youths' commitment to social action? Conversely, might educators relying on problem-posing or habits of mind pedagogies—with their emphases on inquiry and critical thinking—possess distinctive practices for strengthening youths' social analysis skills? Finally, might a "no-excuses" schooling model—which hews far closer to a banking model of education than a problem-posing one— offer an entirely different set of practices that contribute to youth critical consciousness development? Or, to knit all of these queries together, might historian of education Daniel Perlstein be correct in his assertion that "no single pedagogical approach inherently serves the cause of social justice"?[23]

This book seeks to answer each of these questions. To be clear, our goal in embarking on this project was neither to challenge the importance of Paulo Freire's work on problem-posing education nor to identify a particular schooling model as superior to all others in fostering youth critical consciousness. Rather, we hypothesized that a number of different schooling models might prove adept at fostering different dimensions of youths' critical consciousness. And if that hypothesis proved true, we believed reporting on the curriculum and programming underlying those diverse schooling models would broaden educators' understanding of the full range of practices that can contribute to youth critical consciousness development. Certainly, other scholars have studied the ability of specific schooling practices to foster youth critical consciousness of racial inequity; however, we are not aware of previous work that has sought to compare the contributions of different schooling models to youths' developing critical consciousness of racial injustice.[24]

Five Schools, Five Models

Over four years, we compared the critical consciousness development of more than three-hundred Black and Latinx youth in the class of 2017 attending five urban high schools featuring five different schooling models. All five schools are referred to by pseudonyms throughout this book, as are the youth and educators from these schools with whom we spoke and observed.

These five high schools were all located in northeastern cities, served predominantly Black and Latinx student bodies, and cited youth civic development as a core part of their missions. All five schools were also not-for-profit public charter schools that admitted youth in their respective cities via randomized registration lotteries, and approximately three-fourths of the youth attending each of these schools qualified for free or reduced-price lunch—a proxy for low socioeconomic status. In short, these five high schools were highly similar in their size, geography, governance, student demographics, admissions policies, and explicit goals for fostering students' academic and civic development (see table A1 in "A Note on Research Methods").

Yet, these highly similar schools took five different pedagogical approaches to teaching and learning. Specifically, Make the Road Academy featured Paulo Freire's problem-posing pedagogy; Espiritu High School was guided by the Coalition of Essential Schools' habits of mind approach; Harriet Tubman High School featured a no-excuses model; Community Academy followed an expeditionary learning model; and Leadership High School was guided by an action civics approach. Rich portraits of each of these schools, their respective schooling models, and their effects on students' critical consciousness of racial injustice are the focus of the five case-study chapters that follow. By comparing each school's distinctive contributions to students' critical consciousness development, this book offers valuable insights to educators and other stakeholders about teaching tools and school spaces that can be employed to support their own youths' critical consciousness development.

Our decision to focus the five case studies on charter schools—publicly funded schools overseen by their state departments of education rather than by local school boards—was not due to any belief on our part that charter schools are more committed or more effective at fostering youth critical consciousness than district, independent, or parochial schools. Rather, we chose to focus on charter schools for two reasons. First, in order to consider the effects of different schooling models on youth critical consciousness, we needed to find schools that explicitly and unequivocally aligned themselves with a particular schooling model. Because charter schools are typically granted more autonomy than traditional public schools over matters of curriculum and programming, they can more easily affiliate themselves with a singular schooling model or pedagogy. This feature of charter schools made them a good site for investigating the questions motivating this project.

Second, in order to compare the critical consciousness development of youth attending different schooling models, we needed the participating schools to differ in their pedagogical approaches but also to be as similar as possible in every other way—size, geography, student demographics, admissions policies, and school type. For both of these reasons, the five case studies in the ensuing chapters focus on public charter high schools, but that focus by no means signals a belief on our part that the critical consciousness work taking place in these schools is limited to a singular school type. Here, we briefly describe the data we collected over four years at each of the participating schools to compare their respective contributions to students' critical consciousness of racial injustice.

OUR STUDY OF CRITICAL CONSCIOUSNESS

Our study began in August of 2013 just as the three-hundred youth in our study were beginning their first year of high school. All of these teens completed a critical consciousness survey during the first week of their freshman year of high school that included a number of scales associated with the three key components of critical consciousness: social analysis, political agency, and social action. For example, one of the scales included in this survey, Awareness of Systemic Racism, offered insight into youths' social analysis skills by assessing their ability to analyze the systemic factors underlying racism and racial inequality.[25] Another scale, the Youth Sociopolitical Control Scale, assessed youths' confidence that they could effect social or political change in their community.[26] A third scale, the Commitment to Activism Scale, assessed youths' motivation to engage in social action challenging injustice.[27] We administered this survey to youth in their first week of ninth grade to establish their baseline scores on these various scales associated with critical consciousness. Then the youth participating in our study completed these same surveys four more times over the next four years—at the end of ninth grade (May 2014), tenth grade (May 2015), eleventh grade (May 2016), and twelfth grade (May 2017).

Collecting these fives waves of survey data across youths' four years of high school meant that, for any individual student or group of students, we could chart their growth in critical consciousness on each of the scales related to social analysis, political agency, and social action. Then a statistical technique called hierarchical linear modeling (HLM) with effects coding allowed us to identify whether youth attending one of the schools in our study were (a) concluding high school with higher scores on a particular dimension of critical consciousness than their peers across the broader sample, or (b) demonstrating stronger growth over four years of high school on a particular dimension of critical consciousness than their peers in the broader sample.

Those analyses of student surveys could tell us whether students from a particular schooling model were demonstrating outsized scores or growth on a particular dimension of critical consciousness, but they couldn't tell us why or how those results were happening. To answer those types of "why" and "how" questions, we also conducted scores of interviews with students and teachers across the five schools. We also spent hundreds of days observing classes, community meetings, extracurricular activities, and other events at the five schools.

Specifically, beginning in the spring of 2014, we randomly selected twelve ninth graders from each of the participating schools (sixty total students) to sit down with us for one-on-one interviews about their beliefs about racial injustice in the United States, as well as how their respective high schools had influenced those beliefs. Examples of questions that we asked students included: "Do you think society gives people of all races an equal chance to succeed?" and "Are there issues in the news about race or racism that you've been talking about in school?" We then re-interviewed each of these young people again at the end of tenth grade (April 2015), eleventh grade (April 2016), and twelfth grade (April 2017) to consider how their beliefs about racial injustice had changed over the course of high school as well as their beliefs about the most impactful programming and practices at their respective schools.

When youth described particular teachers or administrators as important to their critical consciousness development, we then sought to speak directly with those educators, leading us to conduct interviews with thirty-two teachers and administrators across the five schools as well. All 254 of these interviews with students and faculty were audio-recorded, transcribed, and then coded to seek out patterns and themes that helped us to answer how each of the five participating schools had contributed to their respective students' critical consciousness of racial injustice.

Between the class of 2017's ninth-grade orientation in September of 2013 and their high school graduations four years later, we also spent 334 days observing and collecting field notes at the five participating schools (approximately 17 observation days per school per year). These observations allowed us to supplement students' and teachers' descriptions of the programming and practices at their respective schools with our own first-hand accounts of the schools' academic classes, extracurricular activities, community meetings, field trips, guest speakers, senior talks, and special assemblies. Our field notes from all of these different types of activities focused on how teachers and students communicated formally and informally with each other about racism and other oppressive social forces shaping students' lives as well as strategies for navigating and challenging these forces. These field notes also captured our observations about the distinctive pedagogical features of each school. Similar to the student and faculty interviews, all 334 sets of field notes were then coded to identify specific programming and practices through which these five schools sought to foster their students' critical consciousness development.

Comparison Schools

Our primary approach to investigating the contributions of five different schooling models to youth critical consciousness development was to compare the growth in critical consciousness of youth attending schools featuring these five different schooling models *to each other*. Such a research design has numerous strengths, but a reasonable critique is that it does not include a comparison group. In other words, our investigation of the contributions of various schooling models to youth critical consciousness development would benefit from the inclusion of an additional set of comprehensive high schools that did *not* include explicit goals for youth civic development. Without such a comparison group, this book might simply be reporting on adolescents' typical critical consciousness development rather than the effects of school programming designed to foster such development.

To address this possibility, in the fifth and final wave of data collection in the spring of 2017, we also administered our critical consciousness survey to 275 twelfth-grade students at four additional high schools located in the same northeastern cities as the five schools featured in this book. Two of these additional high schools were traditional district high schools, and two were not-for-profit public charter high schools. The demographic characteristics of the youth attending these comparison high schools closely matched those of the original sample of students in terms of their age, hometown, race/ethnicity, gender, and socioeconomic status. However, neither the mission nor vision statements of these four comparison schools cited explicit goals for youth civic development nor a singular pedagogical approach to teaching and learning. By including these additional youth in our final wave of survey data collection and then comparing their scores to that of youth from the five schools featured in this book, we sought to confirm that our five featured schools had made outsized contributions to their students' critical consciousness development over and above adolescents' typical development.

ORGANIZATION OF THE BOOK

This opening chapter has sought to introduce the concept of critical consciousness and why it matters, as well as our hypothesis that different schooling approaches might prove adept at fostering different dimensions of youths' critical consciousness of racial injustice. The ensuing chapters offer substantial support for this hypothesis. Namely, youth attending this study's problem-posing high school graduated with the strongest ability to engage in social analysis of racial injustice, but youth attending the habits of mind high school demonstrated both the highest levels and steepest growth in their feelings of political agency. Youth attending the action civics and expeditionary learning schools demonstrated the highest levels and steepest growth, respectively, in their commitment to collective social action challenging injustice. Finally, youth attending the no-excuses high school reported both the highest levels and steepest growth in their confidence in navigating settings in which racial inequity is prominent.

The next five chapters offer rich portraits of each of these schools. Each chapter opens with a vignette from the school's ninth-grade orientation for students in the class of 2017, and each chapter concludes with a scene from those same students' high school graduation ceremonies four years later. We book-end each chapter with these events because we believe that each school's approach to welcoming and sending off its students illuminates its culture, core values, pedagogy, and approach to fostering youth critical consciousness. In between these two bookends, we describe each school's distinctive approach to teaching and learning, the particular dimension of critical consciousness on which their students demonstrated outsized growth, and finally the programming and practices that contributed to this development.

The final chapter reviews these promising practices unique to each of the featured schools but then also identifies a number of common teaching tools employed by multiple schools for fostering their students' critical consciousness, as well as the optimal spaces within secondary schools for deploying these tools. Ultimately, we believe both these similarities and differences across the five schools hold important implications for educators, school leaders, and other stakeholders committed to fostering the critical consciousness of the youth they serve.

DANGEROUS TIMES

James Baldwin began "A Talk to Teachers" with the caveat: "Let's begin by saying that we are living through a very dangerous time."[28] Unfortunately, this sentiment remains true for the youth featured in *Schooling for Critical Consciousness* as well. These young people began high school just a month after George Zimmerman's acquittal in the extrajudicial killing of African American teenager Trayvon Martin in Sanford, Florida—a verdict that gave rise to the Black Lives Matter movement. Over the next four years, these young people witnessed the extrajudicial killings of many more young people of color including Tamir Rice, Michael Brown, and Rekia Boyd. In few of these cases were the perpetrators convicted of any wrongdoing.

At the conclusion of tenth grade, these young people listened to Republican presidential candidate Donald Trump characterize Mexican immigrants as criminals and rapists, and then a year and a half later as president of the United States enact a so-called Muslim ban that suspended all immigration from seven predominantly Muslim countries. As these young adults celebrated their high school graduations in the summer of 2017, hundreds of White supremacists descended on Charlottesville, Virginia, to protest the removal of a Robert E. Lee statue wielding torches and semi-automatic weapons, and chanting, "White Lives Matter!" And many of these young people then matriculated to college the following fall just as colleges and universities across the country reported surges in the frequency of campus hate crimes and the dissemination of White supremacist propaganda.[29]

In short, the young people featured in this book have also come of age in an America in which racial injustice remains overwhelming, pernicious, and perhaps even more visible than in recent decades. Critical consciousness can lend these and other Black and Latinx youth the "psychological armor" to resist the negative effects of racial injustice as well as the activist skills and commitments to challenge such injustice. *Schooling for Critical Consciousness* seeks to equip educators and schools with the tools to support their own students' development of such skills, commitments, and armor.

CHAPTER 2

See the Invisible

"GOOD MORNING," said a tall young woman with shoulder-length hair standing at the front of the narrow cafeteria. "I'm Jalissa North, and I'm the student body president. This past summer me and four other peers went to Africa for a service-learning project. We taught math, English, and science."

The ninth graders in the class of 2017 clapped politely, as their first day of high school at Make the Road Academy (MtRA) kicked off. The students were all seated together at long green cafeteria tables. Having come from various district, charter, and parochial middle schools all over the city, only a handful of students knew each other already. One-hundred percent of these ninth graders identified as youth of color, with five out of six identifying as Black or African American. More than three-fourths qualified for free or reduced-price lunch.

Standing at the front of the cafeteria directly behind Jalissa was another upperclassman, Bailey, as well as the school's founder and leader, Principal Yvette Naylor. A dozen MtRA faculty members lined the side walls of the cafeteria.

The second upperclassman stepped forward to join Jalissa. "My name is Bailey," she explained. "I'm the secretary of the student body. Over the summer I worked at an art gallery where we created fancy murals for places around the city." There was another round of polite applause from the new ninth graders.

Because Make the Road Academy had only been founded one year ear-lier with a total student body of fifty ninth graders, Jalissa, Bailey, and the rest of the student government leaders were all just rising tenth graders. In accordance with MtRA's dress code, all of these young people wore white dress shirts with burgundy sweaters and either gray pants or knit skirts. The boys in the audience wore burgundy ties, and a handful wore bur-gundy sports jackets as well.

Now Principal Naylor—a Black woman in her early thirties—stepped forward to introduce herself to MtRA's new ninth graders. "You see," she told them. "We don't just learn about social issues in the world, but we also try to go out and do something about them." She paused. "How many of your know who Paulo Freire is? Who knows from our school's website?"

Only one freshman raised her hand. "He was a man that wanted to find like education for . . ." She paused. "I'm not really sure no more."

"Okay," Principal Naylor said. "Let's give her applause for trying. We're a discussion-based school, so you're going to get used to speak-ing. We dialogue. You're right—Paulo Freire was an educator. He was famous for working on how to educate oppressed populations. What does oppressed mean?"

Another student raised her hand. " Oppressed means being deprived of something."

"Good," Principal Naylor said. "What oppressed means is that there is a group or an institution or a system that is depriving you of privileges or rights. As people of color, raise your hand if you feel like you are sometimes being deprived of rights."

A handful of ninth graders raised their hands. Principal Naylor nodded. "What we do here at Make the Road Academy is talk about oppression in its many forms, and we try to do something about it. And it is my goal that by tomorrow you are more keenly aware of oppression and how it has affected all of us in some way, shape, or form." She paused. "We're going to talk about racism, sexism, homophobia, classism, discrimination—a lot of issues you're passionate about. You may have strong views, and that's fine, but our goal is to challenge your thinking, and challenge our thinking."

ORIGIN STORY: BRINGING LIBERATORY EDUCATION

Make the Road Academy was founded in 2012 by a half-dozen educators, including Principal Naylor and her husband, Mr. Roger Naylor. All were Black, and most had been born, raised, and then become teachers in the historic but struggling city in which MtRA was located.

In their former schools, a number of these educators had incorporated social justice content and a dialogic teaching style into their courses but felt that city- and state-mandated curricula meant they could only do so covertly. As one of those educators, Mr. Bradley Spencer, explained: "I used to get in trouble sometimes for teaching certain things. Like certain historical facts, social justice, Selma riots, ancient history, all types of stuff. And I would tie it into the subject matter, but I would get pushback from administrators."

These educators formed a working group that met every weekend for a year to put together the charter proposal that ultimately led to the opening of Make the Road Academy. In developing the proposal, all the educators had particular elements that they saw as crucial to the success of the new school. Mr. Naylor advocated for an inquiry-based approach that would engage students in dialogue and question asking about the content they were studying. Mr. Spencer wanted students to have opportunities for service and engagement with the community, and Principal Naylor believed that social justice and arts content needed to be infused into every aspect of the curriculum. The group's charter proposal ran nearly 250 pages by the time they submitted it to the state board of education for consideration.

The school's name, Make the Road Academy, emerged from this group's conversations about key dimensions of their proposed school. As Principal Naylor explained, "I remember sitting around the table, and I remember saying, like, I think that what we're doing is bringing liberatory education to our city. . . . What we all have in common is that we believe education is the key to liberation from oppression. That's what brought us to this table, and Paulo Freire is the father of critical pedagogy." As they worked on the proposal, these educators also became increasingly certain that Freire's problem-posing education sat at the nexus of all the different ingredients they wanted to incorporate into their proposed school. So they named the school after a book that Paulo Freire had coauthored with civil rights activist and teacher Myles Horton, *We Make the Road by Walking*.[1]

When the state department of education granted these educators a charter to open their school, Principal Naylor left her job with an education nonprofit to become the school's executive director, and Mr. Naylor and Mr. Spencer left district teaching positions to serve as the school's director of operations and director of community engagement, respectively. Make the Road Academy opened its doors in September of 2012 with a student body composed of just fifty ninth graders. The school was located a few blocks from the city center in a building that had formerly housed a district elementary school. The building itself was nearly one-hundred years old, with unreliable water and heating systems. Its former status as an elementary school was evident in cheerful murals of Dr. Seuss characters decorating the school's walls. Make the Road Academy faculty would quickly paper over these elementary touches with quotations from Malcolm X, bulletin boards honoring notable Black and Latinx Americans, and a mural of the school mascot, the Phoenix, rising from the ashes.

SCHOOLING FOR CRITICAL CONSCIOUSNESS: PROBLEM-POSING EDUCATION

Philosopher-educator Paulo Freire argued that critical consciousness is best engendered through a "problem-posing education" in which teachers and students work together to investigate real-world problems shaping their communities and lives.[2] In his final work, *Pedagogy of Freedom*, Freire described three core principles underlying a problem-posing education: (1) there is not teaching without learning; (2) teaching is not just transferring knowledge; and (3) teaching is a human act.[3]

Paulo Freire also described two tools, codes and culture circles, as central to problem-posing education.[4] A code is any type of image or object that is familiar to students from their everyday lives, which "re-presents" their own reality back to them and allows for an emotional response.[5] In other words, a code can be an object, photograph, text, video, and so on. Such a code then becomes the starting point for a culture circle, which Freire characterized as a "live and creative dialogue in which everyone knows some things and does not know others, in which all seek together to know more."[6] The role of the teacher in the culture circle is to coordinate the circle, rather than direct it, by asking questions and sharing information that promote critical thinking. Through the use of this dialogic strategy, Freire asserted that students begin to take charge of their learning and start to see themselves as social and political beings—an opening step in their critical consciousness development.[7]

DEVELOPING CRITICAL CONSCIOUSNESS: SOCIAL ANALYSIS

Systemic racism refers to the ways in which particular policies, laws, and cultural practices privilege or obstruct the success of particular racial-ethnic groups over others.[8] Whereas interpersonal racism is typically the result of a particular individual's biases or discriminatory practices, systemic racism exists within the policies and practices of different types of institutions.

Scholars have theorized that adolescents' growing cognitive abilities increase their ability to recognize and understand systemic forms of racism as they move from early to later adolescence.[9] Such awareness of systemic racism represents a form of social analysis—one of the three key components of critical consciousness (see figure 2.1).

Accordingly, the critical consciousness survey completed by students at both the five high schools featured in this book and the four comparison high schools included an Awareness of Systemic Racism Scale that served as one measure of youths' ability to engage in social analysis of racial injustice.[10] This scale presented youth with several statements with which they could agree or disagree along a five-point scale such as "Racism in the educational system limits the success of Blacks, Latinos and other racial minorities" and "Many businesses intentionally keep Black, Latino and other racial minorities from gaining positions of power." A score of "1" on

FIGURE 2.1   Components of critical consciousness

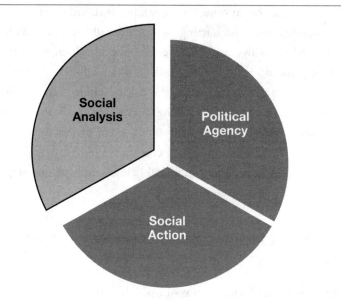

this scale represented a low awareness of systemic racism, and a score of "5" represented a high awareness of systemic racism.

Figure 2.2 reveals that youth across all five of the high schools featured in this book demonstrated growth, on average, in their awareness of systemic racism from the start of ninth grade (Time 1) to the end of twelfth grade (Time 5). Moreover, as they graduated from high school, the students at these five high schools demonstrated significantly higher awareness of systemic racism than their peers at the four comprehensive high schools that served as a comparison group.[11] In other words, the youth attending the five schools featured in this book demonstrated a greater awareness than their peers at several nearby high schools of the policies, laws, and cultural practices that can privilege particular racial groups over others.

Importantly, analyses also revealed that the youth attending Make the Road Academy demonstrated significantly higher awareness of systemic racism at the conclusion of high school than their peers across all five featured high schools.[12] In other words, as the young people attending these

FIGURE 2.2   Youths' awareness of systemic racism from the start of ninth
grade (Time 1) to the end of twelfth grade (Time 5)

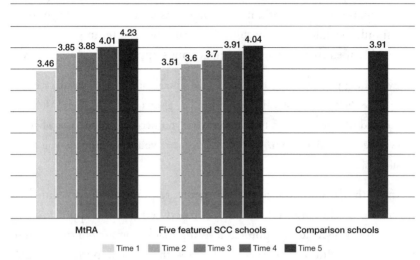

five schools came to the end of high school, students at Make the Road
Academy demonstrated the greatest awareness of the ways in which racism
is built into societal policies, laws, and cultural practices. This ability to
engage in social analysis is one of the key components of critical consciousness of racial injustice.[13]

Developing Understandings of Systemic Racism

Yearly one-on-one interviews with eight youth attending Make the Road
Academy illustrated what their developing social analysis skills looked and
sounded like.[14] Particularly useful was a question that these young people
answered at the end of each year of high school: "Do you think society gives
people of all races an equal chance to succeed?" At the end of ninth grade,
five MtRA students answered "yes" and three answered "no." By the end
of twelfth grade, however, all eight youth were emphatic that the United
States did *not* offer people of all races equal opportunities for success.

An MtRA student that typified this trajectory was Alicia. At the end of
ninth grade, Alicia responded to our question about race and opportunity

by explaining: "The color of your skin doesn't dictate the amount of education you can take in or anything like that. As long as you apply yourself, it doesn't matter if you're dark, if you're light. As long as you apply yourself, you should be able to do anything." A year later as a tenth grader, Alicia still maintained that race did not impact one's opportunities for success:

> Everything you have, you have to take advantage of it. Like, you just have to have the mindset of, "If this is what I'm gonna be given, then just go out and do your research to find out what you need to get and use whatever people is giving you." You gotta use what you have to make you be successful.

In both these ninth- and tenth-grade responses, Alicia seemed to describe what she *wanted* the relationship between race and opportunity to be, given her own vantage point as a young Black woman working hard to become successful. Her perspective aligns with scholarship that has found people from marginalized groups often justify the existing social order so as to maintain hope about their own opportunities for advancement and success.[15]

In her eleventh-grade interview, however, Alicia offered a very different perspective. She stated emphatically that society does *not* give people of all races equal opportunities to succeed and also described two different ways she saw such inequality playing out:

> I think society, when they see a little Black boy, they're gonna think he plays football, he has to play basketball. But if a Black boy says, "I want to be a doctor," I feel like society is gonna look at him like, "What are you doing? That's not what you're supposed to be doing. You're supposed to have a ball in your hand." And I feel like if someone that's Caucasian [says], "Oh, I wanna be a doctor," their parents, okay, if they have money, [they'll say], "I'm gonna pay for you to do this. We're gonna make sure this is here. This is that." People that are Black, they more than likely probably don't have the money [to] get you exactly where you need to be at the right time. It's gonna take like a process to get to where you need to get to. So I feel like, with us, like even if we have the same abilities as somebody that's Caucasian, it just

takes a little bit more time to fulfill what we want to do because [of] like expenses and things like that.

In this eleventh-grade perspective, Alicia described the effect of different societal messages that Black youth and White youth receive about their occupational aspirations. She also noted that White families are more likely to possess financial resources that give their children an advantage over children in Black families—a perspective that finds support in recent studies of racial disparities in wealth and income.[16] In these ways, Alicia demonstrated a growing recognition of the ways in which racism and racial injustice reside, not only in the actions of particular individuals but also in societal institutions and practices.

Finally, as a high school senior, Alicia observed again that society offers disparate opportunities to people of different races. In this explanation, she began to look beyond high school to the world of work that lay ahead:

It's really hard like, if you're an African American that's like in corporate America. Not that I know anybody that's in corporate America, but I feel like it'd probably be really hard just to get there. You'd probably be like six Black people out of twenty-five, and then as a woman you're probably one woman out of twenty-five that's Black. There's probably some White women, but you're probably that one Black woman out of all the women that's there.

In this final interview, Alicia expressed her perception that there are few Black people in elite professional positions in the United States and that such lack of representation presents obstacles for Black people who do manage to obtain such positions. Alicia also expressed a burgeoning intersectional perspective that, as a Black woman, she faced challenges that accompany living at the intersection of two marginalized identities.[17] This increasingly sophisticated recognition of the systemic factors contributing to racial inequity was representative of the trajectory of many MtRA students. In the ensuing sections, we draw upon our interviews with these young people and their teachers, as well as field notes from more than thirty-five observation days at MtRA, to identify the curriculum, programming, and practices that contributed to students' development of the ability to analyze racial injustice.

KEY SCHOOLING PRACTICES FOR SOCIAL ANALYSIS

While children's awareness of interpersonal racism (e.g., biases, stereotypes, discrimination) often develops through social observation and lived experience, a number of scholars have reported that the more covert nature of systemic racism means that adolescents and adults typically develop awareness of systemic racism through explicit learning opportunities that inform lived experience.[18] Accordingly, much of the scholarship on adolescents' developing awareness of systemic racism focuses on the influence of school-based and out-of-school programming. For example, scholars have reported on programming ranging from youth organizing groups to ethnic studies courses to youth participatory action research as capable of fostering adolescents' understanding of systemic racism and other oppressive social forces.[19]

The Three I's

At Make the Road Academy, all ninth-grade students participated in a year-long Social Engagement course that included units on White supremacy, economic inequality, the criminal justice system, and sexism. Such a curricular focus resonates with Paulo Freire's description of problem-posing education as engaging teachers and students in investigating real-world social problems.[20] Mr. Spencer—the MtRA founder who taught Social Engagement during the school's first year of operation—explained of the course:

> That class, it kind of makes the school, to me. Like the other classes are necessary just in order to have a school, to make it functional, for it to be legal, right? But Social Engagement class gives them information they might not ever get in their life. . . . And I've seen students, once they learn about different, like, disparities and criminal justice and all these things, they make better decisions.

For the class of 2017, the Social Engagement course was taught by Mr. Floyd Andrews, a Black man in his mid-twenties who had originally applied to MtRA for a position teaching English. When the sample lesson that Mr. Andrews prepared for his job interview focused on racism in Harper Lee's *To Kill a Mockingbird*, Principal Naylor hired him to teach Social Engagement instead.

Both Mr. Andrews and several of his students described the unit on White supremacy—and specifically the introduction of a "Three I's of Oppression" framework—as the most powerful element of the Social Engagement course. Mr. Andrews explained of the unit's opening lesson:

> I put "Institutional," "Interpersonal," and "Internalized" on one side of the board, and then I put "Oppression." And then I put dictionaries on the kids' desks. And I said, "Define these words individually." And I said, "Now that you know what all these words mean individually, come up with your own hypothesis of what these words mean together." And so they did that, and I had some good responses.

Allowing students to arrive at their own understandings of these terms—rather than "depositing" the definitions into their heads—very much resonates with a problem-posing educational approach.

A few weeks later, Mr. Andrews and his ninth graders reviewed a quiz in Social Engagement class in which students had read ten short vignettes and then identified the form of oppression illustrated within each vignette.

"We're going to start [class] today with reviewing your quiz on the three I's," Mr. Andrews told his students, who were seated in groups around three long tables. "I wanted you to write a sentence explaining why you chose what you chose." He read from the first vignette. "For example, 'African Americans believing their hair isn't beautiful, so they buy quote unquote better hair from other races?'"

"Interpersonal?" one student guessed.

"Internalized oppression," suggested another young woman student, "because it's known for Black people to have coarse or knotty hair, and she believed it."

Mr. Andrews endorsed this second answer. "When any race or group of people start believing the stereotypes about them, it's internalized oppression."

One of his students wasn't so sure. "I put institutional oppression," he insisted.

Mr. Andrews paused. "It would be institutional if you saw lots of stores advertising 'better' hair in Black neighborhoods."

In this unit on White supremacy, Mr. Andrews presented his students with a new heuristic ("the three I's") that they could use as an organizing framework for making sense of the world around them.[21] Importantly, seeking out new perspectives and ideologies for making sense of the world has been characterized as a key developmental task of adolescence.[22] Scholar Theresa Perry adds that, for Black adolescents, such new perspectives and ideologies must offer "an interpretive framework that is capable of making sense of those instances when . . . one experiences discrimination in school and in the larger society."[23] In this way, Mr. Andrews's introduction of the three I's framework represented a powerful contribution to his students' growing ability to analyze how racial injustice operated in both their community and the wider world.

One of the central ideas of the White supremacy unit was that systemic racism can be seen in the different types of commerce present and absent within a community. Numerous MtRA students described these lessons even years later as a powerful takeaway from the Social Engagement course. One student, Janine, explained as a sophomore:

> I remember last year [in Social Engagement] we talked about institutionalized oppression, and it's like when, like you see in my community, they put so many liquor stores and so many things out here because they want us to die. They want us to go off-track, right? But you don't never see liquor stores in Rosefield Hills, like on every corner like that. So I think that's unfair. They don't want us to succeed.

Here, Janine described a newfound understanding of the liquor stores throughout her city as a temptation deliberately placed there to limit the success of the mostly low-income people of color who lived there. When pressed to identify specifically *who* wanted people in her community to go off-track, Janine responded, "The government," but did not offer more detail on the governmental or economic mechanisms at work. In this way, she and a number of her classmates demonstrated a nascent understanding of systemic forms of racism as they came to the end of their ninth- and tenth-grade years.

As a senior several years later, however, another MtRA student, Michael, demonstrated a more sophisticated understanding of such institutionalized forms of oppression, and he credited his ninth-grade Social Engagement course with planting the seeds for such understanding. As Michael explained:

> In this city it's a lot of Chicken Shacks everywhere, but if you go out to like Rosefield Hills or something like that, you're not gonna find one nowhere around. Like you might find a Whole Foods or like a farmer's market or something like that. It's just the options of everything is just much different, and it just seem like certain things are put where they put for a reason . . . Freshman year, when we was in the [Social Engagement] class, it made me think about stuff differently, and once I started thinking about it, you start putting the pieces together, and you start noticing like nothing happens just because. Like, it's all for some reason. Like somebody's benefitting from everything, somebody's not benefitting from everything. It's set up this way for a certain reason.

Michael's words revealed his burgeoning understanding that resources are allocated in ways that benefit the powerful and disadvantage the marginalized. His explanation also illuminates how the Social Engagement course contributed to MtRA students' development of the social analysis skills necessary to recognize and understand systemic racism and other forms of institutionalized oppression.

A Good Community

The three I's framework represented a powerful, but potentially overwhelming, lens through which MtRA students could make sense of the world. Youth learning about interpersonal, institutionalized, and internalized forms of oppression might reasonably come away feeling as if there is little one can do to push back against such powerful social forces. For this reason, within the Social Engagement class's unit on White supremacy, Mr. Andrews shrewdly followed up his students' learning about the three I's with lessons on the Black Panther Party's 1966 Ten-Point Plan for Self-Defense.

To connect the dots between the two sets of lessons, Mr. Andrews first had his students create drawings of a community afflicted by the three different forms of oppression. Students' drawings featured cities with segregated schools and water fountains, discriminatory employers, billboards advertising hair-straightening and skin-lightening products, prisons filled with people of color, and crumbling school buildings. As Mr. Andrews explained, he then told his students:

> This is just a first round of drawings, and in the second round we'll talk about what they can try to do to uplift the neighborhood and what the neighborhood *should* look like. I don't want to just tear them down to the raw meat, to say "I'm Black in America, I can't do anything about it." No, there are things we can do, and this is the way we should go about doing things.

The entry point for these discussions was the Black Panther Party's 1966 Ten-Point Plan for Self-Defense. Part Bill of Rights and part Declaration of Independence, this historical document laid out a vision for a more equitable society for Black Americans that included (1) an educational system which teaches "knowledge of self" to Black students; (2) reparations from the American government to the descendants of enslaved Africans; (3) the release from prison of African Americans who have not received fair and impartial jury trials; (4) the redistribution of properties owned by White landlords who exploit Black tenants; and (5) the formation of self-defense groups within African American communities to end police brutality. In accordance with Paulo Freire's problem-posing approach, Mr. Andrews used this document as a "code" to catalyze students' thinking about responses to systemic racism.[24]

In a subsequent Social Engagement lesson, Mr. Andrews challenged his students to create new drawings of their communities that incorporated points raised by the Black Panther Party's plan. One student, Janine, explained: "My bad community included liquor stores and a whole bunch of people smoking and stuff. And my good community included a restaurant, day care, [and] a building for seniors."

Midway through the lesson, Principal Yvette Naylor, came into the classroom, and youth were eager to share their drawings with her. One young man explained to Principal Naylor that African Americans in his community would be exempt from military service. "Why should we fight for a country that's destroying us?" he asked.

"Tell me your rationale," Principal Naylor challenged him.

Another group of young men had created a drawing in which African Americans had been freed from prison. "Why?" Principal Naylor asked.

One of the young men explained, "Lots of African American males don't go to college after high school and get in trouble because they don't have jobs."

Another group had included a "Do Greater Charter School" and "MLK Jr. High School" in their community and drawn an airplane with a banner advertising available jobs. "How will your schools be funded?" Principal Naylor asked, and the students decided that taxes in their community should be raised for rich people. In another corner of the room, Mr. Andrews chatted with three young ladies about how better housing options could reduce crime in a community. These dialogues aligned closely with Freire's call for a problem-posing education in which teachers and students work collaboratively to investigate real-world problems.[25] Moreover, the elements that MtRA students incorporated into their drawings revealed their growing understanding of the ways in which systemic racism and other forms of oppression shape communities.

Building on a Foundation

The Social Engagement course represented a powerful mechanism for fostering MtRA students' social analysis of racism and racial injustice, but

Principal Naylor explained that she envisioned Social Engagement as an *introduction* to such issues upon which students' subsequent coursework would then expand. From her perspective, such an introduction enabled MtRA students "to be able to go to math class and learn about how to break down the statistics of driving while Black and Brown, and now they see why they need math, and they can go to science class and learn about the Tuskegee experiment, and now they see why we need people [committed to] social justice in science to make sure there's ethics."

In a ninth-grade Spanish class, for example, students worked on their Spanish language skills while simultaneously discussing the interpersonal racism that many people of color experience when shopping at the mall or an expensive store. Working in small groups, students wrote scripts and storyboards for a scene that began with a person of color entering a store and being surveilled by the clerk working there. Their assignment was to complete the interaction with an effective response to this racial discrimination. In so doing, this lesson resonated with the problem-posing emphasis on investigating real-world problems facing one's own community.

In an eleventh-grade English class exploring the theme of the American Dream, students watched a 2014 Coca-Cola commercial—another example of a "code"—that featured Americans of different races and ethnicities singing "America the Beautiful" in different languages. Their teacher, Ms. Daniela Lugiro—a Black woman in her late twenties—then showed the class examples from the thousands of Americans who took to social media to decry the song being sung in languages other than English. MtRA students were outraged by these reactions. "My whole thing," exclaimed one student, "is I thought it was pretty ignorant because they were saying it should have been English, but America is not only English-speaking. We have many races within this country. It's showing selfishness because White people were the only ones who really cared about it. It was pretty messed up."

"America started as a melting pot," another student added, "and we were all immigrants and all came here, but European Americans, when they think of America, they don't think of us."

Finally, the twelfth-grade social studies course—American Social Issues—raised issues of institutional racism in units on the country's immigration policies, war on drugs, and challenges facing college students of color at predominantly White universities (PWIs). At the start of the latter unit, Mr. Craig Davis—a White teacher in his mid-twenties—handed out to the class a letter from an MtRA graduate about her experience as a first-year student at a predominantly White liberal arts college. The letter began:

> Dear MTRA Class of 2017,
>
> Firstly, racism exists. It hasn't gone away. Drill that into your heads right now. Regardless of all the studies that say White students are at their most open-minded while in college, as freshman, they aren't any less racist than their White, middle-class parents. 'Nuff said about that.

The letter—another example of a code—went on to describe this young woman's various experiences with White classmates and professors, and how she had handled herself in those situations. She ended the letter with the observation: "So, overall, PWI's aren't that bad. I love my school, but you just gotta be on your guard more often than you don't."

Mr. Davis assigned his students to read this letter and then to reflect in writing on the offered advice that they would and would not be willing to try if they ended up attending a predominantly White college. In so doing, Mr. Davis sought to build on understandings of systemic racism that MtRA students had developed over the course of high school, as well as their natural interest in looking ahead to the next phase of their lives.

Culture Circles

Make the Road Academy also relied on culture circles—another staple of Paulo Freire's writings on problem-posing education—to strengthen students' ability to engage in social analysis of racial injustice.[26] Art teacher Mary Yagan—an Arab American woman in her mid-twenties—explained that school leaders encouraged MtRA teachers to begin *every* unit with a culture circle:

> And what that is, is a six-step method on how to look at codes. And codes can be found in the media, in a newspaper advertisement, it can be a piece

of artwork, it can even be a song to show that oppression exists. And then the students go through the six-step process of the culture circle to describe what they see, analyze it, look at how this plays a part in real life. What are the related problems because of this? And now what actions can we take to prevent these oppressions from continuing? So we do that at the beginning of the unit to make whatever the unit is relevant, and that's how we connect it to real-life social justice issues.

Ms. Yagan's description reveals that MtRA's culture circles served as a "discourse routine" for promoting the free and open exchange of ideas between students and teachers, which scholars have found to deepen adolescents' understandings of social and civic issues.[27] At the college level, similar dialogic practices have likewise been found to deepen young people's understanding of the systemic factors underlying various types of inequality.[28]

One example of a culture circle came in a ninth-grade Earth Science class beginning a unit on natural disasters. Ms. Niobe Slater, an African American woman in her early twenties, explained to her students that the "code" for the culture circle would be a short clip from Spike Lee's 2006 documentary *When the Levees Broke*, about the impact of Hurricane Katrina on the city of New Orleans, and that the "social justice theme for this unit is whether government agencies are more likely to help certain areas quicker and faster than other areas."

The video clip started with scenes of Louis Armstrong and Billie Holiday performing jazz in New Orleans and celebratory scenes from the annual Mardi Gras parade before switching to footage of the devastating effects of Hurricane Katrina in 2005, and then finally scenes from the city three years later as volunteers continued to clean up and rebuild the city. Students jotted down notes on a handout Ms. Slater had provided them. "What are your immediate reactions to the video?" she asked, after the ten-minute excerpt had ended.

One student raised her hand: "I think the government should have helped them more, because for the city to still look like that three years after it happened, the government should have done more."

A young man noted: "They put so much focus on [Hurricane] Sandy because the places were like New York. And the government looking at New Orleans and acting like it's not such a big place, and that's wrong, that's disrespectful. It shouldn't matter where you live at or how many sponsors your state has. We're all living in America and on earth, so it shouldn't matter what your situation is."

Ms. Slater asked, "What kind of people live in New Orleans?"

"Black," a number of students answered in unison.

"Not just Black," Ms. Slater told them, "but also Caribbean, Haitians, Trinidadians. People of color live in New Orleans. In New York, they got a lot of businesses and private companies, so if a hurricane hits New York, they're going to rebuild as fast as they can because there's a lot of money." She paused. "So what can be learned from Hurricane Katrina? Let's count off by fours for our culture circle."

The students moved into foursomes, and Ms. Slater handed each group a piece of flipchart paper on which to record their responses to the different elements of the culture circle. Students in each group—already highly familiar with the culture circle protocol—divided their paper into six squares and began writing out their Descriptions, First Analysis, Real Life Applications, Related Problems, Root Causes, and Actions. "You can hang your posters up on the front board when you're finished," Ms. Slater told them. One such poster read:

Description: Broken houses, Black people, clouds, people, trees, water, poverty

First Analysis: Government doesn't help people in need; not being prepared because they had storms before; Government doesn't help people without money; Citizens were emotionally and physically hurt; Government shows favoritism. Citizens needed living necessities.

Real Life Applications: Government does not prepare states for emergencies; Do not depend on the government; Be safe not sorry; Previous storms; People that die; People losing their homes

Related Problems: Hurricane Sandy; Education and lives are in jeopardy; People have no place to go; Government didn't think New Orleans was important because of previous storms; Hurricane Irene

Root Causes: Weather in New Orleans, Communities unprepared for storms; Discrimination against poor people and Black people; Government corruption

Actions: Rebuild the community; Volunteer work; Protesting to the government; Be prepared; Build stronger houses; Depend more on ourselves; Do our own hurricane drills

In the final portion of the lesson, each group of students took turns reporting out their thinking to their peers. Their responses suggested a recognition of the role that racism and racial injustice had played in the government's response to Hurricane Katrina, as well as a belief that communities of color needed to heighten their self-reliance as a result. "Government responses can be a little shady depending on who you are and where you live," Ms. Slater told her students as the lesson came to a close. "Keep that in your brains as we go through the unit." In this lesson as well, one could see MtRA students learning to recognize the systemic forces that contribute to racial injustice in the United States, as well as how culture circles contributed to such learning.

MtRA student Zander was one of several MtRA students who characterized the culture circles as one of the most important elements of their school. According to Zander, something that made MtRA special was that "we do learn all of these things about race, you know. We have the Freire Culture Circle, and it's in our faces at that point, you know. So they're not trying to keep it from us; they're not trying to sweep it under the rug. They're trying to teach us about it now so that when we get older, it's not something new to us." In short, many MtRA students recognized their school's culture circles as a valuable opportunity to engage in discussions of race and racism explicitly and directly.

Personal Space

The three I's, codes, and culture circles represented key practices through which Make the Road Academy fostered students' recognition of systemic forms of racism. A fourth practice was creating space within MtRA classes for students and teachers to share their *personal* experiences with the different types of racism about which they were learning. This practice also aligned with a problem-posing approach in that it positioned the cultural knowledge and identities of students and teachers as valuable elements of the learning process and, in so doing, situated students and teachers as *both* learners and knowledge holders.

In a ninth-grade English class, for example, Ms. Lyla Denette concluded a unit on narrative writing by assigning her students to write essays about a time in their lives when they had overcome a struggle. To model this form of writing, Ms. Denette—a Black woman in her late twenties—shared with her students her own narrative writing about a challenge she had experienced during graduate school. She explained, "I chose to write about the classmate who told me I'd never graduate." She handed out copies of her essay and then explained: "It happened on the porch of the graduate school, and it was six o'clock at night. What happened was that I went up to a student and asked if I could be a part of her study group. And she said 'no' because she said no one thought I'd graduate. Imagine someone telling you on the second day of graduate school that you're going to fail. And there will be people who say that to you. And I went home and cried like a little punk, and I didn't even come to class the next day."

Ms. Denette's students were fascinated by this window into their teacher's life. "What race was she?" one asked.

"She was Caucasian," Ms. Denette told them.

"I knew it," the student responded.

"I did allow what she said to affect me for a long time," Ms. Denette admitted to her students. "Because I was the only African American in my class, and I felt like I was there because I had to fill a quota. Like I didn't deserve to be there. And the questions you're asking me about my narrative is exactly how interested I want to be in your narratives."

A young lady in the class raised her hand and shared that she used to volunteer at a nursing home. One day an elderly White lady with whom she was friendly sang at her, "Eeny meeny miny moe, catch a n———r by the toe." The other students in the class pressed their classmate on how she'd responded. "I started laughing," she explained, "because she was always so nice to me, and I didn't want to think she was racist."

Other classes at MtRA were marked by this incorporation of the personal as well. In Ms. Bianca Castillo's ninth-grade Spanish course, one student volunteered midway through a lesson on interpersonal racism, "So yesterday, right, a bunch of us were at the train station waiting for the train with all these White people. Dorinda said, 'Excuse me, sir. I like your hair.' He looked at her and kept on walking."

Ms. Castillo—a Latinx woman in her late twenties—had just divided the students into groups to work on an assignment, but she chose to refocus the class's attention on this student's experience. "So that right there is a person choosing to disassociate himself," she observed, "and you can look at that in one of two ways. We're taught from the time we're little that we keep away from strangers, but this is a grown man, and all he had to do was say thank you. So that man didn't necessarily exercise racism, but what was he doing?"

"Discrimination," a student volunteered.

"Yes," Ms. Castillo agreed.

A few minutes later, as class was winding down, Ms. Castillo shared a recent experience of her own with discrimination. She explained that she had recently walked into a Burberry's—an upscale women's clothing store—to buy a present for her mother, and the salespeople had initially treated her like she couldn't possibly be able to purchase anything in the store. Ms. Castillo added that she wasn't sure if that treatment was due to her looking young, Latina, or a combination of the two. Her students nodded knowingly.

In *Teaching to Transgress,* scholar bell hooks argues, "It's essential that teachers take risks and share confessional narrative surrounding their own identities if they expect their students to do the same."[29] Because both Ms. Denette and Ms. Castillo were willing to share experiences with racial discrimination from their own lives, they signaled to their students that such experiences were relevant and valuable contributions to the learning process, and students responded by sharing their own experiences with racism as well. Ms. Castillo added that making space within academic classes for such confessional narratives "is the key to developing their critical consciousness because once we get the students talking about what is going on in their personal lives, it's almost like a culture circle on their life at that point. Why is that happening to you? Where do you see your role in it? And how can you take what you're going through and kind of come out from the fire?" In short, the inclusion of teachers' and students' confessional narratives represented another feature of problem-posing education through which Make the Road Academy faculty sought to strengthen their students' ability to recognize and analyze racial injustice.

Make the Road Academy's use of confessional narratives to foster students' critical consciousness of racial injustice was unquestionably facilitated by the school's high proportion of educators of color. Approximately three-fourths of the teaching faculty were teachers of color, and all five of the school's administrators—principal, director of operations, director of engagement, dean of students, and director of guidance—identified as Black or African American. A growing body of scholarship points to numerous benefits for youth of color being taught by educators from their own racial-ethnic groups.[30] While we are not aware of previous research that has considered how educators' racial-ethnic identity influences their students' critical consciousness development, the role that numerous MtRA teachers of color played in facilitating confessional narratives about racism within their classrooms suggests that such educators may be uniquely positioned to draw on this pedagogical tool in their work with youth of color.

CHALLENGES FOR MAKE THE ROAD ACADEMY

All of the powerful programming and practices at Make the Road Academy for fostering youths' social analysis skills did not mean this work was seamless. On the contrary, MtRA faculty and leaders encountered multiple challenges in their work to support their students' critical consciousness development. Because we believe these challenges can be as instructive to educators and other stakeholders as a school's successful programming and practices, we conclude this chapter—and each of the case-study chapters—with several examples of such challenges.

Novice Teachers

In *We Make the Road by Walking*, Paulo Freire explained that teaching for critical consciousness requires educators to possess expertise in their content areas but also to be sociologists who can engage students in discussing "exploitation, domination, freedom, democracy, and so on."[31] Put another way, engaging students in powerful learning about racial injustice requires both a deep understanding of this system of oppression as well as the pedagogical skills to incorporate this content into courses focused on biology, history, Spanish, and so on. MtRA faculty members—many of whom were in the beginning stages of their careers—sometimes lacked the deftness to put these two pieces together.

In one MtRA history course, for example, Mr. Roderick Parks—a White teacher in his mid-twenties—framed a lesson around the question: "If you knew you were getting mistreated because of your race, what would you do or say?" After allowing students to share several of their own experiences of racial discrimination, Mr. Parks explained that they were going to watch a short clip from the 2013 film *The Butler*, a biopic loosely based on the life of Eugene Allen, a Black man who had served as the White House butler for eight US presidents. Mr. Parks turned on the clip, which portrayed the protagonist as a young boy watching a White plantation owner shoot and kill his father. MtRA students in the class were understandably rattled by the unexpected violence.

"I don't want to watch that!" one student exclaimed.

"That's not fair," another said.

Mr. Parks turned off the film clip and acknowledged his students' distress. "Obviously, as you were watching this, it is upsetting. That was unnecessary, right? But this is what happened in the 1920s. Obviously today things are very different. So let's think about how we react."

"When someone gets shot?" one young man asked in astonishment.

"I am just saying, we all have a voice," Mr. Parks explained. "Use it. You can educate that person. It may not go anywhere, but you can try." He then played the class another clip from *The Butler* in which a Black character within the narrative was lynched and hung.

The students in this history course clearly regarded their teacher as an ally, but there was also a feeling of anxiety within the classroom. Mr. Parks had skillfully begun this lesson with a warm-up question that allowed students to share their own experiences with racial discrimination, but then students had not been primed for the second half of the class to contend with the emotions raised by watching such racial violence.

Moreover, students ultimately had little time to discuss and process what they had seen. After the second clip from *The Butler* came to an end, Mr. Parks looked at the clock and noted, "Okay, we only have about two minutes. So when you guys come back next class, Thursday, we will discuss what you saw." As a result, his students moved onto the next class in their school day without having had the opportunity to process or reflect on the distressing content they had observed.

If Mr. Parks's lesson focused on important content that needed to be introduced more sensitively, there were also lessons on racial injustice at MtRA in which the content itself seemed more questionable. In an English course, for example, Ms. Carla Dawes—an African American teacher in her early twenties—began a unit on race and America's criminal justice system by explaining to students that private corporations operated nearly 10 percent of the prisons in the United States. Drawing on content from Ava Duvernay's 2016 documentary *13th*, she introduced students to well-known companies that rely on inmate labor to produce their products as well as for-profit prison operators that lobby elected representatives to support laws increasing the inmate population. This opening portion of the lesson effectively engaged MtRA students in identifying systemic factors that contribute to racial injustice in the United States.

In contrast, the second portion of the lesson introduced students to more questionable content. Ms. Dawes asked her students: "What happens to our community when people go to prison?"

"We lose the population," one student volunteered.

"People may riot," volunteered another.

"Those people need to provide for their families," another student suggested.

Ms. Dawes picked up on this last point. "What can happen to their kids and their kids' kids?" She then introduced students to a text known as the "Willie Lynch Speech"—a speech purportedly delivered by a White slave owner named William Lynch in Virginia in 1712 that called for perpetuating slavery by controlling enslaved men and women psychologically and, specifically, by separating family members from one another. Ms. Dawes explained: "Willie Lynch says that when the men are sent away, the women will end up raising the children [to be like] the opposite sex. What are some ways a female could act like a man?"

"Fight?" one student suggested.

"They think they're more powerful," offered another.

Ms. Dawes nodded. "She's not going to stay home to cook. She's going to expect to be treated a certain way." She assumed a loud, exaggerated tone. "I can take care of my own. I don't need you. I can go to work all day long and come home and cook. I open my own doors. I got it." She resumed her normal voice. "Do we see women like that today? So was Willie Lynch's letter correct? Now let's think about the boys. Say Aja is raising her son to have the mentality of a female. What does that mean?"

A young woman volunteered, "He's dependent on his mom."

"Or other women," Ms. Dawes agreed. "He doesn't get his own place. He only moves in with women. He's submissive." Ms. Dawes paused, then continued. "When a woman says jump, he'll go 'How high?' because he is dependent on her. Now when these two people come together, how are they going to raise their children differently? There is going to be a lot of confusion. So similar to back then in slavery times, the cycle has continued. Women are still raising their daughters with the male mentality, not knowing how to be submissive. And women are raising their sons to be females mentality-wise. And these things are problems."

This portion of the lesson raised several red flags. First, the William Lynch letter that Ms. Dawes shared with her class has been identified by historians as a hoax.[32] Columbia University historian Jelani Cobb has written that the text of the speech itself contains numerous phrases that did not exist in the eighteenth century.[33] He further laments that the so-called speech has become a "quick-and-easy explanation" for contemporary disunity within the Black community while ignoring the fact that all racial and ethnic groups contend with internal conflict and divisiveness.

Ms. Dawes's lesson also presented outmoded and essentialist beliefs about gender roles and then characterized resistance to these roles as evidence of dysfunction within the African American community. Whereas Mr. Parks's lesson introduced students to important content with an insensitive instructional approach, Ms. Dawes had her students highly engaged in analysis of questionable content. Both of these lessons were the exception rather than the rule at Make the Road Academy, but they point to the challenge of a school such as MtRA asking novice teachers to introduce students to complex issues of oppression and injustice.

Oppression This, Whites That

Make the Road Academy's commitment to engaging students in lessons on race and racism across the curriculum also sometimes led to students feeling overwhelmed by their learning about racial injustice. Interestingly, students' demands for a respite from such lessons never came in classes such as Social Engagement or American Social Issues that they perceived to be explicitly focused on inequity and injustice but, rather, in courses where students felt as though the content on racism was being shoehorned into the curriculum.

In a ninth-grade English class, for example, Ms. Denette responded to a number of students not having completed their homework by reminding the class that their ancestors had risked their lives to learn to read and be educated. "Why are you always talking about that?" a young man demanded. "That's aggravating. You bring up slavery this."

"Oppression this, Whites that," another student interrupted.

"I just wish our ancestors could hear this discussion right now," Ms. Denette chastised her students. "You don't want to talk about race? When you all get in the real world, you're going to face it, and you're going to think back to these discussions we had. Because if you open your eyes and ears, oppression and racism are everywhere."

Another student raised his hand. "Y'all keep talking about slavery like we need to be prepared for slavery."

"Nobody ever said it wasn't important," the original protestor spoke up. "But if you talk about it twenty-four seven, we're going to stop listening."

"Yes," Ms. Denette told him, "We talk about oppression throughout all areas of the curriculum."

Another student picked up this thread. "We're learning about slavery constantly. Constantly! We know everything down to like everything because like everyday we come in and 'What's a stereotype? Give me a stereotype.' And like we should be against White people because of what they did. There are probably still White people like that, but we shouldn't learn to be racist."

In interviews, several MtRA students voiced similar critiques of what sometimes felt to them like the school's all-encompassing focus on racial injustice. As a ninth grader, for example, Alicia complained of the culture circles: "Every single unit we have to do this. Every single class! And it's just like, 'Oh my gosh.' And then it's always about discrimination or a stereotype, so it's like, 'Are we gonna do anything else?'" As a sophomore, her classmate Michael described more ambivalent feelings about MtRA's focus on racism:

> It's good to teach it, but I feel that they teach it way too much because there would be some days, like, we would be tired of hearing the same thing all day long because we can go to World History and hear it and then science is next and you'll hear it there too. So to hear it all day long, I don't feel like it's necessary . . . especially because it is depressing to hear about all of the obstacles that I'm gonna have to go through because I'm African American. But it's good to know because I wanna be prepared for it.

Michael's comment, in particular, suggests that underlying students' frustration and exasperation with MtRA's curriculum were insufficient feelings of political agency—students' belief in their ability to successfully navigate or challenge such injustices.[34] Put another way, MtRA students' feelings of frustration and inundation seemed to reach a boiling point when lessons on analyzing racial injustice outpaced lessons on coping with racial injustice.[35]

One of the earlier-described lessons from ninth-grade Social Engagement class *did* focus on challenging racial injustice by introducing students to the Black Panther Party's Ten-Point Plan for Self-Defense, and another lesson from twelfth-grade American Social Issues focused on navigating racial injustice at predominantly White institutions. Far more of the lessons at MtRA about racial injustice, however, focused on analytic strategies rather than coping strategies. Scholar Beverly Daniel Tatum has written, "Learning to recognize cultural and institutional racism without also learning strategies to respond to them is a prescription for despair."[36] Perhaps, then, the frustration expressed by MtRA students was not due to the school's emphasis on recognizing racism and racial injustice, but rather an under-emphasis on the skills and strategies necessary to navigate and challenge these inequities. The teaching of such skills and strategies is the focus of subsequent chapters.

GRADUATION: THE FOUNDERS

"Congratulations to the class of 2017!" Principal Naylor exclaimed from the podium at the front of the university auditorium that was hosting MtRA's graduation ceremony. The faculty, clad in caps and gowns, sat behind her on the stage. The guests of honor—the class of 2017—were seated in the front of the auditorium, with their friends and family members positioned behind them. A long central aisle divided the hall down the middle. MtRA's young men sat on one side of the aisle dressed in burgundy robes, and the young women dressed in white robes sat across the aisle from them.

Principal Naylor paused for a moment, choked up by the emotions of the day. "I told the seniors last year that only those who see the invisible can do the impossible. And they were our class that saw the invisible. They were with us when we didn't have a building or teachers, but they believed in our vision, and they signed on to be a part of our school."

Principal Naylor looked out at the class of 2017—MtRA's second graduating class—and then addressed the family members and friends seated behind them. "But what this class has taught me is that not only those who see the invisible can do the impossible, but we must also dare to be bold, dare to be our best, and dare to be the change. It was this class's daring spirit to be bold, to be daring, and to be the change that created school spirit at MtRA. They added our chants and songs. It's because of them that we have a championship sports program at our school. And it's because of this class's daring spirit to be bold, the best, and the change that they surpassed last year's class in receiving over four million dollars in grants and scholarships." Family and friends in the audience applauded enthusiastically.

A few moments later, MtRA's college counselor introduced the keynote speaker, Natalia Steeves. A successful accountant in her early thirties, Natalia had grown up in the city and been a first-generation college student. "I'm a little nervous being back in my hometown," she admitted to the class of 2017, after taking her place at the front of the room. "I speak nationally. I speak internationally. But I've never spoken here in this city. So I looked up Li'l Yachty and Designer. Everyone knows that those folks are really impactful to your generation, and we appreciate that." The audience chuckled. "So I'm part of the millennial generation," Natalia continued. "And I found out that your generation's name is the founders. You are the founders. You're going to solve problems, and you're going to be resolute, and build something better for us. The reason why society has named you that, the founders, is because prior generations have left you a mess. But we're trusting you, and we know that you have the skills and resolve to make it better for the rest of us." An hour later, with diplomas in hand, MtRA's class of 2017 stepped forward into the next chapter of their lives.

CHAPTER 3

Make Your Voice Heard

NOREEN THOMAS and Alanna Mahoney stood at the front of the Espiritu High School "Multi" looking out at 40 incoming ninth graders sitting pensively at round tables. Perhaps befitting a school in a historic New England industrial city, Espiritu High School was located in an old factory building with high ceilings and a large central space. "Multi"—short for multipurpose room—was the nickname for that large central space that served as Espiritu's cafeteria, auditorium, and gymnasium. With a student body of only 160 students, the entire school community could fit comfortably into this single room.

"Good morning, Espiritu High School!" Noreen started. "How is everyone doing today? I'm Noreen, one of your coprincipals. We go by first names here. I'm happy to welcome you to student orientation today."[1] She repeated this welcome message in Spanish, eliciting surprised smiles from the ninth graders, who hadn't expected fluent Spanish from a blonde-haired White woman. "I used to be a Spanish teacher before I was a principal," Noreen explained, "So I do speak Spanish in case you want to let your parents know that."

A number of students nodded their heads. Nearly two-thirds of the Espiritu High student body identified as Latinx, with another quarter identifying as African American. The majority of these students had at least one parent who had immigrated to the United States, primarily from

Colombia, Guatemala, El Salvador, the Dominican Republic, Haiti, and Cape Verde. And a substantial number of Espiritu students had immigrated themselves.

Next, Alanna—another White woman in her forties—stepped forward. "Good morning, everyone. I'm Alanna, your other coprincipal. The two of us, with some of your other teachers, helped to start this school twelve years ago today, which is wild!" She smiled. "You guys come from a really diverse group of schools from three different cities. And you're going to have time today to meet each other. And we also have some older students here today to orient you."

A few minutes later, Noreen and Alanna sent the students off to their advisories—groups of ten to twelve students and an Espiritu teacher, who would meet together every school day for the next four years. For today's orientation, each advisory group was joined by two or three upperclassmen.

In one advisory, Frankie Moore—a White man and veteran science teacher in his thirties—started things off by asking the three upperclassmen in attendance: "Juliana, Gabriella, Mario, what's advisory about?"

Mario took this one. "You'll have Frankie for advisory for all four years. He'll help you with any work, get you ready for college, keep track of your grades. He's like your go-to. Advisory is also like a family. You're going to create a bond."

Gabriella added: "You walk into Espiritu at 8:10 a.m. And what we have here is morning meeting. Everyone gets breakfast free. You sit at your advisory table, so you guys will get to know each other very well."

Frankie asked the upperclassmen a follow-up question. "What else should these guys know about the schedule?"

"Once morning meeting is over, you go to classes," Mario said. "On Monday, Wednesday, Friday you have all your core classes. And then on Tuesday and Thursday, you'll start with English, but then you have CIPs in the afternoon."

"A CIP is a community improvement project," Juliana explained. "So when I was a freshman, I went to a nursing home and hung out with old people. And they were cute and cool."

"And Wednesday afternoons we meet in advisory for long blocks," Gabriella added. "But sometimes we have Facing History assemblies where we discuss bullying, autism, the Sandy Hook shooting, stuff like that."

"Facing History is another CIP," Mario said. "It's a really great class because you have a say over what the issues are you want to bring forth to the Espiritu community." Juliana, Gabriella, and Mario went on to offer tips about the lunch lines, how to play sports for other high schools (since Espiritu didn't field any teams), exhibition night, how to earn senior privileges, and other nuggets of information they thought Espiritu's incoming freshmen should know.

ORIGIN STORY: REAL PROJECTS

A visitor to Espiritu High School might be excused for feeling that the school was *really* a not-for-profit social change organization crossed with a summer camp. Both of those influences were part of Espiritu's DNA.

In the mid-1980s, several elite independent schools partnered with the three struggling industrial cities in which they were located to establish a nonprofit summer program for teenagers from those cities. Influenced by scholar Ted Sizer's work on project-based learning and fostering habits of mind, the Espiritu summer program investigated a single topic each summer through activities, projects, field trips, and civic engagement. The program's teachers came from both the participating independent schools and city schools.

Coprincipal Alanna Mahoney served as director of the Espiritu summer program and observed participating youths' investment in doing "real projects." She recalled how one summer the older teens in the program focused on investigating the tobacco industry. They made a presentation about their research to the city council, and their efforts "got the billboards taken away from in front of housing projects that were promoting smoking Newports."

A number of other Espiritu High faculty members, including coprincipal Noreen Thomas, taught in the Espiritu summer program during those early years. History teacher Deborah Ivey explained:

We found that kids were so successful with that model, exploratory learning, with no books, hands-on with field trips and community connectedness, and then they'd go back to their schools, and we'd hear from their guidance counselors that they were failing their classes, talking back to teachers, and all this stuff. And we would remember them from the summer as the kid who got down in the sand and dug up sand to learn about the animals and water. So we couldn't figure out what the disconnect was.

Coprincipal Alanna Mahoney explained similarly that she felt so "frustrated seeing kids that were so engaged with us in the summer, and then we would see them during the year, and they're like, 'I'm dropping out.'"

When the state legislature passed a law in the late 1990s allowing not-for-profit organizations to apply to open their own public charter schools, Alanna, Noreen, Deborah, and several other educators got to work. Over two years, they developed a proposal for a new charter high school—Espiritu High School—that would engage risk-immersed youth in the same project-based learning and community involvement with which they'd had success over numerous summers. Most of these educators were still working full time as teachers at the independent schools and city schools that had originally collaborated to found the Espiritu summer program, and Alanna suspected that such diversity of experience caught the attention of the state department of education. The state approved their charter application, and Espiritu High School opened its doors to eighty-five ninth graders in the fall of 2002.

SCHOOLING FOR CRITICAL CONSCIOUSNESS: HABITS OF MIND

Teaching and learning at Espiritu High School were guided by the habits of mind approach championed by the Coalition of Essential Schools (CES). Established by Brown University scholar Ted Sizer in 1984, the Coalition of Essential Schools offers a set of ten "common principles" for powerful teaching and learning.[2] The first of these principles is that the purpose of school should be to foster young people's ability to use their

minds well. Emerging from this principle are a set of thinking dispositions—referred to as "habits of mind"—that schools and educators should
cultivate in their students.[3] At Espiritu High School, those habits of mind
included creativity, collaboration, community engagement, gratitude,
humility, integrity, organization, optimism, and self-advocacy.

Another CES common principle calls for students to *demonstrate* their
learning and habits of mind for peers, teachers, family members, and community members.[4] At Espiritu High School, for example, each semester
ended with an "Exhibition Night" (or "X-Night") that Espiritu student
Jada explained entailed "taking one of your best projects in a class. You
basically take it, make it better, and then present it at night to people from
[our city] . . . and they judge you on it." Her classmate Carla added: "We
do presentations every year, so it helps you get over your fear of presenting
in front of everyone, and it's really good."

Other CES principles call for educators to emphasize depth over breadth,
personalize learning for students to the extent possible, and take on multiple roles and responsibilities within the school community.[5] Finally, the
tenth common principle calls for schools to engage youth in "deliberately
and explicitly challenging all forms of inequity."[6] History teacher Deborah Ivey—a white woman in her thirties—explained that she and her colleagues worked to actualize this final principle at Espiritu High School by
making students "aware of social injustice and the power they have, even if
they feel powerless." As described in greater detail in this chapter, fostering
students' recognition of their own power—or political agency—represents
a key dimension of critical consciousness.

DEVELOPING CRITICAL CONSCIOUSNESS: POLITICAL AGENCY

Political agency refers to a person's belief in her ability to effect social or
political change within her community.[7] A robust body of research has
found that political agency is one of the strongest predictors of political
participation, political interest, and attention to current events.[8] Political
scientist Elizabeth Beaumont explains that there are a number of reasons

for these associations.[9] From a motivational perspective, when people believe in their ability to engage in effective political action, they are more likely to perceive politics as important and relevant to their lives. They are also less likely to see social problems such as racism or poverty as permanent and intractable, and more likely to see such problems as capable of being improved through civic and political processes. Finally, people with a strong sense of political agency are more likely to persevere in their civic and political activism, even in the face of difficult circumstances.

Perhaps not surprisingly, individuals from groups with societal power are more likely to have high levels of political agency. In the United States, individuals with the highest levels of political agency are, on average, wealthy, highly educated, White, male, and middle-aged.[10] Notably, the youth attending Espiritu High School and the other featured schools belonged to few or none of these identity categories. This doesn't mean that such youth do not or cannot possess high levels of political agency but, rather, that their families, schools, churches, and other formative influences must work deliberately and explicitly to counter broader societal messages about *who* has the power to influence political change.

Scholars have characterized political agency as one of the three key components of critical consciousness (see figure 3.1).[11] For this reason, the critical consciousness survey completed by youth attending the five high schools featured in this book and the four comparison high schools included a political agency scale.[12] On this scale, students expressed their agreement or disagreement along a five-point scale with statements such as "There are plenty of ways for youth like me to have a say in what our school or community does" and "My opinion is important because it could someday make a difference in my school or community." A score of "1" on this scale represented low feelings of political agency, and a score of "5" represented high feelings of political agency.

Figure 3.2 reveals that youth attending all five of the high schools featured in this book demonstrated growth, on average, in their feelings of political agency from the start of ninth grade (Time 1) to the end of twelfth grade (Time 5). Moreover, as they graduated from high school in the spring of 2017, the youth attending these five high schools demonstrated

FIGURE 3.1   Components of critical consciousness

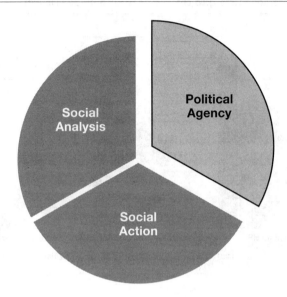

significantly higher levels of political agency than their peers at the four comparison high schools.[13] In other words, the young people attending the five schools featured in this book graduated from high school with a stronger belief in their ability to effect social or political change than their peers at several nearby high schools.

Importantly, Figure 3.2 also reveals that, on average, students at Espiritu High School began high school (Time 1) with weaker feelings of political agency than their peers across all five featured high schools but then demonstrated steeper growth in political agency over four years of high school than their peers across these five schools.[14] As a result, Espiritu students graduated from high school (Time 5) with higher feelings of political agency than their peers in both the featured and comparison schools.[15] In other words, the young people attending Espiritu High School demonstrated both the steepest growth and, ultimately, the highest levels of confidence in their ability to engage in consequential political action—one of the key components of critical consciousness.

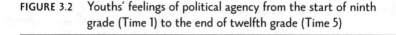

FIGURE 3.2   Youths' feelings of political agency from the start of ninth
grade (Time 1) to the end of twelfth grade (Time 5)

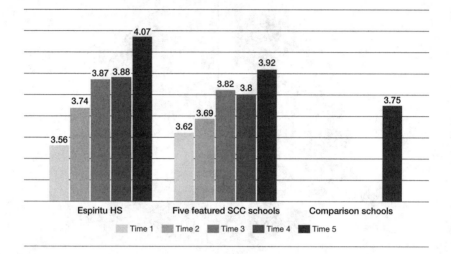

Developing Political Agency

Yearly interviews with twelve of the young people attending Espiritu High School offered a useful window into what such growth in youths' political agency looked like. For example, Espiritu student Carla expressed her belief that she and her classmates possessed the power to advocate for change within their school community: "At Espiritu, if multiple students disagree with something or they want to change something, we usually come together as like a class, and we could write like a paper or make a presentation or something that goes with our point on like what we want to change." She offered several examples ranging from the school's dress code to its technology policy that different Espiritu student groups had successfully changed through such efforts.

Carla's classmate Tiana explained that "the best experience of my life" was joining a group of Espiritu students and faculty attending the 2017 Women's March in Washington, DC, one day after the inauguration of President Donald Trump. Tiana added, "Now that I got to experience that, it's motivated me to do more, 'cause like now I know I can do something about it, even if it's just going to a protest." Finally, a third Espiritu student, Jada, explained that she had gotten involved with a youth advocacy organization, Young Voices, that held its meetings at Espiritu and sought to give teenagers across the state a genuine voice in deciding policy issues. In describing the impact of this experience upon her political agency, Jada explained that now she knows she can "send letters [to my state representative] 'cause I know they read those, and they listen to your calls if you call them. So like having the state representative know you're concerned." Each of these students' explanations revealed their belief that, even as young people, they possessed the ability to influence local, state, and national issues that were meaningful to them.

In terms of what the *development* of such political agency looked like over the course of high school, Espiritu student Adriana serves as a useful example for illustrating this development. Adriana described herself as a smart, responsible, and religious young woman with strong ties to the Dominican Republic, the country from which her parents had emigrated shortly before she was born. As a tenth grader, Adriana cited police violence against people of color as an injustice in her community that concerned her, and she proudly described her role in planning a protest at Espiritu after the 2014 police killing of African American teenager Michael Brown in Ferguson, Missouri. As Adriana explained, "We did a little mini-protest here. . . . I did part of the presentation. And when we walked in, we said, 'Hands up, don't shoot.' And so I was the one leading that. I was up there in front." In terms of the impact of this experience, Adriana added:

> A lot of people might feel like they can't do anything, but, in reality, you can do something. It might be just in your community, but it's better to do something locally than not to do nothing at all. Instead of just standing there, saying, they'll just eventually fix it. How could they eventually fix it if you're not doing something as well?

A year later, as an eleventh grader, Adriana again cited opportunities at her school as having strengthened her feelings of political agency. She explained, "I feel like usually teenagers feel like they can't really do much because they're so young . . . but there's so much opportunities out there."

As examples, Adriana cited both her participation in a recent mission trip through her church but also her work with Espiritu's community improvement projects:

> Like with our CIPs, you can see the poverty class going out and like make a difference [for] those who don't have jobs and like those who are homeless, and things like that. I was in the Facing History [CIP]. That also was a huge part in making change in inequalities because like we were teaching students how we should be thinking of the world instead of being so closed-minded about it.

Importantly, as a twelfth grader getting ready to finish high school, Adriana explained that her sense of agency had now propelled her to engage in social action beyond her school building. As she explained:

> My friends and I, like, whenever there's a march near us, we've been trying to go. And even if we don't know completely what it's about, [they] might as well have two other people to support it, make it bigger, and things like that. Like whenever I hear something like that, I want to join or make a little comment about it and this and that. Just to help with making a difference and making the movement, so honestly wherever I see I can put my voice in, I'm gonna put my voice in.

These descriptions from across her high school years reveal Adriana to exemplify history teacher Deborah Ivey's goal of her students becoming aware "of the power they have" to challenge racial and economic injustice.

KEY SCHOOLING PRACTICES FOR POLITICAL AGENCY

Research on *how* schools and other youth-serving organizations can foster young people's political agency points to three key pathways for such work.[16] The first pathway entails introducing youth to role models that demonstrate how people like them work to effect social and political change. Espiritu student Tiana's participation in the Women's March exposed her to such role models through both the march's featured speakers as well as the adults in her school who had prioritized traveling to

Washington, DC, to attend the event. A second pathway involves offering youth hands-on, guided experiences with political engagement and activism such as Espiritu student Jada's participation in the Young Voices youth advocacy group. Finally, the third pathway entails connecting and including youth in networks of supportive and politically engaged peers and community members. For Espiritu student Adriana, her church and school communities both represented such networks in that she felt surrounded by peers engaged in trying to make a difference in the world.

Over the remainder of this chapter, we seek to unpack the specific programming and practices at Espiritu High School that Tiana, Jada, Adriana, and their classmates credited with the development of their political agency. This important work did not happen piecemeal or by chance. Rather, Espiritu students benefitted from a deliberate sequence of learning experiences—guided by the CES habits of mind approach—that fostered both their belief in their own ability to effect change as well as the necessary skills and strategies to do so.

Community Improvement Projects

Tuesday and Thursday mornings at Espiritu High School featured students' regular academic courses, but the afternoons were reserved for community improvement projects. Espiritu students were required to participate in at least four semester-long projects prior to graduation, though most students completed their CIPs in their freshman and sophomore years, choosing among projects with names like Housing and Homelessness, the Poverty Project, Born to Run, Healthy Teens, Project Earth, Starting a Nonprofit, Diver-cities, Prisoner Pipeline, and Facing History. The focus of so many of these projects on racial and economic inequity resonated with the Coalition of Essential Schools' core principle of engaging youth in "challenging all forms of inequity."

The projects were led by Espiritu faculty and staff. This, too, resonated with the Coalition principle of "teachers as generalists" with multiple types of responsibilities within the school community. Coprincipal Noreen Thomas explained that, when hiring new faculty members, she emphasized that the school didn't view CIPs as extracurricular activities, enrichment experiences, or "extra" opportunities for students. Rather, participating in the CIPs "actually *is* the thing—one of the things—that's helping our students get this sort of understanding of their own power in the society we live in." Here, we offer glimpses into the workings of several of these CIPs.

Project Earth

History and economics teacher Benjamin Harris—a white man in his thirties—led the Project Earth CIP that engaged students in volunteering with organizations working on environmental issues. One Thursday afternoon, for example, two organizers from the Environmental Justice League came to talk to students in the Project Earth CIP and seek their help in raising awareness about an environmental issue playing out just down the street from the school. A local utilities company had spent years manufacturing natural gas at an industrial site just blocks from Espiritu High School, but, in the process, toxic chemicals had seeped into the land and air surrounding the site. The two organizers—Edgar and Maria—explained to Espiritu students both about the issue itself and their own work as organizers.

"When you think of environmentalists," Maria explained, "a lot of people think of rich White people driving around in their Priuses. But environmental justice is saying it's not just about trees and the birds, but it's about people living in communities that make them sick."

Edgar added: "And we know that a lot of times the communities impacted by these problems have less money, and also because of the history of our country, communities that have been most burdened by environmental problems are communities of color. And White communities have been less burdened by these environmental problems." These explanations highlighted for Espiritu students in the Project Earth CIP how racial and economic inequity intersect with issues of environmental justice.

Edgar and Maria went on to explain that a state law required companies to involve local community members in deciding how to remediate environmental issues *if* enough community members signed a petition indicating their concern. They had come to enlist Espiritu students' help in getting out the word about their online petition as well as a series of upcoming community meetings with the energy company. One student asked, "If no one had gotten involved, do you think the energy company would have left the [chemical] materials there?"

Edgar answered, "I think it would have dragged on for years and years and years. But when community residents get involved, it speeds up the process and creates accountability for companies who otherwise wouldn't have to tell anybody about it. So that's the role of you as leaders and organizers to make people feel like, yeah, this matters to me, it does impact my life."

Through this presentation, Espiritu students in the Project Earth CIP gained exposure to two young organizers, Edgar and Maria, who served as role models of individuals working to effect social and political change—one of the key pathways for fostering adolescents' political agency.[17] Importantly, Edgar and Maria also gave Espiritu students the opportunity to play a role themselves in challenging a utility company whose practices were harming their own community. This "real project" through which Espiritu students could demonstrate their learning about environmental injustice also resonated with the Coalition of Essential Schools' habits of mind approach.

Housing and Homelessness

Espiritu coprincipal Alanna Mahoney characterized the CIPs as helping students to develop the skills they would need to be successful in their independent service projects as eleventh and twelfth graders. One example of a CIP actively engaging students in such skill development was the Housing and Homelessness CIP taught by history teacher Agustín Montada, a Latinx man in his twenties. In describing this CIP, Agustín explained, "Every quarter we're looking at housing from a different perspective. In the first quarter we're looking at advocacy, so we're volunteering at the Housing for All Center; we're learning how to engage people that may not know about an issue. In the second quarter, we're looking more at issues of homelessness. And then in the second half of the year, we're going to look at food insecurity and evictions, so they're going to be visiting an eviction court."

To prepare students in this CIP for their volunteer work with Housing for All, an organizer came to brief the students on the organization's campaign to end winter heat shut-offs by utility companies on people behind on their bills. The organizer, Camilo, explained, "What organizing is, it's changing policy. It's rewarding work. [But] it can be challenging. We had a campaign to end child poverty because there was a lot of villainization of people in poverty. But we knew people were less likely to blame children. So we fought for protections for children under six. So little by little we try to organize groups of people. So right now we're trying to organize people with medical conditions, and we think they should be protected [from heat shut-offs]."

Agustín told his class, "We've already done some flyering. And the next step in learning how to be a community organizer is making some phone calls. And Camilo and I will design a training to help you get ready for it, and these skills are going to be valuable for you your whole life."

"We're going to practice making phone calls," Camilo explained, "so it makes it sincere and in your own words. It's going to take a little preparation, but I have total confidence you're going to do a great job. And then you'll help us reach a lot of people."

In reflecting back a few weeks later on his students' advocacy work with Housing for All, Agustín observed, "They were all nervous about phone banking [at first], and then they all loved it. 'Cause they loved the human component, talking to people and hearing people's stories. So I think they like being outside the classroom and like still being in their community. Like we're not taking them to a community that they don't know or they're not familiar with. You know, we're going back into their own communities, and they're seeing people they know . . . and going to places they might walk by on their way to school."

One of the Espiritu students participating in the Housing and Homelessness CIP, Nelson, explained that the highlight of the CIP for him was getting to participate in a state housing summit designed to share best practices for reducing homelessness. As Nelson explained, "The governor spoke, and a bunch of other important people from the state spoke about housing. . . . It was fun because everybody was like at least thirty or older, and I was the only kid at my table. So I had like five other grownups—an accountant, a banker, like real important people, and I was the only kid there. And they were asking me questions, trying to pick my brain, but I answered all of them, and they were all surprised."

Nelson's evident pride in possessing the skills and knowledge to hold his own at a tableful of adults did not happen by accident. In describing his goals for the CIP, Agustín noted that, because the CIPs are intended to prepare students to carry out more independent social action projects, "I designed my class to build in those components. So there's canvassing, there's phone banking, and problem-solving things where you use a problem tree . . . just to kind of help give them tools they can use." Through Agustín's explicit planning and partnerships with organizations such as Housing for All, Espiritu students in this CIP gained hands-on, guided experience with several of the core practices of organizing and activism. Such hands-on, guided experiences represent a second key pathway for fostering political agency and also resonate with the Coalition of Essential Schools' emphasis on giving youth opportunities to demonstrate their mastery of habits and skills.[18]

Starting a Nonprofit

This focus on building students' political agency and activist skill sets was also evident in the Starting a Nonprofit CIP. In describing this CIP, Espiritu student Adriana explained, "You learn about organizations in the world and how they try to help and make a difference in the world. Like how exactly do they work and what you need to do to start off a nonprofit." One key component of this CIP was field trips to local nonprofit agencies such as Avanzar Latino that offered support and resources for people marginalized by inequities in race, ethnicity, and language status. Espiritu student Isaiah explained of Avanzar Latino:

> They help everyone, provide a lot of free services. Like they do day care, and you could take classes there. My mom used to do it when I was younger, and like she used to take me to day care, and she used to take classes to learn English and math. But they also have like computer classes and stuff. So it really helps like Hispanics, or I think anyone, because these are things people need to know, and these are disadvantages they face because they

might not have learned English or might not have learned any math in the country they were born in.

Isaiah's description of visiting Avanzar Latino underscores the point made by Espiritu teacher Agustín that the CIPs were not engaging students in service or field trips into someone else's community but, rather, back into their own. Moreover, through these visits, Espiritu students had the opportunity to engage with activists and nonprofit leaders from their own communities. Such opportunities align with research that has found the most important role models for fostering youths' political agency are those with whom they can personally identify.[19] As political scientist Elizabeth Beaumont explains, opportunities to meet change makers from one's own community "make political efficacy feel like a genuine option and help us imagine undertaking similar activities."[20]

Importantly, the other focus of the Nonprofit CIP was developing in youth the tangible skills that go into running a not-for-profit organization. To do this, students in the CIP envisioned a nonprofit organization they might like to start one day and then learned how to develop materials and resources for that envisioned organization. These materials included a vision statement, budget, donation letter, grant proposal, two forms of marketing, and a press release for an event. Espiritu students developed these materials for organizations that they envisioned offering soccer programs for youth with special needs, support for domestic violence victims, and low-cost fruit and vegetables for families living in urban food deserts.

One of the skill-building lessons in this CIP focused on fundraising. For this lesson, a development officer from a nearby university came to speak to the students about his work. Then Lance Hutchins—an African American English teacher in his early thirties who led the Nonprofit CIP—used a donor letter from a local community center to walk his students through the various components of such a solicitation and assigned them to write their own. In this CIP as well, then, Espiritu students received guidance and practice in the tangible skills necessary for engaging in effective social change work, and, in accordance with Coalition of Essential Schools' principles, they produced products that demonstrated their mastery of these skills.

Looking back as a graduating senior on his high school experience, Espiritu student Luciano cited the Nonprofit CIP as one of his most powerful learning experiences. "That's like the most memorable," he explained, "because it's stuff that I learned like in real life. Like there's nonprofits out there helping people, and all that stuff caught my eye." Luciano's description of the Nonprofit CIP as "real life" may have been due primarily to opportunities to visit organizations such as Avanzar Latino. However, Luciano and other participants in this CIP also worked to develop a very real set of skills around visioning, budgeting, fundraising, and marketing. The development of such skills through guided, hands-on practice once again resonated with both the core principles of the Coalition of Essential Schools and the extant research on fostering youth political agency.[21]

Community Meeting

Another key lever at Espiritu High School for fostering students' political agency was community meeting. Once a month on Wednesday afternoons, the entire Espiritu High School community convened to learn about a topic selected and led by students. According to history teacher Agustín Montada:

> We've done ones on feminism, on Islamophobia, on micro-aggressions, and
> I like those because it facilitates a whole schoolwide conversation. So it's not
> limited to one teacher's classroom or an honors class. It's a more equitable
> way of talking about issues because if everyone is taking part, it's more democratic, and I think that shapes the whole school culture because it leaves
> the students to be the ones to preserve and protect the culture.

Giving students the responsibility for planning and leading these community meetings resonated with the Coalition of Essential Schools' core principles of modeling democratic practices, honoring diversity, and engaging youth in explicitly challenging all forms of inequity. These student-led community meetings also had important effects upon Espiritu students' feelings of political agency.

One of the most powerful examples of these community meetings came in response to the police killing of African American teenager Michael Brown in Ferguson, Missouri, in August of 2014. As the 2014–15 school year began, Espiritu faculty teaching tenth-grade U.S. History incorporated Brown's death and the ensuing protests in Ferguson into the course's opening unit on the civil rights movement.

A few months later, after a grand jury in St. Louis County decided not to prosecute the police officer who had shot and killed Michael Brown, Espiritu tenth graders decided they wanted to voice their concerns, so they requested the opportunity to lead the next all-school community meeting. Espiritu student Destiny explained:

> We had a "Justice for Mike Brown" [event], and it's not just him but everybody who's been killed over time. We did this whole school presentation from the sophomore class [where] we all gathered evidence and our opinions. And it was even from things back back back in the day like the 1940s, from Emmett Till and what happened with him, [to] Martin Luther King, Rosa Parks, Malcolm X. All of those cases came together and [also] the ones that just came up like Trayvon Martin, Michael Brown, Eric Garner, all those. And we put it into one presentation to show that us young children are watching the news, are actually paying attention to what is going on.

Another student, Britni, added: "They had people who made posters and T-shirts, and they walked out into the middle of the Multi in silence, and then they gave a presentation about what happened to Mike Brown, and we just talked to the school about it."

Destiny said of the students watching the presentation: "Everyone was there, everyone was participating, the crowd was participating. Everyone just cared."

Espiritu student Mario was an audience-member for this community meeting. He explained:

> We got to be able to, you know, have our own voice heard by the teachers and our fellow classmates. . . . It kind of gave me an opportunity to actually speak my mind 'cause, you know, I'm usually a bit timorous about things.

But when I finally got the opportunity to, I was finally able to say, "I don't like the way people are taking advantage of their power."

What all of these students' comments make clear is that, for students who participated as both organizers and audience members, this opportunity to teach, learn, dialogue, and protest racial injustice felt like an authentic means of expressing their voice and taking action.

A number of the Wednesday community meetings each year were planned and led by students from the Facing History CIP. History teacher Deborah Ivey, who led the Facing History CIP, explained: "It's absolutely 100 percent student-driven. Whatever we see in the community and want to address, that's what we do. So it's completely focused on whatever they're interested in." Accordingly, one of the Facing History presentations focused on Islamophobia—another form of racial-ethnic bias and discrimination.[22] For this presentation, Facing History students utilized video clips to illustrate the ways in which Muslims in the United States experience unjust stereotyping and racial discrimination. Espiritu student Britni was an audience member for this presentation. She explained: "They showed videos and pictures, and asked, 'What do you think about this person?' And like it showed how you might be stereotyping someone."

Espiritu student Destiny was one of the members of the Facing History CIP who led the Islamophobia presentation. In reflecting on this experience, she explained:

Islamophobia was probably the hardest topic I've ever taught. It was just teaching about how . . . terrorists are nowhere close to being Muslim. If you are a terrorist, you are not Muslim because Allah has nothing to do with violence. He wants nothing to do with violence. . . . So it was really a strong topic, and a lot of kids came up to me and my teacher and said that was amazing to learn about. Just seeing how different it was from what they grew up thinking.

While the process of developing and delivering a presentation on Islamophobia was unquestionably challenging, Destiny also had the powerful experience of hearing classmates tell her how much they had learned from the presentation. In this way, the opportunity for students to lead such presentations—and for other students to see their classmates in these roles—exerted a powerful influence on the political agency of the entire Espiritu student body. Such feelings of political agency represent a key dimension of critical consciousness that allows individuals to transform their ability to analyze oppressive social forces into meaningful social action challenging these forces.

Civics

The 1999 satirical high school film *Election* has a memorable scene that depicts a civics teacher played by actor Matthew Broderick teaching his students about the three branches of government period after period, day after day, year after year. In so doing, the scene takes up a long-standing critique of high school civics classes as a tedious recitation of facts about the three branches of government, how a bill becomes a law, and so on.[23]

Espiritu teacher Deborah Ivey *did* introduce eleventh graders in her civics course to the workings of government, but she also gave them the opportunity to put theory into action by advocating for a policy change within the Espiritu High School community. In explaining the goals of the course to students at the beginning of the school year, Deborah explained: "Later in the year, I'm going to give you the student handbook to see what changes you want to make. The current suspension policy came from suggestions that my civics class had [last year], and the faculty implemented. So you can have a big impact." With this assignment, Deborah simultaneously drew upon the Coalition of Essential Schools' push for students to demonstrate habits of mind such as community engagement and self-advocacy, as well as political science research that has found involving students in school governance to have a strong, positive effect upon their political agency.[24]

A few months later the civics students voted to work on changing the school's electronics policy. As Espiritu student Destiny explained: "The [existing] technology rule is that you can't have headphones, earphones, anything that is powered [unless] you ask a teacher, and you have to have a pass, and it has to be school-related." She then explained of her civics class's proposal: "We're trying to change it to you have your own [media] pass, and you don't have to ask to use any of your stuff. [But] if it's during class, you have to ask the teacher and be like, 'Can I use my media pass?'"

After developing these ideas informally, the civics classes worked for several weeks on writing a formal proposal, seeking out research to support their ideas, and putting together a presentation for Espiritu's administrators, faculty, and board of trustees.

In one class session, having completed a first draft of their PowerPoint presentation, students worked in groups to try to anticipate questions from Espiritu faculty and "fix the potholes" in the presentation. "I thought we said we could have headphones during lunch," one student explained.

"We can't do headphones during lunch," another student countered, "because lunch is supposed to be a social time."

"I think it would be too confusing too," a third student added.

The second student chimed in again: "I think the main thing is that we should say we don't want to change everything completely. We just want more freedom."

Meanwhile, another group of students debated whether students should wear their media passes on lanyards around their necks and, if so, whether students should have to pay for the lanyards. A third group discussed the logistics of how Espiritu administrators should keep track of students whose actions resulted in them losing their media pass privileges.

A few weeks later, the civics class made their pitch to the Espiritu faculty. Students took turns describing the proposed policy revisions, research in support of their proposal, consequences for students who didn't adhere to the new policy, and counterarguments they could anticipate and rebut. "In summary," a young man explained at the end of the twenty-minute presentation, "the technology policy is outdated and incorrect, particularly in regard to tablets. So the media pass allows the use of phones and headphones at certain times. There is no media pass at lunch because this is when we need to be more social and put away electronics. And it helps us prepare for college because in college you have more freedom to decide what you want to do." Espiritu faculty applauded, promised to consider the proposal seriously, and a week later sent a letter to the civics classes requesting answers to several additional questions:

Dear Civics Class:

First of all, congratulations on a very well-done presentation. It was a delight to see you so poised and comfortable delivering your information to the faculty. Thank you! We do find ourselves with a couple of questions which we're hoping you could respond to, largely concerning headphones.

Question 1: While you presented an article about the benefits of headphones, there are many others that indicate students achieved lower test scores with music. Did you do selective research?

Question 2: Why encourage/allow headphones before morning meeting, when this is a good time for students to socialize prior to the start of school?

Question 3: Why encourage/allow headphones usage from 3–4 PM, a time when many students are working on homework often, now, unproductively? Will this improve their efforts, or will time be spent searching for the perfect song?

Question 4: After reading several studies about the benefits of listening to music while working, most discuss classical music or music without words as the best to help people focus. Obviously we will have no way to regulate this, and our concern is that listening to music will be a distraction to people who are already often having difficulty focusing on their work.

In all honesty, you are quite convincing in your presentation, but we are sharing our concerns so that we can continue to think about this before we implement a policy that could change the educational environment we have worked hard to create at Espiritu High School.

Thanks for your efforts!

The Espiritu Faculty

"I think the faculty is in support," Deborah Ivey told her class after everyone had had a chance to read the letter, "but they want you to go another step. I have a lot of ideas, but I'd love to see you work through them. Who wants to look at which question?" The students divided themselves into four groups and got to work on written responses to each of the faculty's queries. Ultimately, Espiritu faculty voted at their next faculty meeting to adopt the class's new technology proposal for the remainder of the school year and, if successful, to make the change permanent in the Espiritu student handbook.

In reflecting on this experience, Espiritu student Jada explained, "I never really thought that schools, like, listened to changes. But Espiritu really listens to its students." Her classmate Carla added: "Being able to make change here, it does impact my future because I believe, like if I can make change within a small group, I can make change over a big group throughout a long period of time." Carla's words align closely with scholar Albert Bandura's explanation that educational practices "that imbue children with a sense of efficacy that they can play a part in influencing their situations are more likely to instill a belief that political systems are also responsive and influenceable."[25] Put another way, Espiritu High School's empowerment of students to change school policy increased the likelihood of these young people perceiving themselves capable of effecting change in the broader society as well. In this way, feelings of political agency serve as a bridge between the social analysis and social action components of critical consciousness.[26]

Senior Project

A final learning experience that contributed to Espiritu students' development of political agency was their senior project. In describing the senior project, Espiritu coprincipal Noreen Thomas explained: "It's totally wide open. They can investigate any issue they want, but there has to be a community connection." Espiritu history teacher Deborah Ivey added: "Then, through a series of steps, like a topic paper and research paper, meeting people in the communities and doing interviews, and working with organizations, they create some project that will address the topic." Importantly, numerous Espiritu students designed and carried out projects focused on supporting individuals and groups marginalized by inequities in race, ethnicity, and language status.

For example, Espiritu student Marco, who had immigrated to the United States as a middle schooler, decided for his senior project to develop a resource guide for teachers at Espiritu and other schools in the city for supporting English learners (ELs). He explained: "So my major goal was to make teachers aware of what is more effective on ELs because I'm an EL too. But I feel like some strategies that maybe the teachers don't know about would have helped me more. And I feel like if they were aware of it, they would do something about it." To carry out this project, Marco not only researched educational practices for supporting English learners but also surveyed English learners at Espiritu High School, soliciting their feedback about curriculum and practices that they had found both helpful and unhelpful. Marco compiled all of these different suggestions and resources into a presentation that he shared with Espiritu faculty, and he later adapted this presentation into testimony for a state congressional committee about the importance of protecting funding for English learners in the state education budget.

Espiritu student Tiana's senior paper and project also focused on immigration and education. Tiana wrote her senior research paper on parental involvement in their children's schooling and, in particular, the challenges facing parents who don't speak English. The topic came out of Tiana's recognition of her own parents' struggles as recent immigrants to navigate the public school system. For her senior project, Tiana explained:

> So right now I'm creating a brochure, a bilingual brochure, because [at] the schools in our cities, many, many of the students are minorities. So we were looking at their websites with my [faculty] coach, and they were out of date and some of them were only in English, and that's not helpful at all for parents if they're trying to figure out what's going on in their child's school, especially if they don't know what's going on because they can't read English. So we were thinking of working to create a brochure and have it in Spanish and English, and telling parents ways they can get involved.

Espiritu coprincipal Alanna Mahoney then recruited Tiana as well to testify before a state congressional committee about the importance of adequate funding levels for bilingual education and supporting youth who are first- and second-generation immigrants.

Finally, Espiritu student Isaiah explained that his senior research paper focused on issues of educational inequality for low-income students and students of color. What particularly caught Isaiah's attention as he researched this topic were issues of inequity and injustice in school discipline systems. He explained:

> If you're a minority, you're more likely to get in trouble. So if you're of darker complexion, then you're more likely to get in trouble and to get suspended. And once you're suspended, you're more likely to get suspended again, and that causes an effect. It causes a cycle, and it doesn't let a child leave or be successful in school because of the cycle that's going on around them, that's happening to them.

To combat such inequitable treatment of students of color at Espiritu, Isaiah and a classmate focused their senior project on developing a plan for incorporating restorative justice circles into the school's discipline system. Isaiah explained, "We think that suspending a student or giving a student detention doesn't help at all, and I think that the solution can be restorative justice and restorative circles. So me and my friend Henry, who is also doing a paper similar to mine, we're doing our project on restorative justice, and specifically like restorative circles in classrooms, and we want to bring it into the school so it's a form of discipline."

Isaiah and Henry worked to develop a multiyear plan for incorporating restorative justice circles into Espiritu's discipline system, presented their plan to faculty, and enlisted younger students to implement the plan for *their* senior projects in the coming year. In developing a plan that he personally would not be at Espiritu to see or benefit from, Isaiah explained, "If you just rush it, then teachers aren't gonna support it because they're just gonna see that they failed once, and they're just not gonna want to do it again. So we want to get them acclimated into the circles and restorative justice, so everyone is on the same page, and it becomes part of the Espiritu culture."

In describing the impact of their senior projects, Espiritu seniors tended to focus on both particular skills they had acquired as well as a heightened belief in their ability to carry out social change work. Espiritu student Tiana explained:

It's been hard, but I'm really glad they make us do this. I just think it made me a better student to not be afraid to go out there and contact all these different organizations, and of course some of them refused to work with me, but that's life. So I think that's a good lesson that things aren't always going to go the way you want them to.

Tiana's explanation revealed how her senior project had allowed her to make use of several habits of mind including organization, self-advocacy, and community engagement that she had developed over four years of high school. Other students such as Britni described their senior projects as offering newfound feelings of political agency regarding what they could accomplish:

The [projects] are basically focused on making change in your community where like it needs change, and that's important to see. They make sure you know that no matter how young you are, [or] who you are, you can make change. So that's important for you to know like as a person.

Finally, a third student, Isaiah, added that watching his entire class complete senior projects "makes it seem easier for me to try to help someone. . . . Seeing people around me do like these important things, it kinda says to myself that I could also do this, and I can do anything." Isaiah's words highlighted the powerful effect of Espiritu students carrying out their senior projects *together*. In so doing, these young people found themselves immersed for the final months of high school in a supportive and politically engaged network of young people all working intently to effect different kinds of social change—a context that Beaumont has characterized as a key pathway for fostering political agency.[27]

CHALLENGES FOR ESPIRITU HIGH SCHOOL

One of the few concerns faculty and students at Espiritu High School expressed about their school's habits of mind approach to fostering young people's political agency and critical consciousness was whether this approach could be sustained in the face of change. In the fall of 2015,

Espiritu's leaders made the decision to double the school's student body from 160 students to 350 students. To achieve this expansion, Espiritu began admitting 90 students into their freshman class rather than the traditional 40. These higher enrollment numbers allowed many more students to benefit from an Espiritu education and brought more resources into the school; however, the expansion also meant expanding Espiritu's building and hiring lots of new teachers.

Students in the class of 2017 were at the midpoint of their high school experience when "the expansion" began, and many believed that it had weakened Espiritu's identity as a caring, supportive, and politically engaged community. Espiritu student Carla explained:

> I feel like two years ago, when it was like every class was small, we used to like—seniors, freshman, sophomores, juniors—we all had this connection with each other, and we all knew each other and, like, if we heard about a march outside of school, we'd go up, and we'd talk about it, and we'd have signups. We'd make an effort for Espiritu to like go out in the community, but now since we're so big, like a lot of people don't like to go up there and encourage going to protests. Or we don't really do anything as much now because . . . now since we're so big we're like not as much of everyone's family.

In this explanation, Carla suggested that the expansion had altered her sense of the Espiritu student body as a supportive and politically engaged social network.[28] While it is easy to look back on the past with rose-colored glasses, a number of Espiritu faculty also expressed similar concerns about the expansion. One faculty member suggested that the community meeting presentations by Facing History and other student groups had not been as effective since the expansion. This faculty member observed:

> Before the expansion, kids were just on board with like Facing History. [A] presentation says we shouldn't do this, we're not doing it, immediately. People are called out. It was beautiful. With larger amounts of a new student population who aren't used to that type of culture, I think it's taken a little while to kind of build that back up. It's not quite there yet, and if you

talk to the seniors about it, they'll tell you about it. They'll be like, "Espiritu before was so much nicer. Everyone was on the same page!"

Even Espiritu's coprincipals acknowledged that the influx of new faculty members required thinking more deliberately about professional development that highlighted the school's practices for fostering students' political agency. As coprincipal Alanna Mahoney explained:

> The people we've hired are incredible, and they are doing it, and a lot of them don't even know, right, all the language and all the theory behind [what we're doing]. . . . One of the teachers just today, you know, kind of whoops, she said something like, "Oh, I didn't know that like a big purpose of CIPs was to get them ready for their senior projects." And you know your first response to someone . . . is just like, "Oh my God, how did you miss this?"

Espiritu High School's curriculum, programming, and practices were originally developed and honed for a tiny student body of just 160 youth that allowed the school to exemplify the Coalition of Essential Schools' principle that "teaching and learning should be personalized to the maximum feasible extent." However, doubling the student body meant that student-led community meetings had a less intimate feel and that students grouped together for a community improvement project might not all know each other from day one. Consequently, some of the powerful practices that Espiritu had always utilized to foster students' political agency may need to be adjusted in the coming years to account for the school's changing context.

Another changing context with which Espiritu High School had to contend was the broader educational landscape. As noted throughout this chapter, Espiritu High School's approach to teaching and learning was built on the Coalition of Essential Schools' emphasis on habits of mind, demonstrations of mastery, and commitments to democracy and equity. These principles were part of Espiritu's DNA. Yet, in March of 2017, as Espiritu seniors were finishing their senior projects and looking ahead to graduation, the Coalition of Essential Schools disbanded as an organization after thirty-three years of work—an acknowledgment that the education reform movement had, in many ways, left it behind. In its wake remained Espiritu High School and a number of other schools that embodied the CES principles and served as evidence of their power to serve students well. That said, one cannot help but wonder whether the end of the Coalition of Essential Schools points, in some way, to the challenge of Espiritu High School holding fast to its founding vision in the years ahead.

GRADUATION: GET PROXIMATE

"A special welcome to the family and friends of the graduates!" Espiritu coprincipal Alanna Mahoney began, after the forty-two students in the class of 2017 had processed into the multipurpose room and taken their seats on the stage across from their teachers. Their other coprincipal, Noreen Thomas, stood up from the piano where she had ushered in the graduates with a buoyant rendition of "Pomp and Circumstance" and joined them on the stage.

Alanna Mahoney continued: "We thank you for the high expectations you have had for these graduates and the sacrifices you have made so that they can pursue dreams that delight and, in many cases, surprise you." She turned to the class of 2017. "Be proud that you are an Espiritu graduate, and that you've already been significant change agents in the world! With forty-two students, you also hold the distinction of being our last small graduating class, and the last class to have your graduation here in the multipurpose room."

Alanna gave way to the class's elected student speaker, Alix, a young man with a bushy beard. "This ceremony marks the start of a new chapter for us all," Alix told his peers, "but it also signifies the end of an incredible journey. None of us was dealt a particularly easy hand in life, but we made the most out of every opportunity to learn, grow, and give back. One of the things that I admire the most about the impact we've had is how diverse our talents and passions are, and how we use them to improve the world around us. From fashion shows at Espiritu to education policy reform in the State House, we've engaged and improved our community in so many unique ways. We are the smallest class this school will see from this point on, but we're also a class of philosophers, linguists, scientists, athletes, activists, and difference makers."

The final speaker—elected by the class of 2017—was their science teacher, Frankie Moore. "As you heard a little bit from Alix," Frankie began, "the class of 2017 has spent four years getting close to the community. Their senior projects, the work that many of them gave well over a hundred hours to, make us all proud as educators. Our seniors have been working with nonprofits, raising money for groups, testifying in the State House, and transforming school culture by leading restorative circles for the underclassmen." Frankie paused, "To put this work in context, back in April, I had the privilege of attending a talk by Mr. Bryan Stevenson, who founded the Equal Justice Initiative in Alabama and works tirelessly for the rights of prisoners. To do this work, to bring justice to those who have been forgotten by society, Stevenson talks about the importance of being proximate. He says if we want to make changes in society, we have to get close to the problems. I love this message, and I see it at work in the class of 2017."

Finally, the two senior advisory teachers took over the podium for the presentation of diplomas. Before handing out each diploma, these educators took turns offering powerful and personal testimony of each senior's growth and development. "Isaiah did amazing work on his senior project," his advisor, Kieren, explained. "A major part of his year was spent on restorative circles. These circles are used to bring people together to force communication to solve conflict. Isaiah used this as a tool around Espiritu to facilitate open and honest discussion between students and teachers, and help to reestablish some of the Espiritu way. For that I will always be grateful." Next up was up Marco. "Marco's journey here tonight has been a great one for me to personally witness," the other senior advisor, Javier, started. "Marco came to the United States from El Salvador a bright student, but he barely spoke English when he arrived at the end of seventh grade. Who would think that a short five years later Marco would be speaking in front of policy makers at the State House? This year,

Marco took on a personally meaningful project studying English learners and their education, culminating with him advocating for guaranteed funds for English learners in our schools." The words—like the graduation ceremony and Espiritu itself—were intimate, personal, and focused on the influence that these young people had already made on the world they would inherit.

CHAPTER **4**

Lift as You Climb

"GOOD MORNING!" Dean Michelle Trotter greeted the ninety ninth graders seated at long tables in Harriet Tubman High School's immaculate gymnasium. A Black woman in her early thirties, Dean Trotter stood at mid-court and spoke into a cordless microphone. "Welcome to Day 2 of your ninth-grade induction." The ninth graders straightened up on their benches and looked expectantly in Dean Trotter's direction. All ninety students were youth of color, and most identified as Black or African American. Nearly 80 percent came from low-income households. They all wore navy-blue polo shirts, khaki pants or skirts, and black shoes.

A large projector dangling from the ceiling beamed an enormous PowerPoint slide high up on one wall of the gymnasium. The slide read "What's Your Game Plan?" and was illustrated by a diagram of a football play complete with Xs and Os.

"Yesterday," Dean Trotter continued, "we talked about the game of practice. Let's do a quick recap to make sure that's in your brains. What's the game?"

A ninth grader raised her hand. "The game is high school."

Dean Trotter nodded. "So you are now in the game, the game of high school. The better you play in high school, the better your opportunities will be in college and beyond. Do mistakes matter and why?"

Another ninth grader raised his hand. "Yes," he said. "It matters because you can't fix everything later."

"What is the result of a mistake in the game?" Dean Trotter asked him.

"That you won't get into a good college."

Dean Trotter nodded again. "Unfortunately, some of the mistakes you might make in high school have severe consequences that you have to face, that can't be fixed. Who are your opponents in this game? Who are we competing against?" This time no one raised a hand. Dean Trotter scanned the gymnasium, then answered her own question. "You're competing against students across the whole world. And who is keeping score?"

Several students raised their hands. "College admissions officers," a young woman volunteered.

"That's right," Dean Trotter told her. "And those people are keeping track to determine whether you've been doing well enough to be admitted."

Principal Frank Pierce joined Dean Trotter at mid-court and took over the microphone. A White man in his late thirties, Principal Pierce exuded the quiet intensity of the soccer coach he had been before moving into education. He explained that next the ninth graders would divide into smaller groups and rotate through three learning stations that offered strategies for success in the game of high school. One of the stations featured a video interview with a Tubman grad who had won the game of high school, gone to the University of Pennsylvania for college, and then found herself failing her freshman biology course. "But rather than deciding the game was too hard for her," Principal Pierce explained, "she took the mistakes she made and made a plan. She's trying to win the game of college so she can get whatever job she wants and have whatever life she wants." Students at that station would identify the steps she had taken to get herself back on track.

After Principal Pierce finished describing each of the learning stations, Dean Trotter reclaimed the microphone and guided the ninth graders through the closing ritual for meetings and assemblies that they had learned the day before. "Education is freedom!" she told the ninth graders.

"Education is freedom!" the ninth graders chorused in unison.

ORIGIN STORY: RIGOR AND SOCIAL JUSTICE

Even this short glimpse into the ninth-grade orientation at Harriet Tubman High School makes clear that the school was quite different in both approach and tone from either Make the Road Academy or Espiritu High School. While both of those schools were guided by progressive schooling traditions, Harriet Tubman High School was established in 2000 as part of a "no-excuses" movement that looked skeptically at both the academic rigor and permissive culture of many progressive schooling models.[1]

The founders of Harriet Tubman High School—a parochial school principal and philanthropist—described their school as built upon the twin pillars of academic rigor and social justice. Specifically, they had founded the school with the goal of offering a highly rigorous academic program that would defy the inequitable educational opportunities afforded too many low-income youth and youth of color in the United States. This dual focus on academic rigor and social justice would continue to define Harriet Tubman High School after the founders handed over the leadership of the school to Principal Frank Pierce and turned their attention to establishing a Harriet Tubman charter *network* that eventually grew to several dozen elementary, middle, and high schools.

From a critical consciousness standpoint, Tubman High School's focus on academic rigor and social justice meant that faculty and administrators explicitly messaged to students that working hard to close racial and economic opportunity gaps was a powerful lever through which they could challenge injustice. Tubman student Tynequa explained of this messaging:

> We talk about it as a whole community in morning [meetings] and whenever we're all together. . . . There's a comparison to the schools that they say have more funding and things like that to show that we actually are making a change between the way that White schools and lower poverished schools have the same education no matter where you are.

In this explanation, Tynequa referred to Principal Pierce's practice of sharing charts and graphs with his student body that showed Tubman students outscoring their peers in wealthy, White suburban communities on a variety of assessments such as the SATs and Advanced Placement exams.

Tubman student Melissa added that this information "makes me realize that what I've been doing, like, is for a reason. . . . You see that it actually makes a change, and it makes you motivated to continue. 'Cause like you're a part of that graph, a little part of it." Likewise, her classmate Allen explained:

> At Tubman we have some of the best statistics in like [test] scores, SAT scores. And those scores coming from predominantly Black or Latino students, I think that really sends a message that racial inequality is something that should not be a part of society because people of any race have the ability to succeed in life. Like we're proving that now.

In short, Tubman students such as Melissa and Allen had learned at Tubman High School to view academic achievement as a lever through which they could challenge racial inequity and dispel pernicious stereotypes about the capabilities of people of color. Another Tubman student, Selena, described this achievement-for-racial-justice approach as "the whole basis of Tubman. Like trying to ensure we all succeed, and we prove all those stereotypes and those statistics wrong."

SCHOOLING FOR CRITICAL CONSCIOUSNESS: NO EXCUSES

Harriet Tubman High School pursued its goals around academic rigor and social justice via a no-excuses schooling model. No-excuses schooling describes an approach to education that seeks to eliminate opportunity gaps facing youth from oppressed racial and economic groups through an intensive college preparatory mission, extended school day and year, strict disciplinary environment, intensive focus on traditional mathematics and literacy skills, and reliance on direct instruction.[2] The term *no excuses* refers to the commitment of educators in such schools not to accept social forces such as poverty or racism as reasons for lowering expectations for what their students can achieve.

Approximately 10 percent of the 6,500 charter schools in the United States follow a no-excuses model.[3] Proponents of this schooling model point to research that has found, on average, youth attending no-excuses charter schools demonstrate "large and meaningful gains" in their literacy and mathematics achievement in comparison to peers at both traditional public schools as well as other types of charter schools.[4] Other scholars have found that youth attending no-excuses schools are up to four times more likely to graduate from college than peers attending other types of schools.[5]

However, critics of no-excuses schools argue that their strict disciplinary conditions and insistence on compliance deprive youth of voice and agency during critical years for the development of such qualities.[6] For example, scholar Joanne Golann reported that youth attending a no-excuses middle school were "taught to monitor themselves, hold back their opinions, and defer to authority rather than take initiative, assert themselves, and interact with ease with their teachers."[7] Still other scholars have criticized no-excuses schools—with their emphasis on direct instruction and hierarchical teacher-student relationships—for embracing the "banking" model of education that Paulo Freire characterized as teaching students to adapt to oppressive conditions rather than challenge them.[8] For all of these reasons, a number of scholars have characterized the no-excuses model as wholly incompatible with critical consciousness development.[9]

DEVELOPING CRITICAL CONSCIOUSNESS: SOCIAL ACTION NAVIGATING INJUSTICE

Harriet Tubman High School's approach to fostering youth critical consciousness also differed substantially from that of the other four schools featured in this book. Whereas the other four schools had developed explicit programming to strengthen students' social analysis skills, feelings of political agency, and commitment to *collective* social action, Harriet Tubman

High School focused on cultivating the academic and navigational skills their students needed to achieve personal success within what scholar Luis Urrieta refers to as Whitestream settings. According to Urrieta, the term *Whitestream* refers to the idea that the vast majority of American institutions and spaces are "principally and fundamentally structured on the basis of the Anglo-European White experience."[10] For people of color to be able to "navigate" such institutions and spaces entails circumventing the obstacles presented by White supremacy and racism.

The development of such navigational skills is crucial to the ability of youth of color to survive, quite literally, in Whitestream communities and spaces. In her study of Black parents' childrearing practices, scholar Raygine DiAquoi reported that Black parents and families have long engaged in teaching their children "survival skills" to navigate life in a racist American society.[11] For many such parents, their "first hope" is that their children will be "able to navigate a racist society successfully and avoid threats to their lives."[12]

Tubman High School science teacher Ms. Rashida Parker—a Black woman in her mid-thirties—spoke similarly of survival in making the case for the school's emphasis on navigational practices. Specifically, Ms. Parker explained, "I think we've always wanted to create the Martin Luther King Juniors of the world and to create the people who can bring about these [societal] changes, but the reality is . . . we want our students to, first of all, be alive so that they can do that work."

Consequently, at Harriet Tubman High School, cultivating youths' ability to navigate Whitestream settings was positioned as both a necessary precursor to engagement in future social change efforts, as well as a form of personal social action in and of itself (see figure 4.1). According to scholars Rod Watts and Carlos Hipolito-Delgado, personal social action—which is distinct from collective forms of social action—refers to the actions of a single individual to resist or challenge injustice.[13] As described in this chapter's opening pages, students and faculty at Tubman High School characterized the academic achievement of Tubman students as a form of personal social action that pushed back against societal stereotypes about their capabilities.

FIGURE 4.1   Components of critical consciousness

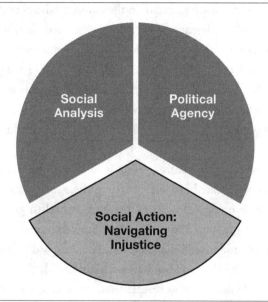

Additionally, the emphasis within no-excuses schools on traditional academic skills and an intensive college preparatory mission came out of a belief that such preparation would allow youth of color to access and acquire power within Whitestream settings that could ultimately weaken more systemic forms of racial injustice as well. In short, then, Harriet Tubman High School's founders and faculty members believed that teaching youth of color how to "play the game" in Whitestream settings was a pragmatic and powerful approach to effecting social change.[14]

Because Tubman High School positioned learning to "work from within" Whitestream settings as a form of personal social action, the critical consciousness survey completed by youth attending the five high schools featured in this book and the four comparison high schools included a Social Intelligence Scale that assessed students' confidence about their ability to navigate various social situations effectively.[15] Scholars have found social intelligence to be a key predictor of both academic and professional success.[16] Other researchers have reported that youth activists demonstrate higher levels of social intelligence than their nonactivist peers.[17]

On this Social Intelligence Scale, youth expressed their agreement or disagreement along a five-point scale with statements such as "In most social situations, I talk and behave the right way" and "I am good at getting along with all sorts of people." A score of "1" on this scale indicated low confidence in one's ability to navigate a variety of situations and settings, while a score of "5" on this scale indicated high confidence in these abilities.

Figure 4.2 reveals that youth attending all five of the schools featured in this book demonstrated modest growth in their social intelligence from the start of ninth grade (Time 1) to the end of twelfth grade (Time 5). However, as they graduated from high school in the spring of 2017, these young people's confidence in their social intelligence was no different than their peers attending the four comparison high schools.[18]

Importantly, figure 4.2 also reveals that, on average, youth attending Harriet Tubman High School began high school with weaker confidence in their social intelligence than their peers across the five schools featured

FIGURE 4.2   Youths' confidence in their social intelligence from the start of ninth grade (Time 1) to the end of twelfth grade (Time 5)

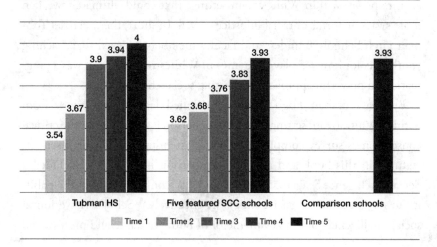

in this book but then demonstrated significantly steeper growth on this Social Intelligence Scale over four years of high school than their peers across these five schools. Consequently, Tubman students concluded high school with significantly higher confidence in their social intelligence than their peers across the five featured high schools and four comparison high schools.[19] In other words, the young people attending Harriet Tubman High School graduated from high school with the strongest confidence in their ability to interact effectively with a diverse range of people and to adapt their behavior to a range of situations and settings. Tubman High School positioned such navigational skills as a key ingredient to achieving personal success and, in so doing, to challenging pernicious racial biases and stereotypes. In this way, Tubman High School faculty and students regarded their efforts as a form of personal social action that represents a key component of critical consciousness.

Developing Social Intelligence

Tubman student Julian offers a useful example of what such growth in social intelligence looked like over four years of high school. As a ninth grader, Julian explained: "I'm, like, passionate to learn about my history [as an African American], but I'm also passionate to learn about other people's history because, like, [then] I understand people more. Like, I understand how different people work because I know their background, or I can understand some of the things that they went through in their background." Here, Julian expressed his belief that greater exposure to the histories of people from other racial and ethnic groups would facilitate his ability to interact with such people.

Three years later as a twelfth grader, Julian explained that Tubman High School had taught him how to deploy different vocabulary and language patterns in different settings:

> We learn a lot of stuff to make us, like, use our vocabulary and things like that. It's kind of like a turn-on, turn-off effect. Like I can turn it on when I want to 'cause I have that vocabulary. Like I have that way that I articulate my words and get my point across because I write, like, in a certain way, and

I speak in a certain way because of the school I go to. But then like my home language is different than my school language. Like, so I think it's just like more of a time and place thing, where . . . you have to know when to use your language and know when to use certain things, or say certain things.

Here, Julian explicitly credited Tubman High School with strengthening his ability to identify and deploy the particular codes and interaction styles relevant to particular situations and settings. Scholars have offered a number of different terms to refer to these abilities including *code switching*, *border crossing*, and *cultural straddling*.[20] In the remainder of this chapter, we describe the specific programming and practices through which Tubman High School faculty and leaders sought to equip their students with such navigational skills. It bears repeating that these educators conceptualized such navigational skills as crucial to their students' ability to excel in Whitestream academic and professional settings and, in so doing, to weaken interpersonal and systemic forms of racism.

KEY SCHOOLING PRACTICES FOR NAVIGATING RACIAL INJUSTICE

Tubman High School's programming included two different approaches to fostering students' ability to navigate Whitestream settings. One approach introduced youth to *conventional* navigation practices for surviving and succeeding in such settings while the other approach introduced students to *critical* navigation practices.

Youth of color engage in conventional navigation practices when their primary goal is to "survive and succeed" in the face of racism and White supremacy, but they hold a limited understanding of the systems of oppression with which they are contending.[21] Consequently, these youths' efforts to strive for success may be hampered by feelings of isolation and self-blame when they encounter obstacles due to these social forces.[22]

Youth engaging in critical navigation practices are also seeking to "survive and succeed" in the face of racism and racial inequity; however, these youths' actions are informed by their recognition of how social, political, and economic forces contribute to racial oppression.[23] Such recognition contributes to youths' resilience, self-esteem, academic achievement, career aspirations, and political engagement by replacing feelings of hopelessness and culpability for obstacles they encounter with a sense of engagement in a broader collective struggle for social justice.[24]

Several elements of Tubman High School's core (i.e., required) programming introduced students to conventional navigation practices for surviving and succeeding within an oppressive social system, and then several elective courses engaged students in learning to critically navigate racial oppression as well. Cumulatively, both sets of programming played important roles in equipping Tubman students to navigate Whitestream settings in which racism and White supremacy remain persistent and pervasive.

Learning Conventional Navigation

Here, we describe several of the core learning experiences at Tubman High School that focused on conventional navigation of racism and racial inequity. These learning experiences included college-readiness class, senior science research projects, corporate internships, and students' core academic courses.

College Readiness

One of the key features of no-excuses schooling models is an intensive college preparatory focus. Accordingly, all Tubman students participated in a weekly college-readiness course during their junior and senior years of high school—taught by the school's college counselors—that prepared them in multiple ways to navigate both the college admissions process and the college experience itself. As part of this programming, Tubman's college-readiness team invited recent alumni back to the school each year to share insights from their first year of college with Tubman upperclassmen.

While alumni participating in these panels spoke about topics ranging from managing their time to the pros and cons of pledging a sorority, they also shared experiences with racism. Tubman student Stephon explained:

We had alumni day, and the alumni was telling us that she had a racist roommate and she, the roommate, used to throw [out] her clothes and stuff, and, like, just say rude stuff to her. And she said she wanted to leave and everything, but like she said the thing is, she got here so far, she wasn't just going to let someone just stop her 'cause of the way she looked. So she's still in that college, and she moved out of that dorm.

Another student, Maria explained:

Alumni day, they was talking about how they go to schools that's like mainly White, and like how to deal with it is just like, they said to just ignore it, and just do what you have to do. And once you get to the top, then they'll notice you more, and then they'll start to respect you more. So I guess you just have to ignore it.

Both of these descriptions revealed Tubman alumni counseling their younger peers on how to "survive and succeed' in college by ignoring, avoiding, and drawing motivation from experiences of racism.[25]

Numerous Tubman students characterized these alumni panels as enlightening and useful in preparing for their own college experience. For example, Diamond explained, "They tell us what's gonna happen and then by telling us that, that's preparing us. . . . And then we're just like, 'Okay, if this happens, I can deal with this accordingly.'" Diamond and other Tubman students' feelings of preparedness for such experiences suggest that youth of color attending many other high schools would benefit from similar programming on navigating encounters with racism at college. Such programming can be characterized as fostering Tubman students' conventional navigation skills because it offered pragmatic suggestions for responding to racial discrimination but did not engage Tubman students in discussion or reflection upon the systems within a predominantly White university that allow such discriminatory practices to persist.

Senior Science Research Projects
Bringing alumni back to campus was one lever for preparing Tubman students to navigate predominantly White university settings. Another

was sending Tubman students out to such universities. Principal Pierce initiated the senior science research program when he learned that only 6 percent of his alumni were majoring in the sciences—a percentage he thought was shockingly low, and which prompted reflection upon ways in which his school might be failing to effectively prepare its students. Through partnerships with several local universities, Principal Pierce arranged for the majority of Tubman seniors to spend every Friday of their final semester of high school as research assistants in university research labs focused on physics, astronomy, molecular biology, botany, neuroscience, and psychology.

Tubman student Julian ended up completing his research project in a neuroscience lab testing the motor responses of males and females over time. He explained that he chose this project because "I want to study psychology [in college], and I kind of wanted to get that insight into the brain and how it works, and like why we make the decisions we make, and how our body works."

In the final weeks of their senior year, Tubman students developed academic poster presentations for their respective research projects and shared their results during a poster session in the Tubman gymnasium attended by both university faculty and Tubman underclassmen. Research projects ranged from "The Role of African American Exemplars in Stigma and Collective Self-Esteem" to "Antibacterial Effects of Turmeric" to the "Neurobiological Basis of Cellular Development in the Central Nervous System in Genetically Designed Mice." The posters themselves looked as professional as those developed by graduate students in these fields, and the Tubman students manning their posters spoke knowledgeably and confidently about the projects in which they had engaged. In reflecting on these projects' effects, Principal Pierce said of his students: "Once they got into the labs and started working with graduate students, most of whom were of color, a lot of them were immigrant students or foreign students. Like once they saw it wasn't just White men in the lab, they were like, 'Oh, this is not terrible!'"

Through these senior science research projects, Harriet Tubman High School sought to foster students' recognition that they belonged and could succeed in such Whitestream academic spaces as well as to gain valuable experiences in actually doing so. Such a practice aligns both with the intensive college preparatory mission of no-excuses schooling as well as scholarship on "role theory" that has found individuals are more likely to adopt an identity such as scientist when they have opportunities to participate in activities that are typical for people in the role.[26] In fact, Tubman High School saw an impressive five-fold increase in the percentage of alumni majoring in the sciences following initiation of the senior science research projects.

Such a sharp increase in Tubman graduates majoring in science suggests the senior science projects achieved the goal of increasing students' comfortability in postsecondary science courses and research spaces. Moreover, the presence of Black and Latinx youth in those academic and research spaces served to challenge the assumptions of other university students and faculty members in those spaces about *who* studies science. When several local media outlets reported on the success of Tubman's senior science research projects, the efforts of Tubman students presented a counter narrative about the interests and abilities of Black and Latinx youth to an even wider audience. In these ways, the senior science research projects seemed to exemplify Tubman High School's characterization of students' individual achievements as a mechanism for challenging racial injustice.

Importantly, the senior science research projects were similar to the college-readiness alumni panels in that they, too, can be characterized as fostering students' conventional navigation skills. In other words, these science projects offered students an opportunity to take on a role—scientist—that they might previously have believed was not meant for them, but Tubman teachers did not formally engage students in discussion about why such racialized stereotypes about scientists exist.[27]

Corporate Internships

An extended school day and school year are also key features of no-excuses schools that educators in these schools believe are necessary to eliminate opportunity gaps between their students and youth from privileged racial and economic groups. Tubman High School utilized its extended school day and year, in part, to foster students' ability to navigate Whitestream professional and corporate spaces. Specifically, Dean Trotter described Tubman High School's emphasis on "getting kids into summer programs . . . putting them in lots of different settings, and getting them internships [because] it's exposing them to these situations." Likewise, Tubman student Julian explained: "We have to do things that other high school [students] won't usually have to do. Like we have to do two summer programs before we graduate. So it's like we have to get out of our comfort zone in order to adjust to the world." Support for this perspective comes from research that a key lever for fostering young people's confidence in their ability to succeed in a particular setting is through guided, hands-on experiences in that setting.[28]

Tubman student Tynequa offered one of the most powerful descriptions of the value of these internship experiences. As a ninth grader, Tynequa explained that the school is "trying to like shape us so that we're not like the little sore thumb in a crowd of people, and we're comfortable with it. When we go in there, [we're] like, 'Yeah, I'm Black, African American,' it's not like *(nervous voice)*, 'Oh yeah, I'm African American. I'm Hispanic.' You're just African American. It's okay." She added: "So I guess just going to places that are like majority White or majority this and majority that is good for me."

As a twelfth grader three years later, Tynequa described how much she and twenty of her classmates had gotten out of a paid internship during her last two years of high school at a prominent technology company located in the same city as Tubman High School. Tynequa explained that she had been assigned to work on the company's financial analytics team and, as a result, was getting to learn "Java, HTML, CSS+, things like that. And I love it." In addition to learning coding, Tynequa added that, "It gives me experience in working in an office because I know how they operate now. I feel like I'm an insider or something now, and it's really cool."

For Tynequa and nearly two dozen classmates, internships at this technology company offered professional experience for their resume, the development of valuable computer programming skills, and the opportunity to feel like an "insider" in a corporate setting. In all of these ways, Tubman's partnership with this technology company served to foster students' confidence, experience, and ability to navigate a high-powered, Whitestream corporate setting. And, similar to the senior science research projects, the presence of these young people of color in a technology company served to counter pernicious but widespread racial stereotypes about who possesses the intellectual capabilities to do computer science. In this way, the internships of Tubman students—as well as the decision of students like Tynequa to major in computer science in college—represent "an act of insurgency in its own right."[29]

Tubman students' corporate internships also resembled the senior science research projects in that they, too, could be characterized as fostering students' conventional navigation skills. These internships offered students hands-on practice at working in a Whitestream setting where they were among the few Black or Latinx employees, but the internship experience did not include explicit discussion or reflection upon the social forces underlying such racial disparities in the technology industry.

Core Academic Courses

Finally, Tubman's focus on conventional navigation practices was evident in core academic subjects as well. In these classes, even when texts raising issues of race and racism were introduced, instruction often focused more on honing the academic and rhetorical skills that students would need for navigating college and professional settings than on analyzing the themes about race and racism raised in the texts themselves. In one of Tubman's English courses, for example, Mr. Alex Landry—a White man in his forties—guided his students' discussion of "Black Men and Public Spaces"—a powerful essay by journalist Brent Staples about the strategies he employs during late-night walks through his city to avoid appearing threatening to White passersby and police officers. "What was our main idea for this essay?" Mr. Landry asked.

One young woman volunteered, "Stereotypes can cause harm for innocent victims."

"I'm writing that down," Mr. Landry told her. "Then I'm putting a semicolon here to add to the main idea. And I want to go stronger than 'to cause harm.'"

The same young woman tried again. "They can become dangerous."

"Good," Mr. Landry responded, "What about the cowbell reference?"

A student waved her hand. "I thought the cowbell was like a warning signal because I looked at the paragraph. He compared bear country to White society and the cowbell to his whistling Vivaldi that he's coming."

"I'm going to switch you to more AP language," Mr. Landry told her. "The word is *analogous*. In the same way he whistles to calm the society who think he's a criminal, a hiker uses a cow bell to warn the bears he is coming. Now let's go back to the paragraph structure. What was going on prior to that sentence?"

The students looked back down at the text, and then a young man offered, "He is writing about how no mugger would be whistling Vivaldi's 'Four Seasons.'"

Mr. Landry nodded. "What is Staples's ultimate message that he says is happening at the end of this?"

"I think he's saying despite all his actions, danger still exists," another young man asserted.

A classmate offered a different perspective: "I thought he was saying that there are dangers, but he is lessening them and changing them. He is changing himself to be more accepted by the society."

"Great!" Mr. Landry said enthusiastically. "We have an argument here, which we love. So let's capture our two arguments." He jotted down both students' perspectives on the whiteboard and then shifted the discussion back toward the essay's diction related to music.

Like many lessons at Harriet Tubman High School and other no-excuses schools, this lesson was an academically rigorous one that offered students terrific practice in traditional literacy skills such as close reading. Moreover, the text itself introduced students to one Black man's strategies for navigating the danger that White people's biases posed to him on late-night walks through his city. Accordingly, lessons like this one both strengthened

Tubman students' academic skills and contributed to their growing understanding of how to "survive and succeed" in Whitestream settings.[30] Yet, this lesson too can be characterized as one focused on conventional navigation of racism because the lesson focused narrowly on Staples's practice of "whistling Vivaldi" to put White passersby at ease and did not take up the interpersonal and systemic racism that rendered such navigational strategies necessary. In fact, when several students began to debate the ultimate point Staples was trying to make about racism, Mr. Landry enthusiastically affirmed their thinking but also immediately tacked away to a new topic. For him, the goal of the lesson wasn't to interrogate the systems of oppression motivating the essay.

Learning Critical Navigation

Each of the schooling practices we have described in this chapter contributed to Tubman students' ability to engage in conventional navigation of Whitestream settings and spaces. In each of these learning experiences, however, educators made decisions *not* to incorporate discussion or reflection on the oppressive social forces necessitating such navigational practices. Importantly, several of Tubman High School's elective courses *did* take up such opportunities for discussion and reflection to engage students in learning to critically navigate racial oppression. Two important examples of such coursework were Community Engaged Theater and African American Literature.

Community Engaged Theater

A key feature of no-excuses schooling is an intensive focus on core academic skills such as literacy and mathematics. In fact, it is not unusual in no-excuses schools for students to take two English/Language Arts courses and two mathematics courses each day at the expense of other content areas. Accordingly, theater was the only coursework in the arts offered at Harriet Tubman High School. Ninth and tenth graders were required to take Theater I and II, and then upperclassmen could select additional theater courses as electives. The school's decision to focus its arts offerings solely on theater emerged, in large part, out of a belief in theater's ability to foster useful navigational skills such as presence, public speaking, and self-confidence.

The head of Tubman's Theater program, Ms. Kara Calderón—a Latinx woman in her early thirties—acknowledged theater's potential to build students' public speaking skills and self-confidence, but she also believed in theater's ability to "empower the young voice" and develop students' "self-awareness" of how they are viewed by others. Toward this end, Ms. Calderón offered a Community Engaged Theater elective for Tubman upperclassmen that introduced Theater of the Oppressed as a powerful practice for learning to critically navigate oppressive situations and settings.

Ms. Calderón began the unit on Theater of the Oppressed by describing Augusto Boal to her students. Boal, a Brazilian playwright and friend of Paulo Freire, became interested in the ability of theater to portray and influence social conditions in his country. "Ultimately, he created Theater of the Oppressed, or T.O.," Ms. Calderón explained to her students. "T.O. relies on presentations of short scenes that represent problems of a given community such as gender or racial stereotyping. Audience members actually interact by replacing the characters in the scene and by improvising new solutions to the problems being represented."

Ms. Calderón explained that Boal sought to turn the spectators into "spect-actors." She added, "In Theater of the Oppressed, if you see a sign of oppression and you want to play the person to make the change in that oppression, you jump in and improvise the character to play what you think they should do to no longer allow themselves to be oppressed. You take control over what is oppressive in the scene. And then ultimately the goal is to go out into the world and act on those suggestions." Boal characterized Theater of the Oppressed as "rehearsal for revolution."[31]

At the end of this introductory lesson, Ms. Calderón told her students, "For homework, I've asked you to identify a personal story of oppression that you're willing to share." One of Ms. Calderón's students, Allen, explained of subsequent class sessions within the unit: "We split the whole class into three groups, and each group put on a scene about what they collaboratively came up with for what their significant oppression would be. One group did racial profiling, the other did body shaming. And my group did misogyny within the business workforce."

Over the course of several weeks, the theater students worked in their groups to develop and workshop scenes portraying their personal stories of oppression, and then they performed these scenes for the entire Tubman community. True to the tenets of Theater of the Oppressed, youth in the audience had the opportunity to enter into each scene. As Ms. Calderón explained:

> We want to allow anyone who is chosen to say, "I'm an audience member. I have a mom who is always like that, and I have an idea of how to deal with her. Can I go in?" And then they jump into the action, and they are improvising right now the dialogue, and they try to see, "Does that work?" It's like practice for real life . . . [And] sometimes in that practice alone, it lets you go home and feel more confident about how you can handle mom.

In this way, Theater of the Oppressed offered Tubman students—both those participating in the course and the spect-actors in the audience— opportunities to reflect on and practice navigating oppressive situations in their lives.

Tubman student Allen explained that, in his group's performance, he had played the oppressor in a scene that involved misogyny in the workplace and that several different classmates in the audience had jumped into the role of the oppressed female employee to try to resolve it. Allen noted: "The last volunteer, he was really good. He stepped in as the role of the woman [employee], and I wasn't the highest of authority, there was somebody over me. So he was able to use that against me to get, you know, the proper treatment in that workforce." In reflecting on his learning from this experience, Allen added, "It opens your eyes even more to not only the wrongs that go on in society but also how you can use theater to both portray those wrongs and find a solution to those wrongs." In this way, Theater of the Oppressed offered Tubman students—both those participating in the course and the spect-actors from the audience—a powerful space to learn how to critically navigate different types of oppressive forces in their lives.

African American Literature

Another elective space that engaged Tubman students in developing critical navigation skills was the twelfth-grade African American Literature course. This elective course was created and taught by English department chair Mr. Dan Kamin—a White man in his mid-thirties—who had been teaching at Tubman for over a decade. In describing his motivation to develop and offer the course, Mr. Kamin explained that the emphasis in no-excuses schools on academic achievement meant that state and national assessments typically dictated the curriculum of the school's academic courses. However, as Mr. Kamin explained, "The value of the twelfth-grade class [is that it] doesn't have a test attached to it. There's no AP, SAT, no state test. There's a vacuum you're in to have this rare opportunity at a high performing charter [school] to do whatever you want with the curriculum." The African American Literature course sought to take advantage of this vacuum and, in so doing, introduced Tubman seniors to ideas about navigating racism, interracial relations, and White supremacy that many described as unique to their years at Tubman High School.

Tubman student Solomon explained of the course: "The first semester, we talked about African American struggles in society, but like we took it to a whole 'nother level. Like binary thinking, I'd never thought about that. Or like solidarity or phallocentrism. Never heard about that stuff. It took an interesting turn to what I usually learn about slavery and all that stuff." Solomon echoed numerous classmates in describing the course as finally extending his thinking about the Black experience in America beyond slavery and segregation. Solomon's classmate Maria added: "I'm interested in like Black power, womanism, and feminism, stuff like that. Like all of this emerged this year, all these feelings, I think because of the class I take, African American Literature. That class, it was very interesting. It opened my eyes for me."

In his classic theory of psycho-social development, psychologist Erik Erikson characterized late adolescence as a period in the life span in which individuals are actively seeking new and different ways of understanding the world and their role in it.[32] Peers, teachers, mentors, celebrities, music, literature, and film all represent sources that can contribute to adolescents' identity exploration.[33] Tubman students such as Solomon and Maria credited African American Literature with having opened their eyes to new ideas about the Black experience in the United States and, in so doing, informed their growing understanding of how to move through the world as Black and Latinx young adults.

One idea that nearly every student participating in the course described as influential and eye-opening was binary thinking. This concept emerged from students' reading of James Baldwin's 1962 novel, *Another Country*—a book which featured both bisexuality and interracial relationships during a time period when both were highly taboo in the United States. As Tubman student Melissa explained:

> Binary thinking is when people label themselves as things, but they're not that thing. Like we call each other Black and White, but we're not actually, like, the colors of black and white. But it's created these like binaries that stop us from unifying. And that's very interesting to me because it's like those binaries are kind of ingrained in us for like so many centuries that we can never stop seeing each other as like different.

Melissa's classmate Julian added: "I just think that [binary thinking] kinda gave me more insight into the world and how reality works because there's a lot of stuff in the book *Another Country*, a lot of interracial relationships, interracial interactions." For Melissa, Julian, and many other students, Baldwin's concept of binary thinking deepened their understanding of the social and historical forces underlying race relations in the contemporary United States.

In one class discussion of *Another Country*, Mr. Kamin and his students considered Baldwin's assertion that the African American musical form, the blues, represents a lever for transforming an America shaped by racial injustice. First, Mr. Kamin played his students one of the songs that Baldwin explicitly referenced—the blues standard "Trouble in Mind" that was first recorded in 1924 but which has roots in spirituals from the 1800s (excerpted here):

Trouble in mind, I'm blue,
But I won't be blue always.
'Cause I know the sun's gonna shine
in my back door someday.

"Why," Mr. Kamin asked, when the song had finished playing, "in this song is the sun gonna come in the back door?"

"The back door represents Black history," a young woman volunteered.

"Black history will shed light on what America is," another young woman added.

"Yes," Mr. Kamin said. "If the house is America, what does the darkness represent?"

"Ignorance?" asked a young man. Mr. Kamin nodded.

Another student waved his hand excitedly. "So the house represents America, and it's filled with darkness, which is ignorance. And Black people will open the back door to bring the truth."

Mr. Kamin nodded again. "Yes. Baldwin believes the blues will bring the truth about the Black experience in America." He gestured at the title on the front cover of Baldwin's novel. "How do the blues help lead Black and White people to *another country* without actually leaving America?"

"The other country is when both Black and White people understand each other," a young man volunteered.

"Yes!" Mr. Kamin said enthusiastically. "But what's getting in the way of reaching this new country?"

"Binary thinking!" a young woman called out.

Tubman student Donnell explained that discussions like this one in African American Literature gave him "an explanation for why I see things and why things happen in the world now. So I've known things that happen in the world. I just didn't know why it happened, a clear explanation. But they give me a good explanation of what's happening."

In short, the twelfth-grade African American Literature course served to strengthen Tubman students' ability to critically navigate Whitestream settings and spaces. Concepts such as binary thinking better equipped these young people to contend with interracial interactions and relationships in their lives, and then, as Julian noted, class discussions provided time and space for Tubman students to reflect on the social forces and dynamics underlying these interracial interactions and relationships.

CHALLENGES FOR HARRIET TUBMAN HIGH SCHOOL

The young people attending Harriet Tubman High School concluded high school with significantly higher confidence in their ability to navigate unfamiliar settings and situations than their peers attending the four other high schools featured in this book. Educators at Harriet Tubman High School supported their students' development of such navigational skills through a number of different types of programming that included college-readiness courses, science research assistantships, corporate internships, community engaged theater, and the study of African American Literature.

In *The Art of Critical Pedagogy,* scholars Jeffrey Duncan-Andrade and Ernest Morrell concluded that youth from marginalized groups are best served when their education offers "a critical praxis that subsumes academic competencies, navigational strategies, critical sensibilities, and collaborative action toward social change."[34] Just as Make the Road Academy excelled at fostering students' critical sensibilities and the upcoming chapters feature schools that powerfully engaged students in collaborative social action, Harriet Tubman High School proved innovative and impactful in equipping students with navigational strategies.

Like all schools and schooling models, however, Harriet Tubman High School's approach to fostering youth critical consciousness came with challenges and shortcomings as well. One such shortcoming was that the school's focus on conventional navigation practices in its core programming sometimes left students feeling as though their school was trying to teach them to "act White."

For example, Tubman student Solomon's internship experience came through a program called the Young Professionals Project—an after-school youth development program that sought to "connect kids to the world of work" through workshops on resume writing, networking, public speaking, and dressing professionally as well as field trips and paid summer internships at companies and corporations. Solomon described the Young Professionals Project as contributing to his growing maturity, but he also expressed resignation about the forms of code switching the program introduced:

> I like to say to my friends, like in order to survive, we got to act White. Because if you go to an interview and act like a Black person, you won't get hired. If you talk to your boss the way you talk to your Black friends, you won't get hired. Like it's sad to say you got to act White, you gotta speak clearly, you gotta do a firm handshake. And I'm learning all this stuff from a White person or maybe a Black person who learned it from a White person. Because I mean it's pretty evident that a Black person should act like a White person when they dress like them, when they speak like them.

In this explanation, Solomon did not question the utility of the strategies he was learning through school and the Young Professionals Project for navigating Whitestream professional spaces, but he simultaneously expressed disappointment that these strategies were necessary for a Black person to succeed in such spaces.

Unfortunately, the conventional navigation focus of Tubman's internship programming did not include explicit opportunities for students to engage in reflection or discussion about having to utilize these navigational strategies, or the social, political, and historical forces that rendered such strategies necessary. Both the Community Engaged Theater elective and the African American Literature elective *did* offer opportunities for Tubman students to engage in such reflection and discussion, but, because these were both elective courses, many students including Solomon were not exposed to a more critical navigation approach that could have spoken directly to his concerns about navigating Whitestream spaces.

Perhaps a related shortcoming was Tubman High School's constant comparisons of its students' academic achievement to that of White peers across the city, state, and country. In this chapter's introduction, a number of Tubman students cited such comparisons as motivating their desire to persevere in their studies, and several scholars have written about critically conscious youth of color taking on such an "achievement-as-resistance" perspective.[35] Yet, the frequency with which Tubman High faculty and leaders publicly compared their students' academic achievement to that of White peers risked conveying the message that *the point* of Tubman students' achievement and success was to prove they could surpass White youth. One student, Selena, even referred to such a goal as "the whole basis" of Harriet Tubman High School. At times, such a preoccupation with using White students as the yardstick for success seemed to paradoxically (and unintentionally) contribute to notions of White supremacy.

A third challenge for Tubman High School was negotiating the balance between the school's programming focused on conventional and critical navigation practices. Namely, one might describe programming focused on conventional navigation skills as both the long-standing norm at Harriet Tubman High School and one that was built into the school's no-excuses roots. In fact, the no-excuses model guiding Tubman High School tended to view discussion and reflection on social inequity as a distraction from the intensive focus on academic achievement that could *really* support both student success and meaningful social change. As Dean Michelle Trotter explained of this philosophy:

> I feel like the way we empower our students is to prepare them for college, and to be prepared for college you have to do more than be able to talk about the civil rights movement and social justice. You have to be well educated in math, in science, in history, and literature. So that decision is intentional because we want them to be prepared for college so that they can go and make these changes they want to make in their community.

In this explanation, Dean Trotter voiced the no-excuses rationale for emphasizing programming focused on conventional, rather than critical, navigation skills. At the same time, Tubman High faculty such as Ms. Calderón and Mr. Kamin had begun to utilize their elective courses to usher a more critical navigational stance into the school's culture and curriculum. Moreover, students participating in those elective courses then carried a more critical orientation with them into their other academic courses, extracurricular activities, and interactions with Tubman educators.

If Principal Pierce had been determined to maintain Tubman's emphasis on conventional navigation of racial injustice, he possessed the authority and force of personality to push back on this elective programming encouraging more critical navigation practices. But he did not. In fact, just the opposite. As the class of 2017 entered its final year of high school, Principal Pierce shifted Tubman High School's use of morning advisory periods to include opportunities for small-group discussion about injustice in the news and on social media. The school also piloted a weekly "Project" period in which regular classes were suspended, and students chose from a menu of special projects that included producing a podcast about gentrification taking place in their city and raising awareness of LGBTQ rights within the Tubman community. These projects also created spaces for discussion of the oppressive social forces underlying the navigational skills that students were learning.

In short, Tubman High School was shifting slowly but perceptibly from an emphasis on conventional to critical navigation strategies. This shift was by no means a shortcoming, but managing that shift represented a challenge for the entire school community, as it involved tacking away from the no-excuses "DNA" that had guided Tubman High School for nearly twenty years.

Finally, Tubman High School's overarching focus on teaching navigational skills—whether conventional or critical—seemed at times to limit students' understandings of the full range of opportunities for social action available to them. For example, in responding to an interview question about *how* to challenge racial injustice either now or as an adult, Tubman student Allen explained: "The first thing is to get a good education, and so that way you can prove to people that minorities are successful. . . . Then second, maybe I might be some sort of activist. I never really thought of it like that." Similar to many of his classmates, Allen had internalized Tubman's messages about the importance of striving for academic and professional success within an unjust social system, but he had engaged in little reflection about other approaches to fostering social change. His classmate

Selena expressed frustration that she and her classmates had been exposed to such a narrow vision of how to effect change:

> It's like the only thing we really do is prove ourselves through education. But like I never really see us take part in marches and stuff like that. . . . We're always like those silent workers. We just work with education, or we work to prove to people that we all go to college. I think that's as far as we go. I wish we did more.

In short, Tubman's intensive focus on fostering students' navigational skills meant that many of its students possessed little experience with collective forms of social action. In the chapters ahead, we feature two high schools—Community Academy and Leadership High School—at which students demonstrated substantial growth in just such a commitment to activism and *collective* social action.

GRADUATION: FIRST STEPS

Tubman faculty and students processed into the auditorium to the same African drum beat that had begun their morning meetings since the fifth grade. First came the faculty with brightly colored sashes atop their royal blue gowns. When they reached the front of the auditorium, they took their seats in the roped-off rows of seats beside the stage.

The audience's volume shifted from cheerful to raucous as the Tubman seniors began processing down the center aisle and onto the stage. They too wore royal blue caps and gowns. A few students wore sneakers underneath their gowns—a uniform violation that indicated their time as Tubman students was nearly over. When the graduates arrived on the stage, they swayed in unison until the drumming came to a dramatic close, and the class of 2017 valedictorian, Olajide, took her place at the podium.

Olajide welcomed family, friends, parents, teachers, and her fellow graduates to this celebratory day. "There was once a time in history," she reminded them, "where African Americans were stripped of education and humanity, but never stripped of hope. Like African Americans during slavery, we all definitely struggle. Of course I am not comparing the horrors of slavery to what we have today. However, many people have doubted our intelligence and ability. They have doubted us because of the color of our skin or where we came from. Sometimes we have even doubted ourselves. But at the end of the day it is Harriet Tubman High School that has kept us together and refueled our hope."

Olajide paused for a moment. "During slavery, no slave escaped from freedom alone," she told the audience. "They had to rely on a network of others—other slaves who kept their secrets, former slaves or abolitionists like Harriet Tubman who lent a hand or shelter. African Americans could not have resisted slavery if they could not have a sense of hope from the people around them. We, too, have gained hope from the people around us. This hope comes from our parents and guardians who literally helped us take that first step when we were younger, and the other first step of fighting for our education. This hope also comes from the graduating classes who came before us. They are constant reminders that they have made their path forward, and now it is our turn."

The audience and her classmates applauded enthusiastically. Then Principal Pierce took the stage. "Let me give you some of the context for this graduating class," he told the family members and friends in the audience, and then he went on to describe the class of 2017's work to outperform peers in their city, state, and nearby suburban communities. "This level of achievement is important for what it leads to for individuals," Principal Pierce told the audience. He gestured at the graduates sitting behind him on the stage. "Brandeis, Notre Dame, Davidson College, Bowdoin, Emory, Pomona, Howard." The audience started to applaud and whistle. "But it's also important," Principal Pierce continued, "because these students show America what students of color are really capable of." The cheering and affirmations grew even louder. Principal Pierce paused for emphasis and looked back at his graduating seniors. "And that is being the best. That you are equal or superior to anyone, and America needs to know that."

"That's right!" exclaimed several audience members.

"Lift as you climb!" called another.

Both Principal Pierce's words and the accomplishments of the graduating seniors seemed to exemplify Tubman High School's vision of personal achievement as social action.

Principal Pierce turned to address the graduates. "Tubman High School is not an easy place to go to school," he told them. "Or to work. It's not an easy place to send your child to school. Tubman asks a lot. Tubman is rigorous. Sometimes, unpleasant. Your own hard work and experience are the reasons you're sitting here now at the end of your Tubman experience. You didn't give up, you persevered, you kept working even when you did not want to, and that is a life lesson."

Principal Pierce looked out at the hundreds of family members in the audience. "The second reason you've been successful is because of your parents and your families. They did not have to send you to this school. And in many ways, their lives would have been easier if they had decided not to send you to Tubman or to keep sending you to Tubman. Parents, how many of you have ever argued with your children about homework?" Hands shot up across the auditorium. "How many of you have ever received a detention phone call?" The hands stayed up. Principal Pierce nodded. "You don't have to raise your hand for this one, but how many of you ever sat up late at night and questioned whether Tubman was the right place for your child?" A clamor of affirmation reverberated across the auditorium. "Well, that's what your parents went through," Principal Pierce told his graduates. "Parents persevere too. And they didn't do it to make their lives easier, but they did it to make your lives better. Because they love you." A number of the graduates on the stage applauded for their parents, and Principal Pierce brought his speech to a close. "And you parents," he told them, "you did this, you persevered, so that you could sit here and look up at your child as he or she is about to leave and know that you did everything possible to prepare them for life. And you did." Principal Pierce paused to let that acknowledgment sink in. "You did everything possible." Parents in the audience nodded somberly, contemplatively. Several clapped emphatically.

Principal Pierce gave way at the podium to Tubman faculty member Ms. Stacy Jones who restored the energy level in the room when she exclaimed, "Now for the moment you've all been waiting for!" After the whooping and cheering from both graduates and their families had settled down, Ms. Jones continued: "It is one of the many African traditions that have permeated through many different countries and lands, influenced by the African diaspora, including the United States and Latin America. Today the families of our graduates will bestow a Kente cloth upon their child to mark this momentous occasion in which we celebrate our students' completion of high school and their transition to college. As elders, you are passing your legacies, your supports, and your love to your child on this important day. Students, we ask that you wear your Kente with pride. Pride in yourself, pride in the beautiful heritage of which you are a part, and as a symbol of your lasting connection to the Harriet Tubman community." Ms. Jones began calling out names, and Tubman students in the class of 2017 stepped forward to receive their diploma from Principal Pierce and Kente cloth from their parents and to begin the next chapter of their lives.

CHAPTER 5

Take a Stand

"WHAT A WEEK!" Community Academy teacher Casey Washington exclaimed, looking out at the forty-five ninth graders assembled in the school's black box theater. A White woman in her late twenties, Casey had already started getting to know these new ninth graders in her three sections of freshman humanities.[1] "We've done a lot of things! And this is our last thing of the week."

The ninth graders murmured appreciatively. For the past five days, these new high schoolers had had Community Academy to themselves as they got oriented to high school, their classes, and teachers. On Monday, the upperclassmen would join them, and the school year would commence in earnest.

Principal Klarens Hill joined Casey at the front of the small theater. "Good afternoon, class of 2017!" he called out. An Afro-Latinx man in his late thirties, Klarens had been one of the five teachers who founded Community Academy thirteen years earlier. He had been principal for the past six. "This is Community Circle," Klarens told the ninth graders. "We have this meeting every week where we share things, and it's amazing." He looked out at the ninth graders sitting in five neat rows of plastic folding chairs. All forty-five students wore the Community Academy school uniform—khaki pants and a polo shirt with the Community Academy seal over the heart. The majority of these young people identified as Black or

African American, with a smaller percentage identifying as Latinx. Three out of four came from low-income families. Klarens looked over at Casey. "I heard there's going to be some audience participation today!"

"That's right," Casey told him. "Earlier today, each crew got together and put together something artistic that represents our motto: 'To learn, to lead, to serve.' Every crew is going to present what they did for the rest of us. First up is the Spelman crew."

Community Academy's crews were groups of seven or eight students from all four grade levels, intended to be single-sex, and led by a teacher. The crews met for half an hour three times per week, and students stayed in the same crew for all four years of high school. Each of the crews was named after a historically black college: Hampton, Spelman, Shaw, Wilberforce, Morehouse, and so on.

Three young women who comprised the Spelman crew came to the front of the theater to share a drawing they had worked on together. One of the young women explained, "Right here we have the question, 'What does it take to be a professional leader?' As you can see, she has on the Community Academy uniform. Her shirt is tucked in. She has on the black belt, khaki pants, and shoes. She has her Community Academy water bottle, and she's thinking: 'I love school. Did I bring in my homework today?' The audience applauded lightly.

Next up was a young man representing the Wilberforce crew who recited a spoken word poem that began, "Anybody can say there ain't no 'I' in team, but those are just words." The young man went on to exhort his new classmates to help out the 'new girl' who needs help and to remember that teachers need help too. He concluded the poem with one of the core mantras of expeditionary learning: "Remember, we're all a crew, not passengers!" The ninth graders applauded more enthusiastically this time.

Several more crews shared drawings. Finally, Casey called up four girls from two different crews—Bennett and Tougaloo—who had been paired together for this activity. All four young women came to the front of the room but faced away from the audience. Marcella, the teacher leading the Bennett crew, explained, "Alright, I know everybody out there heard of Mary and her little lamb. Right now, we're going to tell you a story about

Bennett, Tougaloo, and a little lamb." The four young women swung around in unison, and one of them started a beat. The other three girls started rapping: "Bennett had a little swag, a little swag, and so did Tougaloo. And every day they came to school, they aimed for honor roll. They really rocked those polo shirts, and those khakis too." This last line got the audience laughing and cheering. "And every crew want to be like us 'cause we're Bennett and Tougaloo!" The clapping and cheering escalated several more notches as the four young ladies signed off, took their seats, and brought the class of 2017's first week of high school to a close.

ORIGIN STORY: EXPEDITION INTO THE UNKNOWN

Community Academy opened its doors in September of 2001 with just five staff members and thirty-two ninth graders, but the school's small size belied its big plans for influencing public education. In fact, the school's founders—an educator, technologist, and health professional—wrote into their original charter application: "While our core mission is the education of our students and their families, we also aspire to serve as an innovative laboratory for rethinking urban secondary education." There were several different dimensions to this rethinking.

First, Community Academy became one of the only public schools in the United States located inside a community health center. This partnership and colocation came out of a fundamental belief—held by both the school's founding educators and the health center's medical professionals—that "healthier people learn better, and people with greater access to education are healthier." Through this collaboration, the health center sought to close health disparity gaps facing the community of color it served through regular presentations, communication, and check-ins with Community Academy students and their families.

At the same time, the partnership allowed Community Academy students valuable opportunities for internships and job shadowing at the health center as well as guest lectures and workshops from health center professionals. The school's founding director, Anne Nelson, a White woman in her fifties, explained that such opportunities were crucial to her vision for Community Academy because "I didn't want the kids to feel like they were going to school. I wanted it to feel more professional, and for them to be immersed in a professional environment." She added: "I really wanted to change the experience of going to school."

Accordingly, Community Academy's culture had a looser feel than the four other schools featured in this book. There were no bells to signal the start of class, and, in fact, teachers often started teaching their lesson with just a handful of students in the room. The rest of the class would then trickle in over the next several minutes, having stopped to pick up something at their lockers or to chat in the hallway with a friend. In most Community Academy classrooms, students sat together in groups of four or five at large rectangular tables, rather than at individual desks arranged in neat rows. This configuration aligned well with teachers' frequent incorporation of group work into daily lessons but also enabled students' side conversations with one another. For both reasons, Community Academy classrooms were noisy places, filled with a low but constant hum of chatter.

Community Academy also became the first expeditionary learning high school in its city.[2] Expeditionary learning schools were built on Outward Bound founder Kurt Hahn's belief that learning should be an active and engaging process that feels like an expedition into the unknown and that develops in students the "curiosity, skills, knowledge, and courage needed to imagine a better world and work toward realizing it."[3] From Hahn's overarching philosophy came ten core principles of expeditionary learning. Several of those principles emphasize the importance of students being given the time, space, agency, and autonomy to "explore their own thoughts, make their own connections, and create their own ideas."[4] Community Academy teacher Joshua Burriss explained that what this looked like on the ground was that the school's curriculum at each grade level was composed of several expeditions—"a trimester-long investigation into something, and the goal is to go depth over breadth. To really spend time digging into an issue, a place, a theme." Such expeditions typically include guiding questions, learning targets, case studies, fieldwork, and a major project or product.[5]

Expeditionary learning schools also emphasize the importance of fostering school and classroom cultures in which both students and teachers trust each other, feel comfortable taking intellectual challenges and risking failure, value each other's diverse histories and talents, and demonstrate empathy and caring. At Community Academy, efforts to foster such a culture ranged from teachers going by their first names to thrice-weekly crew meetings to a whole-school camping trip at the start of each school year. As Community Academy student Tatyana explained of crew: "We talk about, you know, highs and lows, something good that happens, something bad that happens. . . . It's like really a chill-out place for us to get to know each other more and gain a closer bond with each other."

With a student body of fewer than two-hundred students, Community Academy was also just really small. This, too, was by design. Founding director Anne Nelson explained that, prior to starting Community Academy, she had lived for a number of years in a tiny Vermont town of just a few hundred people and that, "I really wanted that village feeling [for Community Academy] where there is no crack to fall through. Someone is going to notice you."

The tenth and final principle of expeditionary learning focuses on service and compassion, and is summarized by the short phrase: "We are crew, not passengers."[6] In other words, the ultimate purpose of learning is to develop the skills and commitment to engage in "consequential service" in the wider world rather than to float along as a passive observer. Community Academy incorporated this principle directly into both its mission of equipping students "to engage deeply and productively in community life" and its motto: "To learn, to lead, and to serve." In describing this mission, Community Academy student Angelina explained, "They want us to go out into the world knowing who we are and where we're coming from, and they want us to know like some things are unjust . . . and how we could change the system." Over four years, Community Academy students in the class of 2017 demonstrated greater growth in their commitment to social and political activism than their peers across the other schools featured in this book. Here, we describe what this growth in students' commitment to activism looked and sounded like, as well as the programming and practices at Community Academy that contributed to such growth.

DEVELOPING CRITICAL CONSCIOUSNESS: SOCIAL ACTION CHALLENGING INJUSTICE

A commitment to activism refers to an individual's propensity to engage in a wide range of social action behaviors such as writing letters to newspapers, contributing to a political campaign, engaging in protests, or boycotting particular businesses or products.[7] Paulo Freire characterized challenging oppression through such collective social action as the ultimate goal of critical consciousness development (see figure 5.1).[8]

Accordingly, the survey completed by youth attending both the five high schools featured in this book and the four comparison high schools included a Commitment to Activism Scale that served as one measure of the social action dimension of critical consciousness.[9] On this scale, youth

FIGURE 5.1   Components of critical consciousness

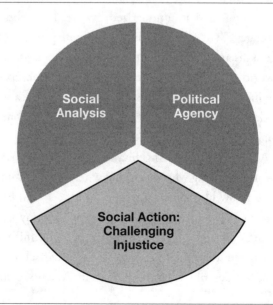

expressed their likelihood along a five-point scale of taking part in a variety of activist activities including signing a petition about a social or political issue, taking part in a protest or demonstration, and campaigning for a political candidate or cause. On this scale, a "1" represented a low commitment to activism, and a "5" represented a high commitment to engaging in activism.

Figure 5.2 reveals that youth across all five of the high schools featured in this book demonstrated modest growth in their commitment to activism from the start of ninth grade (Time 1) to the end of twelfth grade (Time 5). Moreover, as they graduated from high school in the spring of 2017, these young people demonstrated a significantly higher commitment to activism than their peers at four comparison high schools.[10]

Figure 5.2 also reveals that students at Community Academy began their first year of high school with a substantially weaker commitment to activism than their peers across all five featured high schools. However, Community Academy students then demonstrated significantly steeper growth in their commitment to activism over their four years of high school such that, by the end of twelfth grade, there was no significant difference on this

FIGURE 5.2   Youths' commitment to activism from the start of ninth grade (Time 1) to the end of twelfth grade (Time 5)

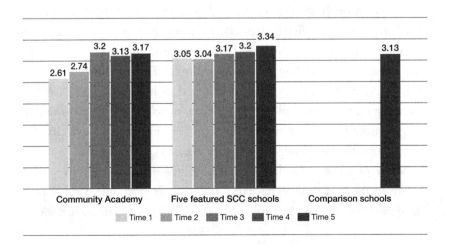

scale between Community Academy students and their peers across all five featured schools.[11] In other words, Community Academy students began high school far behind their peers in their commitment to activism but then caught up over the course of high school.

A closer look at Figure 5.2 also suggests that Community Academy students did much of their catching up over their first two years of high school (Time 1 to Time 3). Specifically, the commitment to activism of youth from all five high schools featured in this book increased very gradually during this time period, but Community Academy students' commitment to activism increased, on average, by nearly 25 percent. In fact, at the midpoint of high school, Community Academy students' commitment to activism had nominally surpassed that of their peers across the five featured high schools. One can also see that this trajectory then leveled off during Community Academy students' final two years of high school. Consequently, this chapter focuses particularly on the programming and practices during the first half of high school through which Community Academy sought to foster students' commitment to activism challenging racial injustice.

Developing a Commitment to Activism

Few students attending Make the Road Academy or Harriet Tubman High School were involved in any activist activities at all, and the activism of youth attending Espiritu High School and Leadership High School came primarily through their respective school's programming. Community Academy students differed dramatically from their peers at these other schools in the extent to which they sought out and engaged in social activism outside of school hours or sponsorship. In fact, of the twelve Community Academy students who participated in interviews, ten described engaging on their own volition in protests, marches, and demonstrations ranging from the 2017 Women's March in Washington, DC, to a citywide youth protest against budget cuts facing the city's high schools.

Many of these examples of youths' engagement in collective social action focused on challenging racial injustice. For example, Community Academy student Leondra explained as a tenth grader that she had joined a citywide youth protest after the police officer who killed Michael Brown in Ferguson, Missouri, was not indicted:

> I decided to participate when I found out on the news that he wasn't gonna get punished for it. The only punishment he got was like a paid vacation, they called it. And I felt like just empathetic for Michael Brown's family, and I felt really bad. So I feel like me going out there would be helping at least a little bit just to show that I care.

Leondra's classmate Janelle explained that she had joined this same protest "because it started to get tiring like hearing the police doing this. And [I wanted] for us to go out there and actually do something about it."

Another classmate, Ronald, described going as a twelfth grader to a Black Lives Matter protest. He explained: "I went to a protest, like it was a huge protest. It looked like a concert. . . . I was planning to just go link up with my boy, you know, [but then] I told him, like, yo bro, you gotta meet me, they're doing a protest. I kinda wanna go." Finally, a fourth classmate, Brittany, explained that, on the evening during her senior year in which President Trump announced a travel ban on visitors from five Muslim-majority countries, she took public transportation out to her city's international airport to join a protest of this new policy. Brittany explained, "I went to the airport, to the march, [and] we got to meet a Muslim man who was really happy that we was out there helping him and all his people. And I got to learn that what they're going through is really no joke and they're really trying to fight for their lives, but no one's trying to help them."

This out-of-school activism by Community Academy students far outpaced their peers at the four other schools featured in this book. Engagement in such activism can have a dramatic effect upon an adolescent's civic trajectory. Adolescence represents a peak period in the life span for seeking out new and different ways of understanding the world and one's role in it.[12] Consequently, opportunities to engage in activism during adolescence—and exposure to activist mentors and organizations—can have a profound effect upon an individual's self-concept and worldview, and greatly increase the likelihood of future civic and political involvement.[13]

KEY SCHOOLING PRACTICES FOR CHALLENGING RACIAL INJUSTICE

Community Academy's expeditionary learning model contributed in multiple ways to youths' engagement in out-of-school activism challenging racial injustice. First, expeditionary learning comes out of Outward Bound's experiential education model that prioritizes an "active" approach to learning, or "learning by doing."[14] For such an educational model, classroom learning about social change efforts and social justice issues must necessarily be accompanied by opportunities for active participation in such efforts and issues. Accordingly, both faculty and students immersed in Community Academy's expeditionary learning culture came to see engagement in out-of-school social change work as a natural extension of their in-school curriculum.

Second, expeditionary learning schools are guided by ten core principles. One of these principles calls for youth to take increasing responsibility for their own learning, and another encourages youth to engage in "consequential acts of service to others."[15] Community Academy's commitment to these principles contributed as well to a school culture and ethos that catalyzed youths' interest in participating in a number of different forms of collective social action. Here, we describe the specific programming and practices through which Community Academy educators brought these principles to life within their school community and, in so doing, fostered students' commitment to challenge racial injustice through social and political activism.

Learning Resistance

Recall scholar Beverly Daniel Tatum's warning to educators doing critical consciousness work: "Learning to recognize cultural and institutional racism without also learning strategies to respond to them is a prescription for despair."[16] Community Academy faculty sought to avoid this "prescription for despair" by explicitly pairing lessons on racial injustice with lessons on resistance to such injustice.

This pairing of oppression and resistance began in the opening weeks of students' ninth-grade humanities course when they learned about

Christopher Columbus's fifteenth-century enslavement and genocide of the Arawaks he encountered on the island that includes modern-day Haiti, as well as the successful Haitian uprising against French colonial rule in 1791. One of the big "learning targets" for this expedition was that students would be able to "explain how colonialism led to injustice *and resistance* in the Caribbean" (italics mine). In describing this approach to studying injustice, Community Academy educator Jill Solomon observed: "It's a pretty good balance of, here's a colonial power, and here's how people resisted that power. . . . Here's what we experience today that's a result of that resistance, and not just to that power. I think that framing is really important." In other words, Community Academy's humanities curriculum sought to give as much "air time" to marginalized people's efforts to challenge oppression as to the oppression itself. This framing contributed to students' commitment to activism by introducing them to numerous tactics for challenging oppression as well as by strengthening their conviction that such tactics can pay off.

In terms of the effects of such programming, Community Academy student Angelina explained at the end of ninth grade that she felt like she had benefitted from learning in humanities class "about people who faced that [racism]. They spoke up about it and actually did something." Three years later as a senior, Angelina declared that the most memorable learning in which she had engaged at Community Academy was that very first ninth-grade expedition on the Haitian Revolution:

> That was really cool how it was like a whole bunch of Haitians, like Black people, starting their own revolution, and I think the only nation that actually like, built themselves after the Europeans left, and built from there. Like they strictly took out all the White people, all the French people, I mean, from Haiti. The Haitian revolution was dope, like I wish I was [alive] back then. Not really but I do.

For Angelina and several other students, learning about the Haitian overthrow of French colonial rule—and its ripple effect throughout the Americas—was inspiring and refreshing.

This pairing of racial oppression and resistance continued in ninth graders' next humanities expedition on apartheid South Africa. Humanities teacher Casey Washington explained:

> The South Africa unit is really focused on forms of resistance. We open with a history of colonialism [in the country], and how did they get to this place, and then we go through civil disobedience, militant resistance, Black consciousness. We talk about truth and reconciliation, so trying to frame it through, "What power do people have?" Because I think ninth graders especially feel like they are very powerless, and that things are just going to happen to them, and there's nothing people can do.

In one lesson during this expedition, ninth graders learned about a protest in 1960 in Sharpeville, South Africa, against the apartheid government that highlighted how different political groups in South Africa had favored different approaches to challenging apartheid policies. Specifically, the African National Congress and Pan-Africanist Congress advocated for civil disobedience while the paramilitary branches of these groups—Poqo and MK—sought to overthrow the apartheid government through violence against individuals and installations associated with the government.

"Pretend it's 1960," humanities teacher Danny Green—a white man in his twenties—instructed his students, "and Sharpeville has just happened. The activists could choose between militant resistance and civil disobedience. So you guys are going to have that debate that they had in 1961."

One student started: "I think we should do militant resistance because of what just happened at the Sharpeville Massacre. They tried to be peaceful and whatnot, and people ended up dying and stuff."

Another student disagreed. "I say civil disobedience because it will make the apartheid worse, all the drama and fighting."

"My opinion is militant resistance," said another student. "I say that because Poqo and MK really touched the government on some basics like shutting off their power or like attacking government buildings and power stations. And I feel like that was important because it was like sending the government a warning and getting their point across."

Another young woman spoke up. "In India, Gandhi used civil disobedience, and it takes time, but they got what they wanted in the end."

Another student's hand shot upward. "But you know what happened to all those people trying to be peaceful? Sixty-nine of them got killed."

A young man who had thus far been quiet raised his hand. "If civil disobedience doesn't work and militant resistance doesn't work, then what will work?" A couple students snapped their fingers to "second" this question.

Their teacher, Danny Green, nodded too. "I think that's a good question for us to leave on and you to start thinking on," he told his students. "Is there a middle ground?"

In this debate, one could see the emphasis within the expeditionary learning model on learning experiences that "provide something important to think about, time to experiment, and time to make sense of what is observed."[17] Community Academy student Janelle added that learning about "the South Africans made me want to stand up for what I believe in because they did the same thing. That made me stand up for what I want to do." For Janelle, learning about the resistance of Black South Africans—and their ultimate success in ending apartheid—inspired her to seek out opportunities to engage in activism against contemporary injustices facing her community.

Another Community Academy student, Tatyana, explained as a tenth grader that she had recently participated in a march in her community one Saturday night to protest police violence against African Americans in Ferguson, Missouri:

> [At] first I was like, I don't know what me marching out here is gonna do 'cause they can't personally hear what I want to say. But it takes time. But civil disobedience will actually get us to where we want to be if we do it without violence and with words. . . . If you kill them with words, you will get what you want. It's gonna take time, so you have to be patient.

Tatyana's words suggest that learning about civil disobedience in apartheid South Africa had strengthened her belief in the ability of political activism to topple racial injustice and, in so doing, had motivated her participation in this citywide protest. Scholar Bettina Love has lamented,

"Too often in schools we learn and teach about oppression and injustice, but rarely are we taught or do we teach about how ordinary people fought for justice."[18] Tatyana's words reveal the powerful effects that can come about from youth engaging in such learning.

Standing in Solidarity

The ninth-grade expeditions on racial injustice and resistance in Africa and the Caribbean connected, broadly speaking, to many Community Academy students' own racial-ethnic backgrounds. Several of the expeditions in the later grades sought to foster youths' sense of solidarity and commitment to activism on behalf of other racial-ethnic groups contending with oppression and injustice. In so doing, these expeditions resonated with another expeditionary learning principle emphasizing the development of empathy and caring.

A tenth-grade expedition, for example, focused on the historical and contemporary displacement of Native Americans in the United States.[19] Humanities teacher Joshua Burriss observed that this expedition did a good job of "bringing students into a space of compassion and empathy and solidarity" with the experiences of Native Americans.

The expedition began with tenth-grade humanities teacher Jabari Dymon—a Black man in his late twenties—asking his students to "imagine that your family's history is in danger of being completely wiped out of memory and lost. How hard would you fight to preserve it?"

One young woman raised her hand. "My family is from Cape Verde, and if they were to be wiped out, I'd try my best to preserve it because I know my ancestors worked hard to make what we have now. So I wouldn't want that to go to waste because that would be a terrible loss, and I'm pretty sure no one would want that to happen."

"My family originated from Haiti and the DR," volunteered another student. "I would fight to the extreme by bringing back all the wonderful traditions like drinking soup on New Year's Eve, and the music [that] is very important to us."

"My family is from Jamaica," said a third student, "and I would go to the ends of the earth to keep Jamaica alive. Because who doesn't like Jamaica?"

"My family originated from Haiti," explained another young woman, "and we were the first Black independent nation. And that was huge back then. That's when slavery, the foundation of it, really started, and most slaves tried to kill their masters and rebel, and it didn't happen. And Haiti was the first to do it."

"You guys have some incredible minds," Jabari Dymon told his students. "I asked you that question because as we learn more about Native Americans, their plight, and how they revive their culture, think about how these authors—Sherman Alexie, Leslie Silko, N. Scott Momaday—they're really trying to bring up their culture through literature. Mary Crow Dog, she is actually out there fighting for equality. So to hear you guys say you'd fight to the extreme, it's clear it's really important to you, and it's really important to them." In this and many other lessons throughout the expedition, Jabari drew upon literature as a "mutually humanizing experience that can spur social action."[20] In other words, Jabari drew upon literature to help his Black and Latinx students see their own experiences of racial injustice reflected in those of Native Americans and, consequently, to strengthen their commitment to engaging in activism on behalf of—and alongside— other marginalized peoples.

Later in this same expedition, Jabari engaged his tenth graders in reading several short stories by Native American author Sherman Alexie that emphasized similarities between the injustices facing Native Americans and African Americans. In one of these stories, a police officer pulled over a Native American motorist because he didn't fit the profile of the neighborhood he was driving through. In the discussion that followed, a number of students reported on their own negative experiences with law enforcement.

One student observed, "If you have a smart mouth or a smart comment, they'll make up something so you can get arrested, or will keep bothering you."

"You don't have to even have a smart mouth," added another young man. "Sometimes just because they're in authority, they want to do what they want to do."

Jabari asked: "Okay, how many of us feel that way sometimes? I mean, we're Black, Latino, and he's Native American, but there are probably some similar experiences. Do people feel like they have to keep their guards up sometimes?" Nearly the entire class nodded their heads. Jabari added: "The other day, I shared with some of you after the Mike Brown incident about an experience that I had recently. I had just come from getting some food, and an officer pulled me over and was asking me a bunch of questions about my food that just had nothing to do with anything. I know not all police are bad, but some like to harass." Through discussions like these, Jabari helped his students to connect their own experiences with racial injustice to those of Native Americans, and to see issues such as racist policing practices as extending beyond their own Black and Latinx communities.

In describing the impact of lessons like these, Community Academy student Angelina explained, "When I learned this, I'm like, wow, like it expanded my mind. It blew my mind because I'm over here only talking about Black and White issues, but Native Americans, they have it just as bad. Like they're forgotten. They're not even talked about." Her classmate Tatyana explained similarly: "We learned about the Indians too, about their reservations, and . . . I was like, wow, Blacks aren't the only ones who go through this. There's other races that go through this as well." For both of these students, the expedition opened their eyes to connections they shared with Native Americans as racially marginalized groups in the United States. These young people's words and experiences resonate with social critic James Baldwin's observation: "You think your pain and your heartbreak are unprecedented in the history of the world, but then you read. It was books that taught me that the things that tormented me most were the very things that connected me with all the people who were alive, or who had ever been alive."[21]

As described earlier in this chapter, numerous Community Academy students participated on their own time and volition in protests against injustices ranging from police violence to President Donald Trump's Muslim ban. A number of Community Academy students also described their interest and support for the 2016 protests at Standing Rock Reservation against the construction of the Dakota Access Pipeline through Meskwaki and Sioux reservation land. Expeditions on the displacement of the Native

Americans in the tenth grade and then the Syrian refugee crisis in the twelfth grade contributed to such demonstrations of solidarity with other marginalized racial-ethnic groups.

Decades of research in moral psychology have demonstrated that—perhaps for evolutionary reasons—people's feelings of obligation for the welfare of others tend "to be limited to our kin, and to those with whom we are in cooperative relationships, and perhaps to members of our own small tribal group."[22] Yet, philosopher Peter Singer has observed that, while evolutionary understandings of human nature might *explain* people's tendency to feel obligations to a relatively small circle of individuals, such an explanation does not justify those feelings or make them morally defensible.[23] Through its humanities expeditions, Community Academy sought to foster not only students' commitment to activism but also their motivation to deploy their activism on behalf of marginalized groups beyond their own.

Teaching Activist Skills

In addition to engaging students in learning about oppression and resistance in a variety of contexts, Community Academy faculty also actively sought to teach their students how to make use of tools employed by activists. For example, Community Academy's physics classes carried out a research study focused on whether a street near their school where a classmate had been hit by a car would benefit from school zone signage. These young people then presented their findings to a municipal transportation board that subsequently voted to post the additional signage. Likewise, as part of their expedition on mass incarceration in the contemporary United States, students in twelfth-grade humanities learned about—and then published their own—political cartoons and viral videos to convey their perspectives on racism in the criminal justice system.

Several other courses at Community Academy engaged students in writing letters to politicians and other government officials to challenge injustice. For example, the final expedition of the year in ninth-grade humanities explored America's colonial relationship with Puerto Rico, and the culminating assignment for this expedition engaged students in writing a letter to an elected official expressing their opinion about what Puerto

Rico's relationship to the United States should be. Likewise, students in twelfth-grade humanities concluded their exhibition on the Syrian refugee crisis by writing to an elected official about what role the United States should be playing in the crisis. As the senior humanities teacher Sarah Singer told her students, "In our current political system, the most effective way that people like us can make change is by contacting our elected officials because we elect them, and they care about what we have to say. If they're not doing what we want them to do, we vote them out of office. So they listen. They really do." In reflecting on this assignment, Community Academy student Dana explained: "I feel like it gives us a voice 'cause we're writing letters to the senators and representatives, and I feel like, if we send out these letters, that it would make some type of improvement to what's happening." For Dana and a number of other Community Academy students, these opportunities to express their perspectives to elected representatives about America's treatment of oppressed racial-ethnic groups felt like purposeful forms of political activism.

Perhaps the most dramatic example of youth at Community Academy learning to use the tools employed by activists occurred when a European foreign ministry issued a travel warning advising tourists not to visit the predominantly African American neighborhood in which Community Academy was located due to higher poverty and crime rates. One of Community Academy's foreign language teachers shared the travel warning with her classes, and the teacher and students decided to write a letter protesting this warning. The final version of the letter—addressed to that nation's local consul-general—read in part:

> [We] personally invite you to visit our school as soon as possible in order to address a very serious misrepresentation made by the foreign ministry of the neighborhood where our students live and learn. Specifically, we are asking you to come so that after your visit, you will request that the foreign ministry apologize and retract its disparaging characterization of our community.

Community Academy students alerted local newspapers and news stations about their plans to hand-deliver this letter, and the news outlets began to cover the story. The students also wrote letters to their pen pals in the country from which the travel warning had been issued—and who had visited them the previous year—asking for their help as well in pushing back against this hurtful travel warning.

As a result of this multifront campaign, the local consul general ended up accepting Community Academy students' invitation to visit their school and community. During his visit, the consul general engaged in a frank discussion of the travel warning with the entire student body and accompanied a smaller group of students on a tour of their school and neighborhood. As Community Academy student Tatyana explained:

> They, you know, walked [him] around the neighborhood to show that it's really not that bad. We got local stores, we got bread for y'all, you know. We got restaurants, and, you know, we do have security around so don't ever think you're not safe. So they really did something about what they felt wasn't right, and now that country has a whole new spin of what our neighborhood is really about.

Tatyana was one of several students who had not been enrolled in any of the foreign language classes leading this protest but who remarked that the whole episode had taught her something about what could be accomplished through activism. One of the students who did take a leading role in this activism described the experience in an interview with a local news outlet: "At first I was nervous, but I felt like I had power, and I felt like a leader because I was setting an example for plenty of other students who feel this way also."

As described earlier, expeditionary learning emerged from Outward Bound founder Kurt Hahn's belief that learning should prepare students to contribute meaningfully to the world, and that the learning itself should be engaging, productive, and tangible.[24] One can see such philosophical underpinnings in these various assignments and activities that engaged students and their teachers in applying activist tools in the real world. Such an approach also resonates with sociocultural theories of learning that conceptualize learning as situated in community practices.[25] In other words, learning entails novices engaging in real-world practices under the guidance of seasoned mentors such that they gradually master the content and skills necessary to engage independently in these practices. By actively guiding Community Academy students in practices ranging from writing letters to elected officials to engaging with the media to publicize a protest, Community Academy faculty sought to equip their students to graduate from high school with the knowledge and skills to engage in meaningful and productive activism for the causes they championed.

Supporting Activism in School

In addition to giving students opportunities to practice using the tools employed by activists, Community Academy faculty and leaders also explicitly supported their students' deployment of these tools both inside and outside of school. This practice, too, aligned with the active approach to learning that is at the foundation of the expeditionary learning model.

For example, one of Community Academy's extracurricular clubs was the "Student Advocacy Club," which Community Academy student Taty-ana explained was a space where "we can talk about things that the school does and how it affects us in a good way or a bad way. Then like we try to work around it to see how it can benefit us." Several Community Academy students described this club's efforts during their ninth-grade year to change the school uniform policy to allow students to wear shorts. As Community Academy student Leondra explained of this effort, the club "did a proposal and [included] a whole lot of paragraphs of reasons why we should be able to [wear shorts], and everybody signed petitions and every-thing like that. And they changed it, so now we're just free." A few years later, Community Academy student Aimee explained that she and other members of the club had successfully campaigned for additional adapta-tions to the uniform policy including the right to wear colorful headbands and sweaters over their uniforms. In reflecting on these efforts, Commu-nity Academy teacher Casey Washington observed that she and her col-leagues felt gratified to see that their students have "taken these ideas about forms of resistance and fighting for justice and have used them."

Additionally, at the outset of the class of 2017's senior year, Community Academy teacher Jill Solomon formed an Equity Club that met weekly during students' study-hall period. At the group's first meeting, Jill—a white woman in her forties—opened up the floor for students' perspectives on what issues the group should focus its efforts.

Twelfth grader Ronald spoke first: "Community Academy felt like a family when I first came here, but now we don't support each other. We need more togetherness. Nobody really wants to care."

Another student, Igor, added, "People are putting each other down. If you know there's someone in need and there's something you can do to make them feel better, help them."

The students decided to plan an initiative to foster more togetherness and less bullying within their community, and they agreed to present a challenge at Community Circle related to this initiative for each crew to accomplish.

Two Thursdays later, three of the students in the Equity Club—Ronald, Jimmy, and Eunice—took center stage at the school's weekly Community Circle. They began with a short skit in which Jimmy made fun of Eunice's clothing and accessories. "What are those?" he asked incredulously. "You look like Velma from Scooby Doo!" The students in the audience reacted raucously to this insult.

Then Igor entered the scene. "Are you serious, bro? You're judging her based off her appearance?"

Ronald added: "You don't know the half of what that girl goes through. Maybe she can't afford new clothing. Y'all are both human, right? Aren't you the same?"

"Nah, she's dusty, and I'm not," Jimmy declared, to more laughter from the audience. But, as the skit continued, Jimmy's character began to reconsider his perspective. In the skit's final scene, he and Eunice were holding hands, and he apologized for his hurtful comments.

When the skit ended, Ronald turned toward the audience. "As a community, we need to do more to support one another. That was a skit about bullying, and now we have a challenge for every crew. Everyone—you have to make three people smile by the end of tomorrow." There was murmuring in the audience about that challenge being an easy one. "It may be corny," Ronald continued, "but if we're gonna do positive things as a community, we need to do it together. Now here's what we're gonna chant:

'Peace! Positivity! Unity in our community!'" He began the chant. "Peace! Positivity! Unity in our community!" About half the audience joined in hesitantly. "Yo," Ronald called, "we need two representatives from each crew up here right now!"

A handful of students began moving slowly toward the front of the theater to join him, but then another senior stood up and marched up the center aisle to join Ronald, waving his arms emphatically. The entire room exploded with noise. "Peace! Positivity! Unity in our community!" Students started screaming out the chant and jumping up on their chairs. The black box theater felt like it was shaking. Ronald called out above the commotion: "We're gonna check in with the teachers to see who has the most positive crew!"

From a sociocultural learning theory perspective, these opportunities for youth to engage in school-based activism through the Student Advocacy Club and Equity Club represented important intermediate steps in their development as activists.[26] Specifically, these experiences allowed youth to engage with increasing autonomy in enacting the activist practices to which their teachers had introduced them and in which they were now mentoring them.[27] Prioritizing such opportunities for student autonomy—or "self-discovery"—also represents a key principle of expeditionary learning. As Principal Klarens Hill explained:

> If I can take a step back in some moments, not be the authority, and really trust that students can carry the day, I end up seeing beautiful things. It takes so much longer . . . and sometimes what they want to say is not what I would say, but it's also very important for me to step back and accept what they have to say because they can speak to their peers in a way I can't.

More than any of the other high schools featured in this book, Community Academy faculty and leaders demonstrated the patience to allow their students to do beautiful things. As Principal Klarens Hill noted, this approach was not an efficient one. Granting students the autonomy to take the lead on activities ranging from community meetings to class projects to extracurriculars meant that the planning and execution of these activities were often flooded with students' tangents, side conversations, teasing, flirting, and restlessness. But sticking with this autonomy none-theless meant that students at Community Academy also felt genuinely empowered to take ownership for effecting change within their school community. That empowerment led to beautiful, astounding moments like an entire student body raucously chanting "Peace! Positivity! Unity in our community!"

Supporting Activism in the World

Importantly, Community Academy faculty's support for student activism extended beyond the school walls as well. A number of Community Academy students participated in protests and marches after the 2014 decision not to indict the police officer who killed Michael Brown in Ferguson, Missouri. In describing her teachers' responses to such activism, Community Academy student Angelina explained: "The teachers, you know, they're not supposed to like openly say it, but they'll [say] like, 'I think it's really good what people are doing. I think you should do that, and it's good for people to do that.'" She added: "They was like telling us just be safe, they support us, and in fact, like, a few teachers went too."

A year later, youth across the city planned school walkouts to protest proposed budget cuts to the city's district high schools. As a charter school, Community Academy was not directly affected by these budget cuts, but a majority of Community Academy's class of 2017 decided to walk out in solidarity with their peers across the city. Community Academy student Brittany explained that teachers not only supported students' decision to walk out but also actively engaged them afterward in thinking about how these proposed budget cuts related to institutional forms of racism:

> Our teachers was talking of it being related to the Black Lives Matter move-ment and all that. . . . They wanted [us] to see that most of the people that's in the [the city] public schools are Black. We discussed the reasons of going and why we did the protest.

Both Angelina's and Brittany's comments echoed those of their class-mates in characterizing their teachers as encouraging their activist efforts. Such affirmations aligned with the expeditionary learning principle encouraging youth to be "crew, not passengers"—to engage actively in the world rather than float along as passive observers. Moreover, such affirmations from trusted adult mentors played an important role in Community Academy students' growing confidence in their own ability to engage independently in activist practices and to incorporate such commitment to activism into their developing adult identities.[28]

Finally, Community Academy faculty also reinforced the school's "crew, not passengers" mantra by sharing their own activist commitments with their students. At an equity-focused professional development session, faculty member Jill Solomon handed out Black Lives Matter and Safe Space stickers to her colleagues, and nearly every faculty member pasted the stickers onto their classroom doors and laptop computers. Faculty members spoke up at Community Circle about their attendance at protests for gay marriage, against police violence, and to halt construction of the Dakota Access Pipeline. They invited activists from local organizations like Families for Peace and Justice to come to Community Circle to speak to students about their work and about opportunities to get involved in it.

Additionally, Community Academy student Brittany explained that her participation in the Women's March and in protests against President Trump's Muslim ban came about, in large part, because her twelfth-grade humanities teacher, Sarah Singer, shared that she would be attending these protests. During a Community Circle discussion after the protests in Ferguson, Missouri, about what such activism can accomplish, Principal Klarens Hill described attending a protest for political prisoner Mumia Abu-Jamal during college and "feeling like I was making a change." Two years later, after the election of President Trump in 2016, Klarens told the entire school community: "President-elect Trump has said many terrible things about us, and the 'us' is not just Black people and people of Latino descent. But he spoke about Muslims, he spoke about the LGBT community, he has not recognized all we can offer the world." In this very personal talk to which students listened attentively, Klarens acknowledged that everyone in the room "will continue to be under attack for who we are" but pushed them to commit to "fighting for the liberation we all need." In all of these different ways, Community Academy faculty displayed their own commitments to activism to their students. For young people explicitly seeking out new and different ways of understanding the world and their role in it, such modeling contributed enormously to their beliefs about the importance of activism challenging racial (and other forms of) injustice.[29]

CHALLENGES FOR COMMUNITY ACADEMY

Community Academy's commitment to expeditionary learning and its core principles contributed to a school culture that provided students with opportunities to exercise agency, autonomy, and leadership. Numerous examples throughout this chapter make clear that this student-centered culture played a central role in Community Academy students feeling empowered to engage in activism both inside and outside of their school community. However, every one of the schools featured in this book demonstrated both strengths and challenges in its work to foster youth critical consciousness, and we have also sought to acknowledge that Community Academy's culture was also one in which students regularly came late to class, spent instructional time on their phones or talking to peers, took long "bathroom breaks" to wander the halls, and exerted less-than-maximum effort in carrying out class activities. In so doing, Community Academy students often avoided fully engaging in the learning necessary to develop deep understandings of the complex social and political issues included in their curriculum.

For example, as part of a humanities expedition on the American labor movement, students learned about twenty-thousand immigrant factory workers striking in Lawrence, Massachusetts, in 1912 in response to a cut in pay for women and children factory workers. After reading an article about the strike, the students engaged in a simulation in which they took on the role of the workers planning to strike. Teacher Johanna Henes—a White woman in her late thirties—set up the activity and then added: "There are some real challenges to pulling off this strike. Your job right now is to figure out how you're going to solve these challenges. I'm staying out of this one. You guys are going to lead the charge, and we have twenty minutes for this discussion. Begin."

Per Johanna's suggestion, the students circled up, but then one young man asked his group whether anyone had watched the television show *Power* the previous night. A short discussion ensued about who had and had not watched the show, and then who did or did not watch television at all.

"We need to vote for a leader," a young woman interjected, bringing the group back to the simulation.

"We need a bilingual leader," a young man added, recognizing that the workers involved in the strike had come from more than a dozen countries.

"Anybody Cuban?" a young woman asked. "Anybody speak Patois?" This latter question sparked a side conversation among several students about whether there was a difference between Haitian and Creole.

After this side conversation had petered out, one young man asked: "Should we allow women in the strike?"

A young lady bristled. "If I'm in the factory and making coats, why can't I walk and freakin' yell?"

Another young woman told her male classmates: "Y'all wouldn't be here without women, so . . ."

A young man countered: "Well, I came from my father's sack, so none of us would be here without men."

Teacher Johanna Henes interjected. "Okay, we are at eleven minutes and fifty seconds. So what's been challenging so far about having the discussion in this way?" The students noted language barriers and the absence of a clear leader—two genuine challenges faced by the striking workers in 1912. Johanna reset the students, but this time told them they could assume they were able to communicate with one another.

A young man restarted the simulation: "We all have family we want to provide for. What does everyone think? Go back to work or continue to protest?"

Another student advocated for going back to work and striking again in the spring when the weather would be warmer. A third student suggested taking a vote.

"Honestly, I'm just moving," a young lady interjected.

"I'll be a bank robber," a young woman beside her added. Her peers laughed, and the simulation got side-tracked again. The vote about whether or not to continue the strike never happened, and a few minutes later Johanna brought the simulation to a close.

In this activity, Community Academy students arrived at some genuine insights about how language barriers and squabbling about leadership had posed obstacles for the striking workers in 1912. At the same time, all of the off-track comments and side conversations limited the depth with which students engaged in this learning activity. Such off-track comments and side conversations occurred frequently in a number of Community Academy classrooms during many different types of instructional activities. In some ways, Community Academy's pedagogical orientation exacerbated this problem in that the expeditionary learning emphasis on providing students with time to "explore their own thoughts, make their own connections, and create their own ideas" meant that teachers often favored instruction with large blocks of time for students to engage in independent or group work.[30] This approach had many strengths, but it also allowed students in a school like Community Academy with a looser culture to opt out of taking full advantage of their work time. In short, the lack of structure in many Community Academy lessons meant that students often did not fully access the school's rich curriculum.

The upshot of these challenges was that, for many Community Academy students, their school's curriculum exerted a more powerful influence on their emotions and worldview than their analytic skills. Put another way, Community Academy students emerged from expeditions on the American labor movement and Syrian refugee crisis with heightened feelings of empathy for the oppressed groups about whom they had learned and a desire to engage in activism challenging such oppression. However, their understanding of the social forces underlying these historical events and social issues often lagged behind that of peers at the other schools featured in this book. Specifically, our survey and interview data revealed that Community Academy students completed high school with a significantly weaker understanding of systemic forms of racial and economic inequity than their peers in the other four featured high schools.[31] Often, the curriculum and content at these other schools were less rich than at Community Academy, but these other schools had established classroom cultures that allowed teachers and students to dig more deeply and intellectually into that curriculum and content.

In his foundational work on fostering critical consciousness, Paulo Freire argued for an egalitarian relationship between teachers and students such that both are teachers and both are students.[32] Yet, in his conversations with civil rights activist Myles Horton almost twenty years later that were chronicled in *We Make the Road by Walking*, Freire also observed:

> Without the limits of the teacher, the students cannot know. That is, the teacher has to enforce the limits. For example, how is it possible for a teacher to teach if the students come and go from the room at any time they want on behalf of "democracy." What if the teacher is not able to say on the first day, "No, it's impossible. You can come here on time, and you leave here on time as well as I do."[33]

In other words, Freire recognized that the pursuit of egalitarian teacher-student relationships should not serve as a justification for allowing students to disengage from their learning. Community Academy's culture and philosophy, despite many strengths, sometimes contributed to such student disengagement.

GRADUATION: YOUR VOICE IS A WEAPON

Friends and family members started cheering raucously as the first notes of "Pomp and Circumstance" filled the Wilmington Theater, and Community Academy seniors began processing down the center aisle. "That's my boy!" one mother called out audibly above the cheering. Other audience members laughed.

When the final graduate reached the stage, "Pomp and Circumstance" faded away, and all thirty-one young adults—clad in blue and white caps and gowns—took their seats. Principal Klarens Hill approached the podium.

"Seniors!" he began. "You made it here tonight. Your efforts, your years of effort have actually paid off right here right now in this moment. It was hard. It was maybe seeming impossible. But it was possible. You all did it." He paused. "I think our job, as faculty and staff, is to set up obstacles for you all to overcome. And you have done that. We've watched you grapple with concepts, hard curriculums, and hard conversations. You raised your voice, often. This class has raised their voice to say, 'We want this to change. That to be better for our school.' I am grateful to you, seniors, for both your words and your actions." Klarens looked across the audience. "For those of you who are new to our graduation, this is unusual. We have a lot of awards to give out here tonight to people who supported these seniors. So we're going to go right into it."

Over the next half hour, Community Academy faculty members presented awards to a dozen recipients including the school's volunteer librarian, a recent alumnus, a grandmother of one of the graduating seniors, and a nearby college that had demonstrated extraordinary support for Community Academy students who joined their student body. The dean of students presented a "good neighbor" award to an organization—Families for Peace and Justice—that had partnered with Community Academy to improve the school and community.

After all of these accolades had been offered, four members of Community Academy's award-winning slam poetry team marched onto the stage in a single-file line wearing military-style camouflage uniforms. Speaking in unison, their voices took over the entire theater as they emphatically called out wrongs perpetrated—and still being perpetrated—against people of color in the United States. Redlining, gentrification, cultural appropriation, police violence, genocide. "This is war!" the young poets declared. A number of audience members applauded emphatically. "We will no longer sit silently while you take everything that belongs to us!" The applause grew even louder as the performers put America on notice. They pledged to rewrite President Donald Trump's laws, tear down walls built to keep out immigrants, eject police from city street corners, and do whatever is necessary to preserve their heritage from attack. The poem ended with a final, powerful admonition: "America, you're on notice! We're coming!"

The entire theater exploded with cheering, whooping, and hollering. The applause continued for over a minute, and when it finally subsided, Principal Klarens Hill returned to the podium to present the diplomas. "This is what it's all about," Klarens began. "We gave kudos to alumni. We thanked community partners and family members. Now it's your turn. I know y'all can't wait to cross this stage, but, before you do, one more thing. You're always welcome back. Text, email, drop by, stay in touch. We'll be here to celebrate when you succeed and pick you up when you struggle." In the front row of the theater, several Community Academy teachers nodded emphatically. On stage, several graduates smiled. And with that, Klarens began calling up the thirty-one seniors who represented the newest graduates—and next generation of activists—from Community Academy.

CHAPTER **6**

Be the Change

"GOOD MORNING, class of 2017!" Principal Rochelle Andrade told the ninth graders seated in front of her in the Leadership High School auditorium. A handful of students murmured "Good morning" in response, then waited expectantly for Principal Andrade to continue. All ninety-five young people wore light blue dress shirts and gray pants. The boys wore gold-and-blue striped ties. This was the first day of these teenagers' high school careers, but also Principal Andrade's first day as principal. A woman of color in her early thirties, Principal Andrade had worked as an English teacher and assistant principal for several years before taking over this fall as Leadership High School's head of school.

"Welcome to ninth-grade orientation!" Principal Andrade continued. "Today and all this week we're going to introduce you to our school's core values, and we're going to start with respect." She clicked on a large screen positioned on the stage behind her that displayed in a stark, bold font: "Respect This House."

"I was watching *Martin* reruns last weekend," Principal Andrade told her students, "and there's this funny one where Martin has a fight night in his apartment. And he's charging at the door for people to come in, and he's watching the fight and sees that one of his neighbors is going into his fridge; another has his feet up. And then he goes into a tirade where he says, 'You need to respect this house!' And so I was thinking about that in the context of us here. So, in the context of using 'respecting this house' as a metaphor: what are the rules of this house?"

There was a long pause; then a young woman in the middle of the auditorium raised her hand. "Wear the proper uniform every day."

Principal Andrade nodded. "Yes, and the purpose of that is that we respect the learning space. So if you're in the uniform every day, it's not about Jordans; it's about learning. How about another one?"

"Stay quiet in the hallway?" suggested another young woman.

"Good," Principal Andrade told her. "On this floor and in the stairwells we're silent so that we're respecting the other schools in the building." Leadership High School and its three-hundred students were crowded into the top floor of a school building that housed two elementary schools on the first and second floors. The three schools shared the auditorium and cafeteria on the ground floor. "We're also respecting our teachers because they're driving us forward," Principal Andrade added. "And, as adults in the building, we're going to be respectful to you. We're also going to celebrate our achievements and have fun." Several ninth graders snapped their fingers in support of this last point.

Fast-forward three Augusts.

Principal Andrade—now starting her fourth year as principal—was back in the auditorium orienting the newest group of ninth graders. Sophomores and juniors were still home enjoying a final week of summer vacation. And three floors up, students in the class of 2017—now seniors—were cycling through workshops being held in four different classrooms as part of their "Twelfth-Grade Academy." The Twelfth-Grade Academy was an orientation to students' final year of high school and included workshops entitled Academic Maturity, Civic Skills, College Counseling, and Academic Integrity.

In the Civic Skills workshop, history teacher Mr. John Thomas—a White man in his late twenties—had projected onto the classroom whiteboard the civic skills that seniors needed to demonstrate to earn a Leadership High School diploma:

Public oral testimony
Public relations and marketing
Volunteering
Cause-related fundraising
Voter registration
Teaching and mentoring
Canvassing
Prepare a piece for publication
In-person lobbying

"Most of these skills you're going to be able to demonstrate through Seminar on American Democracy, your Be the Change projects, and Get Out the Vote," Mr. Thomas assured the seniors. "The only two you're asked to do totally on your own are the last two. And you'll do so much writing in your classes this year that you'll probably write something that you could turn in for the piece for publication." Mr. Thomas gestured at the last civic skill on the list. "Anyone know what lobbying is?"

A young woman raised her hand. "When you present your ideas to a high-up person."

"For the purpose of what?" Mr. Thomas asked.

"For change."

Mr. Thomas nodded. "That's a pretty good definition. We've sent kids up to the state capital to argue about charter schools in the past, but that's not the only type of lobbying. There's even internal lobbying here. There have been people in the past who have come up with ideas for rule changes here that they took to the principal. With your Be the Change project, you're all going to be working on a social cause. As you build that out, think about how you might lobby for this cause. This one is going to take some legwork on your end to find someone you can talk to."

Another student raised her hand. "Is the requirement that you succeed in making the change?"

Mr. Thomas shook his head. "No, it's about making a concerted effort."

ORIGIN STORY: LEARN TO BE THE CHANGE

Leadership High School opened its doors in the fall of 2009 with seventy-five ninth graders. The school's founder—Mr. Nate Herman, a White man in his late twenties—had written the original blueprint for the school as a college senior interested in both progressive schooling approaches and the role of schools in preserving democracy. After several years teaching abroad and a fellowship year with a charter school incubator, Mr. Herman dropped the progressive pedagogy in his original proposal in favor of a no-excuses approach but maintained his vision for a school explicitly committed to fostering students' civic skills and commitments. As he explained, "I sort of wiped out most of the [original] pedagogy, but I kept the part I cared about most, which was, 'How do you educate citizens for a democracy to be sustainable?'" This revamped proposal won Mr. Herman the opportunity to start Leadership High School in the same northeastern city in which he himself had grown up.

Then Mr. Herman set about recruiting students. As he recalled, "I was this White guy with a pamphlet I printed on my home computer, walking around to street fairs and community centers and churches and hair salons, being like, 'Hey, I'm opening a school. You should come.' And that still blows my mind, as a parent today, that the parents were willing to do that, and I am grateful for it." In fact, more than three-hundred families entered the lottery for the seventy-five seats in that first cohort of Leadership students.

Per Mr. Herman's revamped proposal, Leadership High School adopted many of the practices of no-excuses schools: a longer school day and year, uniforms, demerits, an unequivocal college preparatory mission, and, most of all, an intensive focus on academic rigor. But layered on top of—or perhaps alongside—that no-excuses foundation were programming and practices connected to the school's mission of preparing active and engaged citizens necessary for a sustainable democracy. For example, Leadership students participated each year in Get Out the Vote campaigns in which they led voter registration drives in their own community to strengthen its representation and voice. As seniors, Leadership students participated in a year-long Seminar on American Democracy—originally cotaught by Mr. Herman and an attorney—that deepened their understanding of the processes by which laws and policies at every level of government are drafted, lobbied for, interpreted, and implemented.

Finally, the capstone project for all Leadership students was the development and execution of a "Be the Change" project. As Mr. Herman explained, these Be the Change projects were among the holdovers from the school's original proposal and came out of his belief that "by the time you are seventeen or eighteen years old, you need to [be able to] conceive your topic, design your intervention, whatever that's going to look like, execute it, write about it, [and] analyze it . . . before we're going to give you a diploma." In considering the effects of such programming on Leadership students' civic development, one recent study found that graduates of Leadership High School were significantly more likely to have voted in the 2016 presidential election than peers who had entered the lottery to gain admission to Leadership High School but had attended high school elsewhere.[1]

After more than a decade at the helm of Leadership High School, Mr. Herman moved on to a new opportunity to shape education policy across the United States, and Ms. Andrade took over as principal. If Mr. Herman's original vision for Leadership High School had focused on fostering in students the civic skills, knowledge, and dispositions necessary for *sustaining* the American democracy, then Principal Rochelle Andrade's tenure as principal shifted students' deployment of those qualities toward recognizing and challenging injustices embedded within our democracy. As Principal Andrade explained:

> Understanding how this stuff works in terms of power and equity and race and all this stuff was really empowering for me as a college student 'cause I could finally say, 'Well now I can get fired up about how to change that,' and like there's this whole history that's happened that is fucked up but, like, I now can get fired up about where to go. And there have been a lot of change agents along the way who have tried to get the country to move in a certain direction.

Prior to taking over as principal, Principal Andrade had advocated for Leadership High School to take on this more critically conscious orientation but had gotten some pushback from colleagues and leaders worried about disrupting faculty and students' intensive focus on academic rigor and achievement. From Principal Andrade's perspective, however, the two went hand in hand. She explained:

> As a student myself, I needed to know what that story was about race in this country, and equity, and how folks have gotten empowered, to feel fired up about getting an education. Without that narrative, there were multiple times where I would have just pulled back and not gotten the education, and just gone home to a life that felt familiar.

Several research studies offer support for this connection Principal Andrade recognized between students' critical consciousness, academic motivation, and academic achievement.[2] After taking over as head of school, Principal Andrade explained: "I've been articulating that to staff overtime!" Moreover, her goal of infusing a more critically conscious flavor to Leadership's civic programming led to the addition of two powerful new learning experiences for students: a menu of theme-based English seminars and a Sociology of Change course. In this chapter, we describe both of these learning experiences in greater detail as well as their roles in fostering Leadership students' developing critical consciousness.

SCHOOLING FOR CRITICAL CONSCIOUSNESS: ACTION CIVICS

Civic education has been part of public schooling in the United States since its inception. Two of the founding fathers of public education in the United States, Thomas Jefferson and Horace Mann, regarded universal public education as a key lever for preparing citizens to take on their civic duties and responsibilities within a democracy.[3] That ethos lives on in mandates across forty states that require adolescents attending public schools to take stand-alone courses in civics or government.[4]

The predominant focus in such civics and government coursework, however, has been civic *knowledge* delivered primarily via textbooks and teacher lectures. A growing number of scholars have characterized this approach as the "old civics," and they have questioned the ability of "old civics" to foster in students the civic *skills* and *dispositions* necessary for engaging effectively in the contemporary political system.[5] Civic *skills* refers to the capacities necessary for genuine civic involvement, such as running a meeting, giving a speech, and writing a letter or email about a civic issue.[6] Civic *dispositions* refers to the ability to look beyond one's self-interest to the greater good of one's group or community.[7]

Action civics—or "new civics"—seeks to foster youths' civic knowledge, skills, and dispositions by supplementing textbooks and lectures with more experiential approaches to civic learning such as simulations of democratic processes, classroom discussions, community service learning projects, youth participatory action research, and meaningful student governance opportunities.[8] A growing body of scholarship suggests that such approaches to civic education have a powerful effect on young people's commitments and abilities to engage in civic and political processes.[9] Accordingly, states such as Massachusetts have begun to amend their civic education mandates to require school-based civics curricula to include student-led projects and opportunities for experiential learning.[10]

Although the term *action civics* wouldn't be popularized for several for more years, this idea of a more experiential approach to civic education was present in the original Leadership High School proposal that Mr. Herman authored as a college student as well as in programming such as the school's yearly Get Out the Vote efforts and Be the Change capstone projects. Leadership faculty and leaders referred to these types of learning opportunities as "authentic civics" and cited their place in the school's programming as a distinguishing feature of a Leadership High School education.

Pairing the strict, achievement-oriented culture of no-excuses schooling with action civics was an unusual marriage. Both Mr. Herman and Principal Andrade explained that, for a number of years, the way that marriage had played out in practice was that Leadership High School was effectively divided into a lower school and an upper school. Faculty in the lower school focused intensively on no-excuses-style structure, discipline, and academic skill building, while upper-grades teachers worked to incorporate more creativity, freedom, and opportunities for authentic civic engagement into students' learning experiences. But Principal Andrade explained that ushering in a more critically conscious approach to civic education also meant starting to tack away from a strict no-excuses model for the younger students as well. As she explained:

> I think over time we have become an organization that is still focused on real results for kids and wants to push academic rigor at all times, but we also want to explicitly teach kids how to get empowered in their communities, and you can't do that, and say to a kid that they're not allowed to talk back to an adult ever. . . . So I think we're starting to get into really great territory where we kind of want some rebels. We want kids pushing back. So how do we explicitly teach that, and how do we shift the systems we use around culture and discipline at the school to allow for that?

Principal Andrade acknowledged that Leadership High School was still at the beginning of this process of transformation. In the remainder of this chapter, we present the effects of Leadership High School's action civics approach on students' developing critical consciousness and, in particular, upon their commitment to activism challenging racial injustice and other forms of oppression.

DEVELOPING CRITICAL CONSCIOUSNESS: SOCIAL ACTION CHALLENGING INJUSTICE

A commitment to activism refers to an individual's propensity to engage in a wide range of social action behaviors such as writing letters to newspapers, contributing to a political campaign, engaging in protests, or boycotting particular businesses or products.[11] For Paulo Freire and other scholars, engagement in such collective social action represents a key dimension of critical consciousness and also the ultimate goal of critical consciousness development (see figure 6.1).[12]

FIGURE 6.1   Components of critical consciousness

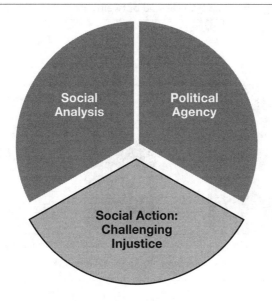

Accordingly, the critical consciousness survey completed by youth attending the five high schools featured in this book and the four comparison high schools included a Commitment to Activism scale as a measure of students' commitment to social action.[13] On this scale, youth expressed their likelihood of taking part in a variety of activist activities including signing a petition about a social or political issue, taking part in a protest or demonstration, and campaigning for a political candidate or cause. Youth evaluated their likelihood of engaging in such activist activities along a five-point scale in which a "1" represented "No Way!" and a "5" represented "Definitely!"

Figure 6.2 reveals that youth attending the five high schools featured in this book demonstrated modest growth in their commitment to activism from the start of ninth grade (Time 1) to the end of twelfth grade (Time 5). Moreover, as they graduated from high school in the spring of 2017, the youth attending these five featured high schools demonstrated significantly higher commitment to activism than their peers at the four comparison high schools.[14]

FIGURE 6.2   Youths' commitment to activism from the start of ninth
              grade (Time 1) to the end of twelfth grade (Time 5)

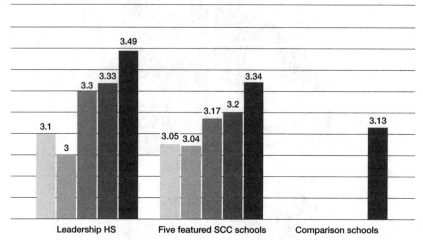

Importantly, further analyses revealed that the youth attending Leadership High School finished high school with a deeper commitment to activism than their peers across all five featured high schools at a level approaching statistical significance.[15] In other words, as the young people in these five schools came to the end of high school, Leadership students were more likely than their peers to cite a commitment to participating in social action ranging from mass protests to letter-writing campaigns. Finally, one can also see in figure 6.2 that this stronger commitment to activism demonstrated by students at Leadership High School began to emerge at the conclusion of tenth grade (Time 3) and then widened over the course of students' final two years of high school (Times 4 and 5).

To clarify, then, youth attending Community Academy demonstrated the steepest *growth* in their commitment to activism among the five featured high schools in this book. These Community Academy students began high school with, on average, very low commitments to activism and then demonstrated impressive growth over their subsequent four years of high school. In contrast, youth attending Leadership High School began high school in the middle of the pack in terms of their commitment to activism but then concluded high school four years later with the strongest commitment to activism across the five featured schools.

Developing a Commitment to Activism

In addition to a different growth trajectory, Leadership students' commitment to activism also took a different form than that demonstrated by Community Academy students. Scholars Roderick Watts and Carlos Hipolito-Delgado offer a useful framework for considering the differences between these two sets of students that distinguishes between personal action, group action, and the mass action of social movements.[16] Personal action describes the actions of a single individual to protest a policy or practice (e.g., writing a letter to a newspaper) while group action describes the efforts of an organization or collective to stage a similar protest (e.g., college students protesting the invitation of a campus speaker). Finally, the mass action of social movements involves the coordinated efforts of multiple groups and stakeholders to collectively challenge institutional practices or policies (e.g., Occupy Movement, Black Lives Matter).

The majority of Community Academy students described participating in citywide protests against gentrification and reduced funding of public schools (e.g., "group action") as well as nationwide protests against the police killing of teenager Michael Brown in Ferguson, Missouri and President Donald Trump's Muslim travel ban (e.g., "mass action of social movements"). In contrast, very few of the young people attending Leadership High School described participating in such citywide or nationwide activist efforts. Instead, beginning in the ninth grade, Leadership students cited their engagement in activism as coming primarily through their participation in twelfth graders' Be the Change projects (e.g., "personal action").

For example, Leadership student Daryl explained as an eleventh grader: "[For] everybody's Be the Change project, they need people to come support them, and sometimes people just do it because they feel like, this is going to be me next year." Daryl explained that a senior whose Be the Change project had focused on combatting sex trafficking "emailed me personally, and she said that she thought I should be involved in this."

Another senior enlisted him in her campaign to convince the city's department of education to treat the Muslim holiday of Eid as a public holiday similar to Christmas or Yom Kippur on which all city schools were closed.

Daryl's classmate Venice offered a similar description of her involvement in older students' Be the Change projects:

> We're basically helping them by giving them money that they need, giving them the clothes, the food, anything that they ask. Like the food drive, that's someone's Be the Change project. So like whenever they need help, we all help them because we know that when it's our turn, we're going to need that help to change it. Because no one can really change the world on their own. Because you need the backup. And I guess the eleventh, tenth, and ninth graders are the backup for the twelfth graders.

Within Watts and Hipolito-Delgado's framework, one might characterize these Leadership underclassmen as supporting the school's twelfth graders in carrying out "personal" forms of sociopolitical activism—that is, the efforts of a single individual (or very small number of individuals) to challenge an unjust policy or practice.

Watts and Hipolito-Delgado characterized personal forms of activism as generally less impactful than group action or the mass action of social movements; however, Leadership underclassmen described these opportunities to participate in twelfth graders' projects as having a substantial impact on their own developing commitment to activism.[17] For example, Leadership student Samuel explained as a ninth grader that supporting a senior's project to supply hiking products to a program serving low-income youth "makes me think that I can actually do something in the community." He added: "It allows you to think that you have a way to change the world." Samuel's classmate Soccoro similarly described the impact of helping out a senior whose Be the Change project culminated in a bottle drive to raise funds for the homeless. Soccoro explained: "I feel like if the twelfth graders are able to make a change for people that they've never even met before, then I could do the same thing when I get there." She added that participating in the seniors' projects also meant "that they're teaching us their ways so that we're able when we get to twelfth grade to have a Be the Change project that actually means something."

Of the twelve Leadership students who participated in yearly interviews, seven described the impact on their commitment to activism of participating as tenth graders in a particular Be the Change project challenging police violence against African Americans. As Leadership student Kelly explained:

> Many of the seniors did their Be the Change project on police brutality. . . . Instead of being violent, like we had a walk, and they just laid down in front of the [police] precinct. Like they all went in front of the precinct, made signs, laid down, made like basically a silent protest. That was like a big move. [There was] a lot of discussion on how we feel about it, and how to like approach a situation without being too violent. 'Cause like I think that's probably the best way to do it. 'Cause like no one gets hurt. No one wants to end up the next person on the news.

Her classmate Daryl explained: "We went out to the police station over there, and everybody just laid down . . . and it was like a good five-minute silence to show that Black people, like they should care about our lives, and not just go off the stereotypes that we're a certain way." Finally, a third Leadership student, Alvin, added: "So students actually like went in front of the police station and had a die-in, in a sense. So in it, we just laid down on the floor. I forget how long it was, but we just laid down on the floor . . . and said, 'If you want to take my liberty, you might as well kill me.' Because that's the only way that we're going to give in to your oppression."

In reflecting on the experience a year later, Alvin added that he and his classmates were "not only just sitting back and saying they shouldn't do that, we're actually like taking action." His participation in Be the Change projects such as this one had contributed to his sense of himself as already engaged in taking action to challenge injustice. In fact, when asked as a tenth grader about whether he looked forward to future opportunities to engage in activism, Alvin echoed a number of his classmates in explaining that, by virtue of his participation in the police die-in and other seniors' Be the Change projects, "I think I started already." Such a comment revealed the extent to which Leadership students' participation in these various Be the Change projects had contributed to their growing civic identities.[18]

Looking Forward

Participating in seniors' Be the Change projects gave Leadership under-classmen an opportunity to start conceptualizing themselves as activ-ists, but these opportunities also started underclassmen thinking about the projects they would carry out during their own senior year of high school. Leadership ninth grader Soccoro was by no means the only student who explained that helping out with seniors' projects started her think-ing about what kind of project she could lead that would "actually mean something." Her classmate Kadeem explained as a ninth grader: "I think my Be the Change project might be able to find a solution to help end racism." Leadership student Anajah—whose family was Indian and Jamai-can—explained as a ninth grader that she wanted her project "to end the racial differences between Indians and Blacks." Finally, as a senior carrying out a Be the Change project focused on shutting down websites contribut-ing to sex trafficking, Leadership student Jaclyn explained: "I wanted to do my Be the Change project since like ninth grade on this."

Leadership students' participation in interviews at the end of each year of high school also revealed the evolution in their thinking about their Be the Change projects. For example, Leadership student Lionel explained as a tenth grader that police violence against Black teenagers was an issue that mattered to him, and that he thought his role as a star football player in the city league might position him well for a Be the Change project that involved talking to younger football players about "staying off the streets and out of the cops' way." A year later as an eleventh grader, Lionel explained that a social issue on his mind was young people's lives being cut short by violence and that, for younger kids in his football league, "I am kind of taking [on] mentoring. I'm probably going to do it for my Be the Change project next year. I just got to like keep processing and figure out exactly what I'm going to do." Finally, as a twelfth grader actu-ally carrying out his Be the Change project, Lionel explained that he had sharpened his focus to supporting youth in his football program struggling with academic eligibility. Lionel added that low grades could have dire consequences for youth in his football program by preventing them from winning athletic scholarships that offered a pathway into college. According to Lionel:

> I took five [players] out the middle school and five out the high school. And we had practice Monday, Wednesday, and Friday. [Then] game on Saturday or game on Sunday. So out of those days, two [players] from the middle school, three people [from the high school] had to come early two days. And then like we would make sure they knock their homework out first before practice starts. . . . And then when you finish practice, you don't have homework instead of that being the reason why your grade is going down. And I seen improvements across the board.

With these improvements in his teammates' academic grades, Lionel made good on a commitment to support youth in his football program that he had first begun contemplating as a tenth grader. While, again, such efforts represented a form of personal action that was perhaps less impactful in scope than various types of group action or mass action, they served to strengthen Lionel's civic identity and, in so doing, his commitment to engaging in other forms of activism going forward.[19]

KEY SCHOOLING PRACTICES FOR CHALLENGING RACIAL INJUSTICE

Leadership High School's Be the Change projects were a quintessential example of the action civics emphasis on experiential civic learning and unquestionably exerted an outsized influence on participating youths' developing commitments to activism. However, Leadership High School's programming also featured several other learning experiences that scaffolded students' civic development as well. Two of these learning experiences, in particular, seemed to represent the foundational work on which the Be the Change projects rested.

Thematic Seminars

The first of these learning experiences was a menu of semester-long English seminars—Black Experience, Chicano Literature, Postcolonial Literature, Multicultural Literature, Deconstructing Masculinity—that Principal Andrade had established for eleventh- and twelfth-grade students in her second year as principal. In explaining why she had replaced the school's traditional eleventh- and twelfth-grade English courses with these thematic seminars, Principal Andrade explained:

> I think the important transition we've made is to talk about justice and equity through the English and history courses specifically. . . . So an English course was like very grammar-heavy when I [first] came to this school, very writing-mechanics heavy, not enough text and not enough meaty texts and not enough diverse texts were taught. And it was framed as 'we're going to build skills as readers,' less about 'we're going to interrogate the world through this piece of literature.'

Principal Andrade gave her English teachers the autonomy to propose the themes and critical lenses upon which each of these seminars would focus but also acknowledged that, "For me, that's always [going to be] race and justice." Toward this end, she developed and taught the Black Experience seminar herself for the first year of the new seminar system, and it was also notable that nearly all of the other seminars focused on issues intersecting with race and ethnicity as well.

In one class session from the Black Experience seminar, Principal Andrade and her students discussed author William Faulkner's decision in *Light in August*—a novel set in 1920s' Mississippi—to have a Black character, Joe Christmas, castrated and shot by White authorities for his affair with a White woman.[20] "What does that say about the racial climate in the 1920s, and what might Faulkner be trying to do in this book?" Principal Andrade asked her students.

"Probably the disadvantages Blacks are faced with," one student volunteered. "He is setting Christmas as an example."

"An example of what?" Principal Andrade prodded.

Another young man raised his hand. "You know how people say that people are innocent until you are proven guilty? Black people are guilty until they're proven innocent." A number of other students nodded vigorously, and the entire energy in the classroom shot upward. A young woman waved her hand.

"This is like public humiliation for Black men," she observed. "Christmas becomes a figure for Black men of, if you continue to have relationships with White women, you will be subject for castration and maybe even death."

Through readings and discussions like these, the Black Experience offered Leadership students the opportunity to consider the long and violent history of racial oppression in the United States. For this reason, Leadership student Venice explained that seminars like Black Experience "opened my mind to the world because I knew there were problems going on in society, because you know nothing is ever perfect. But, like knowing these specific things and the way that people are treated. . . . I feel like I learned that all from my literature class and my books." Another student Christian—who identified as Latinx—added: "I feel like it affects my mind greatly because our perspective is still around our own personal lives . . . so there's not a lot of room to build a bigger perspective for yourself. But literature allows you to see, for example, Black men. I'm not a Black man, but it allows me to see what they're going through." Both of these students' words revealed how literature seminars such as the Black Experience played an important role in deepening youths' understanding of how oppressive social forces influence individuals and, in so doing, catalyzed their thinking about the forces in the world that need to be challenged and changed. In this way, Leadership High School's thematic seminars exemplify scholar Nicole Mirra's call for secondary literature courses to foster youths' "critical civic empathy" by connecting "their subject matter to the world outside the school doors and position[ing] their students not simply as children, but as developing citizens of a democracy badly in need of their energy and leadership."[21]

A year later, Ms. Janelle Wilson—a Black woman in her mid-twenties—took over as the instructor for the Black Experience seminar and incorporated into the course Michelle Alexander's *The New Jim Crow: Mass Incarceration in the Age of Colorblindness*.[22] In one class session at the beginning of this unit, Ms. Wilson asked her students to share examples of the annotations they had made as they read the book's introduction.

One young woman shared a quote and then explained: "That quote is the whole basis of this book. It's talking about how the actual crime system and the war on drugs, it's a system created just to have control over us."

Another student agreed. "When they were describing what happens after you've been labeled a felon. Every time that is happening, it's different ways that people are getting unjust treatment."

A third student added: "The government does such a good job of hiding it that people aren't really seeing it." As Leadership students dove deeply into this text, Ms. Wilson pushed her students to make connections between the contemporary forms of racial injustice highlighted by Alexander and the legacy of slavery and Jim Crow featured in Faulkner's novel and other literary works.

The Black Experience was by no means the only English seminar that provided space for Leadership students to deepen their understandings of racial injustice. In Chicano Literature, for example, students read works from the Farmworker's Theater (*El Teatro Campesino*) of Luis Valdez that portrayed both the exploitation of Mexican immigrants and the activist efforts of the United Farm Workers to challenge such exploitation. Leadership student Erik explained, "In Chicano Lit I actually learned a lot about how immigrants are treated. . . . It got me thinking that they deserve opportunities just like us. Because if they're coming to America to seek a dream, [and] we're not giving them the dream, then it's kind of unfair." Likewise, in Post-Colonial Literature, students read works such as Zadie Smith's *White Teeth* that portrayed the lasting effects of European colonialism on Africa, Asia, and the Caribbean.[23] Reflecting on this and other texts from the seminar, Leadership student Kelly observed: "I know racism still lives, but when we're reading a book, I'm like, wow, like this really does still exist from happening really, really long ago."

Over the course of their final two years of high school, Leadership students had the opportunity to take four of these English seminars and, in so doing, to dive deeply into the nature and effects of racial injustice in the United States and abroad, in the past and the present, and in concert with other social forces such as sexism and economic inequality. In this way, Leadership High School drew upon literature to deepen students' understandings of the many permutations of racial injustice. Author Salman Rushdie has written: "In this age of information, in this age of information overkill, literature can still bring the human news, the heart's and mind's news."[24] Through portraits of injustice that reached Leadership students' hearts and minds, these seminars represented a powerful influence on these young people's developing commitment to change the world and also contributed to the decision of so many Leadership students to focus their Be the Change projects on issues of racial injustice.

Sociology of Change

Principal Andrade and her faculty also added a semester-long Sociology of Change course to students' twelfth-grade program of study that served as a ramp-up to their Be the Change projects. Principal Andrade explained that the course was intended both to provide more structured time for students to plan and execute their Be the Change projects as well as a space "where we talk about revolutions and grassroots and nonprofits" that push and prod governments toward social change. If the English seminars provided an opportunity for students to think deeply about how oppression shapes individuals, the Sociology of Change course offered a nuts-and-bolts investigation of how social change *happens*. Such a focus on civic skills within the Sociology of Change course—rather than simply civic knowledge—exemplifies an action civics approach to youth learning and development.

One way the Sociology of Change course sought to foster such civic skills was by introducing students to the writings of activist Marshall Ganz who had worked as a community organizer for the United Farm Workers alongside Cesar Chavez and then later helped to develop Barack Obama's grassroots organizing model for the 2008 presidential campaign. In one class session, Sociology of Change teacher Ms. Rachel Fuller—a White woman in her mid-twenties—asked students about what they had learned from a Ganz article about five key components of a successful social change movement.

One young man explained, "He's talking about like building relationships with the community. Can I give an example? He talks about Barack Obama and how he was involved in his community as an organizer. People began to support him because they saw him as someone who was supportive."

Ms. Fuller nodded. "Why is this important for creating a change movement?"

Another student raised his hand. "People are going to listen to you if you have a relationship with them."

Ms. Fuller shifted the conversation to another of Ganz's key components. "Storytelling. What is it? Why does it matter?"

A young man spoke up. "You gotta convey a message to the people. Like telling them a story, how it affected somebody."

Another classmate agreed. "Engaging people to be a part of it. Appealing to their emotions."

A third student added. "If you feel sorry for a person, you'll want to help them out."

As the discussion continued, Ms. Fuller and her students unpacked other key elements of Ganz's framework for social change such as strategizing and mobilizing resources. Importantly, as the semester moved forward and students continued developing their own Be the Change projects, Ms. Fuller regularly pushed students to consider whether and how their own projects were taking up these various components of effective social change. Leadership student Jaclyn said of reading social change theory by Ganz and others:

> It's very helpful because some of the stuff I actually didn't know, you know, Ganz's theory, Hirsch's theory. And looking at it from different perspectives allows you to communicate with different people, which is good, 'cause it all comes back to the people who support you. 'Cause you can't do it by yourself. So the class has definitely helped.

As noted by Jaclyn, Leadership seniors also learned in Sociology of Change about scholar E. L. Hirsch's work on the role of consciousness raising and collective empowerment in successful social change movements, as well as the difference between proactive and reactive social change efforts.[25] Through each of these readings, Ms. Fuller introduced Leadership students to theoretical frameworks for understanding what makes some social change efforts successful and others unsuccessful. In this way, these readings by Ganz and others came to serve as "mentor texts" for Leadership students' own developing activist efforts.[26]

Sociology of Change also engaged Leadership students in considering specific tools through which activists have sought to effect social change ranging from nonviolent protest to micro-finance loans. Over several class sessions, for example, Leadership students considered the role of social media in contemporary social change movements such as Black Lives Matter, the Arab Spring, and the 2015 Ice Bucket Challenge, which raised funds for amyotrophic lateral sclerosis (also known as ALS or Lou Gehrig's disease).

Regarding this latter example of social media and activism, Ms. Fuller began by showing her students a video compilation of celebrities dumping buckets of icy water over their heads to raise money for ALS research and then challenged her students to come up with criteria for evaluating whether this online activism had or had not been successful. After students had identified three key criteria for a successful social media campaign—money raised, awareness of ALS, and participation in the movement—Ms. Fuller assigned her students to find data relevant to judging the success of the Ice Bucket Challenge along these three dimensions. Twenty minutes later students began sharing out their findings.

"Since the beginning of the challenge, the ALS association gained 1.7 million donors," one student shared, reading these statistics from a website he had pulled up on his Chromebook.

"And they gave about $115 million," another student added. "Definitely successful."

A third student debated this last point by quoting an article she had pulled up on her laptop screen. "It says, 'When the Ice Bucket Challenge started, the people who were challenged to participate had 24 hours, or else they had to donate a hundred dollars. However, it says a lot of people instead bought bags of ice and poured it on their heads. And then it says although the ALS association has seen as much as four times as many donations compared to last year, just imagine for one second, what if the thousands of people who spent money on buying one or two bags of ice actually gave the money to ALS? It would be out of control."

"What about raising awareness?" Ms. Fuller asked.

A young man raised his hand. "I would call it a temporary success because, like, when the Ice Bucket Challenge was a thing, and people were doing it, it's like the searches of what ALS is went up a lot. But after a while people started forgetting about it. Like it was just a trend that people did." Through lessons and discussions like these, Sociology of Change sought to expose Leadership students to different levers for effecting social change, as well as an opportunity to evaluate the effectiveness of such levers.

Recall that critics of "old civics" have argued that curriculum and programming focused on civic *knowledge* do not sufficiently prepare youth to engage effectively in the political system.[27] In Sociology of Change, one can see another example of how Leadership High School's programming aligns closely with new civics or action civics in its emphasis on introducing students to civic *skills* that they could then apply themselves in executing their Be the Change projects.

Be the Change Projects

As noted throughout this chapter, Leadership High School's Be the Change projects aligned closely with the action civics emphasis on experiential civic learning, and the effects of these projects permeated the entire school's programming and culture. Programmingwise, the theme-based English seminars and Sociology of Change course had been established, in large part, to develop in students both the understanding of racial injustice and activist skill set necessary to carry out meaningful Be the Change projects. Culturewise, numerous Leadership underclassmen described their participation in older students' Be the Change projects as having catalyzed their belief in their own ability to effect social change as well as their thinking about the types of projects they would one day carry out themselves.

The projects themselves also sought to influence the world beyond the walls of Leadership High School. Leadership senior Lionel was the football star described earlier in the chapter whose Be the Change project focused on supporting the academic development and eligibility of younger players within his city football program. To measure his impact, Lionel kept track of his mentees' report cards and was thrilled to see evidence of improvement over the course of the academic year. In reflecting on the project, Lionel acknowledged, "I didn't think I could do that, but it just happened. I was like more determined to do it because I know somebody in that situation. . . . He's like a really great player. When he was fourteen, he had acceptances from college recruits and stuff, but [then] he was stuck in ninth grade for two or three years." Lionel's project potentially diverted several younger players from a similar predicament and also strengthened his own belief in his ability to effect such positive change.

A few weeks before graduation, Leadership seniors in the class of 2017 gave presentations on the results of their Be the Change projects to their teachers and peers. Principal Andrade sat in on many of these presentations as well. Reflecting on that experience, she observed: "I was trying to take off my principal hat . . . and just listen. One of them was our student who was homeless and like living in shelters, and her whole project was about creating this [support] group for homeless kids, or kids who had ever been out of permanent housing, and, looking at it through fresh eyes, I was like, 'This is pretty freaking impressive.'"

Another impressive Be the Change project was Leadership student Zoli's organization of a community dialogue on gentrification within her historically Black neighborhood. In describing her motivation to focus on gentrification, Zoli described "seeing the stores change [in my neighborhood], and there's a lot of condominiums being built." She also added, "My mom, like her relationship and experiences with the city housing system has been, like, crazy, so I guess just seeing my mom struggling with that and then seeing other groups benefitting off of that made me want to focus on it this year."

Zoli's event took place on a warm spring evening in the final month of her senior year in the courtyard of a local middle school. She and a few classmates had set up approximately forty folding chairs facing a long, rectangular table reserved for the invited panelists. In one corner of the

courtyard sat a DJ table flanked by two large speakers on stands and operated by an eleventh-grade Leadership student and his older brother. They
played a reggae remix of Rihanna's "Work" as both Leadership students and a
number of adults—primarily African American but also an older White couple—trickled into the courtyard. Zoli wore a dress and heels, and she greeted
each arrival at the entrance to the courtyard. The students headed straight for
the refreshments table arranged in another corner of the courtyard.

Shortly after 6:30 p.m., Zoli kicked off the panel discussion by explaining how she had come to this project. "I want this to be an informative
event," she told the audience. "It's not to attack gentrifiers, but to engage
in conversation. I believe that young people have a voice. We don't have to
be old and educated to make change in our community."

Seated beside her were three panelists, who then introduced themselves.
Alexis, a Black woman in her late twenties, worked as a community liaison in the mayor's office, and she explained that she saw the purpose of
tonight's event as addressing questions such as "What can we do to ensure
that affordable housing is available? How do we make sure your grandma
doesn't get evicted?"

A second panelist, Jacy, a gender nonconforming Black person in their
mid-thirties, worked as an organizer for a racial justice organization. Jacy
explained:

> Gentrification makes me extraordinarily angry because it reminds me of
> being gentrified out of my own neighborhood when I was ten. It was the
> first time I experienced eviction. So the experience of having some muscular
> White people come into my house and take all my stuff out and put it on
> the street is, like, not fun. Experiencing homelessness with my mother for
> a number of months is not fun. Having our rent tripled on us in the next
> place we lived so that we had to move out within a month is not fun. All
> those things make me angry. Seeing increased police presence in the neigh-
> borhood to protect White people, and never the people who actually lived
> there forever and ever is not fun. I don't really know what else to say about
> that except that it needs to stop.

The third panelist, Dr. Monroe, a Black man in his late fifties, had lived in this community for thirty-five years and ran an organization that advocated for affordable housing in the city. Dr. Monroe expressed doubt that gentrification could be slowed or the culture of their historically Black community be preserved. "What we have to begin to do," he explained, "is realize that change is inevitable. I don't know anything that stays the same unless it's rooted in deep economic roots."

Over the next hour, the panelists took questions from the audience, and Zoli skillfully moderated the conflicting perspectives offered by Jacy and Dr. Monroe in response to many of them. At the close of the discussion, Zoli shared her own perspective: "As you can see, there is a difference of opinion on this panel. And everyone's gonna have a different opinion. But the purpose of today is to just make you all aware of what's happening. It's to get your mind thinking, get you aware, and also get you outraged. If you're upset about this, then you're going to do something about it." And, with that, Zoli brought to a close an event that had drawn upon the civic knowledge, skills, and dispositions that she and her classmates had spent the past four years developing.[28]

CHALLENGES FOR LEADERSHIP HIGH SCHOOL

Of the five schools featured in *Schooling for Critical Consciousness*, Leadership High School's programming and practices may have been the most adept at addressing all three dimensions of youth critical consciousness: social analysis, political agency, and social action. Like all of the featured schools, however, there were also drawbacks and challenges to the various decisions Leadership High School faculty and leaders had made about *how* to foster students' critical consciousness.

Mandatory Social Action

As described in this chapter's opening pages, Leadership High School's action civics model articulated a number of specific civic skills that students needed to develop over their four years of high school and then required students to make use of these skills in their own, small-scale social action projects as a prerequisite for graduating. Leadership faculty and administrators took this final graduation requirement very seriously. In fact, Leadership founder Mr. Nate Herman acknowledged that there had been Leadership students "who did everything else, passed their classes, passed their tests, and they didn't do either a sufficient or complete job on their Be the Change project, and I didn't let them graduate."

Such prioritizing of the Be the Change projects came out of Mr. Herman's conviction that a central pillar of Leadership High School's work was cultivating students' development of the civic skills necessary to be effective sociopolitical actors in the various communities they would join as young adults and adults.[29] At the same time, making the Be the Change projects mandatory meant there were some Leadership students who confessed to merely going through the motions in carrying out their particular projects. In other words, just as there were unquestionably Leadership seniors such as Anajah and Jaclyn who regarded their Be the Change projects about race relations and sex trafficking as a long-awaited opportunity to address social issues about which they felt passionate, there were also seniors who regarded the capstone project as merely a final hoop through which they were required to jump.

Leadership student Kelly, for example, explained that she thought the Be the Change requirement was "supposed to make me feel empowered to do things," but, in terms of its actual effects, "I feel like it's bad to say nothing, [but] I just don't feel, like, this energy to go outside and hang up signs and post on Twitter, and movements and stuff." She added that the process of Leadership students carrying out their Be the Change projects "was helpful. Maybe not for me exactly because I don't feel this empowerment, but, you know, [for] other people that are in my grade like Jaclyn. 'Cause I feel like that's something she's really gonna do, and now she has like the foundation to really go forward." Kelly's point here was that her school's capstone project was a far less consequential experience for her than for some of her other classmates. Perhaps as a result she spoke dismissively of her own Be the Change project as "just me putting out words."

Overall, Leadership High School's Be the Change project seemed to be a powerful opportunity for students to carry out a project about which they felt passionate and a catalyst for future activist involvement. Nonetheless, Kelly's perspective revealed that the school's practice of *requiring* youth to engage in social action diminished the authenticity of the experience for some of these youth. The concern, then, is that such youth may be dissuaded from participation in future social action opportunities because they experienced such opportunities during high school as extrinsically mandated rather than intrinsically motivated.[30] Especially given that prior research on the effects of such mandatory high school service and social action projects are inconclusive, educators at Leadership High School and elsewhere must keep attuned to the possibility of the Be the Change projects having unintended, negative effects upon students' future civic and political engagement.[31]

White Teachers

A second challenge to Leadership High School's efforts to foster youth critical consciousness lay in the lack of racial diversity of its faculty. Specifically, at a school where nearly three quarters of the students identified as Black or African American, there were only five Black teachers among the thirty-person faculty during the class of 2017's senior year. Consequently, several Leadership students expressed their belief that this lack of faculty diversity had negatively influenced their learning about issues of racial injustice. For example, Leadership student Erik explained as an eleventh grader:

> Like the teachers I've had, I feel like they do care about race, but it doesn't affect them. So like even though they do care, they kinda don't care 'cause [in] their life they're kind of like privileged. They grew up not being Black. They didn't have to go through what a Black person has to go through, so . . . they try to understand, but like it's really hard 'cause like they didn't grow up around our situations.

A year later, as a graduating senior, Erik expressed his belief that Leadership High School would have engaged students even more deeply and frequently in considering issues of race and racism if there were more Black teachers among the faculty. He explained of his mostly White teaching faculty: "If we had more African Americans as teachers, then maybe we would be talking about it just like more . . . Like we have a very hard stigma as African Americans, and I feel like we just don't talk about it 'cause like it makes them uncomfortable, and like they just don't understand what I feel."

Another Leadership student, Jason, offered a similar perspective on the influence of the school's faculty demographics. "It's crazy how this school, mostly the teachers are all White. I'm not saying there's no Black teachers, but the population of it is that a minority of the teachers are Black and Spanish, so I feel like it's built in[to] the way that we learn and what they allow us to learn, the important issues that we touch on." Jason went on to express his belief that his teachers' relative lack of knowledge about Black history meant "we spend a month or so learning the same things every single year about MLK and Malcolm X." Both Erik and Jason were measured in their critiques of the Leadership faculty in that they acknowledged their teachers' genuine commitments to engaging with them around issues of racial injustice and inequity. Nonetheless, both of these young men perceived the shortage of Black teachers among the Leadership faculty to have limited the depth of their learning about these issues.

Several Leadership teachers directly or indirectly acknowledged this critique as well. One of the school's five Black teachers observed that, in her work with students, her same-race identity "definitely [has] a positive effect on them. They feel like they can talk to me about stuff, or they feel comfortable talking about things in class when I bring up things like stereotypes or racial issues." Relatedly, several of Leadership's White teachers acknowledged their own hesitation, at times, to bring up issues of race or racism with their students. For example, in response to a question about discussing harmful racial stereotypes with students, one White faculty member explained: "I do think that it's definitely addressed, [but] I think it's always a hard line to walk because, for the most part, it's a bunch of White teachers that are saying this, so we don't want to be, um . . . " This teacher never finished her sentence, but the implication was that she and other White teachers feared that bringing up such issues of race or racism with their students might be inappropriate or unproductive. Such a perspective aligns with previous scholarship that has found teachers feel "extraordinary pressure" *not* to talk about race.[32]

For her part, Principal Andrade acknowledged that, while she had taken explicit steps to infuse Leadership High School's programming with more critically conscious curriculum on race and racism, she "hadn't done enough yet" to support her teachers in developing the skills and comfortability to lead such programming. In short, then, all of these educators' comments resonated with the points raised by students like Erik and Jason that being taught by a predominantly White faculty had substantively influenced the treatment of race and racial injustice in the curriculum.

Ultimately, even the most critically conscious curriculum and programming requires teachers ready, willing, and able to engage students in meaningful discussions of inequity, injustice, and oppression.[33] Increasing the racial diversity of one's faculty is an important piece of this work, as is substantive professional development around the role for both White teachers and teachers of color in fostering the critical consciousness of Black and Latinx youth. Both of these steps could further amplify the effects of Leadership High School's programming and practices on the critical consciousness development of its students.

GRADUATION: FIRED UP AND READY TO CHANGE HISTORY

Leadership High School's graduation took place in the most historic theater in the city. Family members and friends filled up the mezzanine level while Leadership underclassmen took over the balcony, looking down from the top of the house on the proceedings that would one day be for them.

Several hundred side conversations hushed abruptly when the first strands of "Pomp and Circumstance" floated out from the theater's sizeable speakers, and, clad in gold caps and gowns, Leadership High School's seventy-five seniors and thirty-plus faculty processed down the center aisle. At the end of their walk, they found seats in the theater's first several rows.

Principal Andrade appeared on stage—clad in a gold cap and gown herself—and took her place at the podium. She began her remarks with a story. "The other day, my husband started to tell me about something that happened on the subway. I was only half listening until he said something about Leadership High kids. Then my ears perked up. As a principal, I was on full alert. 'What about Leadership High kids?' I asked. 'Were they misbehaving or something on the train?' I was ready to take thorough mental notes. Whatever he told me might need to be followed up on tomorrow. 'No!' he said, 'it was some other teenagers talking about Leadership kids.' Now a different alarm bell goes off. 'What did they say?" I asked. "Did it sound like there was any tension between them and our kids? Like a possible fight?' 'No, no, no,' he said. 'It was clear that they have some friends at Leadership High. One was saying, you know, he wanted to hang out with someone, but the kid he wanted to meet up with attends Leadership. So his friend started teasing him, 'Oh, then you know you can't see her *anytime* soon. She goes to Leadership. She's going to be at school for *a while*.'" The crowd laughed knowingly.

Principal Andrade admitted to her audience. "I've been wrestling for weeks with what I wanted to talk to you about today." The theme she had ultimately settled on was *boldness*. First, Principal Andrade addressed her faculty. "You are fierce activists," she told them. "You are standing up for the kind of education you will hope to secure for your own children one day. And that makes you bold. It makes you a bit of a problem for the status quo." She paused, then added. "It is my honor to stand shoulder to shoulder with you, disrupting right alongside you."

Principal Andrade looked out at the audience. "Parents, thank you for being bold in your own right. Thank you for eschewing the advice of friends who meant well, who advised you not to put your child in that charter school. Thank you for embracing high expectations, learning through failure, and the teamwork it was going to take to see this thing through. As one of our students, Keona, said last week at the senior dinner, 'This diploma is for you too.'"

Finally, Principal Andrade looked down at her graduates in the front of the theater. "I realized when my husband told me about the kids who had to wait until late in the evening to see their friends who attend Leadership High School, it isn't only the adults who work at Leadership High who have answered a call, who are doing important work. Work that feels bigger or more significant than the individuals. These young people sitting right in front of me, they have answered a call. They are doing important work. They are world changers." A number of audience members applauded.

After a pause, Principal Andrade continued. "My favorite writer of all time is James Baldwin, as our staff knows. In *The Fire Next Time*, in 1963, he wrote, 'If we—and now I mean the relatively conscious Whites and the relatively conscious Blacks, who must, like lovers, insist on, or create, the consciousness of the others—do not falter in our duty now, we may be able, handful that we are, to end the racial nightmare, and achieve our country, and change the history of the world.'" Principal Andrade smiled at the graduates in front of her. "These graduates are not only conscious, but equipped, fired up, and ready to change that history. I am so proud of you, I am so honored to have known you, and to have played a role in your education." The audience applauded raucously, and Principal Andrade made way for the graduates' elected student speaker, Zoli. An hour later, Leadership students and their families spilled out of the theater and into the city streets, diplomas in hand, fired up and ready to change the world.

CHAPTER 7

Tools and Spaces for Youth Critical Consciousness

OVER THE PRECEDING five chapters, we have sought to portray how Make the Road Academy, Espiritu High School, Harriet Tubman High School, Community Academy, and Leadership High School excelled at fostering different dimensions of youths' critical consciousness of racial injustice. Youth engaged in Make the Road Academy's problem-posing educational model finished high school with stronger *social analysis* skills than their peers in the other schools while the young people attending Espiritu High School—with its habits of mind approach—demonstrated both the steepest growth and highest levels of *political agency*. Youth participating in Community Academy's expeditionary learning model demonstrated the steepest growth in their commitment to challenging racial injustice through *collective social action* while the young men and women participating in Leadership High School's action civics model concluded high school with the highest commitment to engaging in such collective action. Finally, the young people participating in Harriet Tubman High School's no-excuses schooling model demonstrated both the steepest growth and highest levels of confidence in their ability to successfully navigate Whitestream spaces and settings—a skill that Tubman educators framed as a form of *personal social action*.

The preceding five chapters offered case studies of each of these distinctive trajectories of youth critical consciousness development as well as the curriculum and programming at each of the five schools that had contributed to these distinctive trajectories. We believe descriptions of these practices can be useful to educators and other stakeholders invested in supporting their own students' growth in the various dimensions of critical consciousness.

That said, what also emerged from the five case studies were a number of common teaching tools employed by multiple schools for fostering their students' critical consciousness of racial injustice. We begin this chapter by describing these common teaching tools in greater detail, and then we turn to the spaces within secondary schools where these tools can be deployed to support youths' critical consciousness development. Finally, we conclude *Schooling for Critical Consciousness* with some thoughts about how educators and other stakeholders might draw on the programming and practices featured throughout the book to support their own critical consciousness work with youth.

TEACHING TOOLS FOR YOUTH CRITICAL CONSCIOUSNESS

Over four years investigating youth critical consciousness at five distinctive high schools, we observed a number of common teaching tools across these schools, including theoretical frameworks, youth teaching youth, opportunities to effect school change, real-world assignments, and teachers getting personal. We describe each of these tools in turn.

Theoretical Frameworks

Students at several different schools cited their learning about various theoretical frameworks as having powerfully influenced their critical consciousness of racial injustice. Perhaps the most notable example was the Three I's framework—that oppression can be interpersonal, institutional, and internalized—introduced to youth attending Make the Road Academy in their ninth-grade Social Engagement course. Numerous MtRA students described this framework as having opened their eyes to the multifaceted workings of racial injustice within American society. In so doing, the framework strengthened these young people's ability to analyze the causes and consequences of racial injustice in their lives and community.

If the Three I's framework contributed to MtRA students' ability to engage in social analysis, then students at Leadership High School described their twelfth-grade Sociology of Change course as introducing them to a valuable framework for engaging in social action. Specifically, Leadership students cited organizer Marshall Ganz's components of a successful social change movement as having bolstered their knowledge of how to recruit allies and partners for social change work challenging racial injustice. Students explicitly drew upon Ganz's framework in developing and executing their own Be the Change capstone projects.

Psychologist Erik Erikson has characterized the central task of adolescence as moving beyond a strict adherence to the worldviews of one's family members and home community, and seeking out new and different ways of understanding the world.[1] These new understandings can come from peers, popular culture, adult mentors, and so on.[2] Moreover, these examples from Make the Road Academy and Leadership High School reveal the power of theoretical frameworks such as the Three I's to deepen adolescents' understandings and commitments. Scholar Bettina Love makes reference to the power of such frameworks when she notes: "Theory helps explain our reality and our students' realities. . . . Theory does not solve issues—only action and solidarity can do that—but theory gives you language to fight [and] knowledge to stand on."[3]

Another example of the power of such frameworks occurred in Ms. Natalie Morales's tenth-grade US History class at Espiritu High School during a unit on the civil rights movement. At the outset of the unit, Natalie pointed out to her students that, when one looks at all of the books written about the civil rights movement, there are more books about Martin Luther King Jr. and Rosa Parks than every other activist combined. "What does that tell us?" she asked her tenth graders. "Does it mean MLK and Rosa Parks are more important?"

"It might mean what they did had the biggest impact on people," volunteered one student.

"Possibly," Natalie said. "But I also want to question why other people aren't talked about as much. Lee Anne Bell at Barnard College talks about the stock story, the concealed story, and the resistance story." Natalie went on to define the stock story as the story offered by the dominant group to maintain the status quo, while concealed stories are those circulated and told and retold by people on the margins, and resistance stories are those that challenge stock stories. "We often hear a stock story about Rosa Parks," Natalie observed, "that she sat in the front of the bus because she was tired that day. The concealed story is that she was actually involved with the NAACP, so she was fighting for civil rights before she made that decision not to move to the back of the bus." As the lesson continued, Natalie gave her students an opportunity to think about how this framework applied to other stories involving race and racism that they had grown up hearing.

"Like the Native Americans and Pilgrims coming together to celebrate," one student volunteered. "That's a stock story we're told about Thanksgiving." In this and other examples, Espiritu students embraced this stock-concealed-resistance-story framework as a new tool for making sense of the world.

Youth Teaching Youth

A second theme that emerged in the critical consciousness work of several schools was the powerful effect of youth teaching youth. For example, nearly all of the interviewed students from Leadership High School described the powerful influence of the school's Be the Change projects on their commitment to engaging in social action. In making this point, however, Leadership students just as often pointed to their participation *as underclassmen* in an older student's Be the Change project as they did to the project that they themselves had designed and carried out as seniors. Such participation highlighted for Leadership ninth, tenth, and eleventh graders what young people can accomplish, and jump-started their own thinking about the types of projects they might one day carry out themselves.

A similar pattern of youth teaching youth emerged at Espiritu High School. Espiritu held a monthly, extended community meeting with an agenda planned and led by rotating groups of students. For example, after the police shooting of African American teenager Michael Brown in Ferguson, Missouri, Espiritu tenth graders used this community meeting to hold a "Justice for Michael Brown" event in which they drew parallels for the rest of the student body between Michael Brown's death and that of Emmett Till in Jim Crow era Mississippi in 1955. Likewise, Espiritu students participating in the Facing History community improvement project took responsibility each year for leading several of these community meetings on topics ranging from Islamophobia to bullying to racial microaggressions. In interviews, Espiritu students described the powerful influence on their feelings of political agency of taking on an instructional role in these community meetings *as well as* being an audience member for other students' presentations. Similar to the Be the Change projects at Leadership High School, these student-led community meetings served as a powerful example to the entire Espiritu community of what young people can accomplish when given the chance.

As noted earlier, adolescence represents a peak period of identity exploration in which individuals are actively seeking out new and different ways of understanding the world and their role in it.[4] Because such a process explicitly entails adolescents pulling away from one's parents and close family members, many scholars have written about the ways in which adolescents' peers take on an outsized influence on their developing worldviews.[5] In fact, parents and educators often bemoan the effects of such outsized peer influence on adolescents' ideas and actions. However, both Espiritu High School and Leadership High School offer examples of how the outsized influence of peers can be directed toward positive and powerful outcomes as well. Namely, the students attending Espiritu High School and Leadership High School both described how learning from their peers about different forms of racial injustice had strengthened their feelings of political agency and commitment to social action, respectively.

Another powerful example of youth teaching youth was the "senior talk" delivered by each member of Community Academy's senior class at the school's weekly Community Circle. As principal Klarens Hill explained to the entire student body before the first senior talk of the year: "A tradition at Community Academy is to have seniors give an apologia, and it is based on Socrates's apologia where he defended his life. The idea is that if you were put on trial and defending your life, what would you say, and what would you share?" The senior talks typically lasted ten or fifteen minutes. They were highly personal and often emotionally wrenching. Seniors opened up about topics ranging from painful relationships with their parents to experiences with bullying to challenges that had influenced their goals and trajectories. Quite often, these topics intersected with issues of race and racism.

The talks typically concluded with lessons learned and advice for the underclassmen coming up behind them. One Community Academy senior concluded her talk: "When people are confident in their own identity, it takes away the stress of following the stereotypes society has embedded on our race." Another young woman finished with the explanation, "Now I know I don't need a man to be successful. And I don't try to force a relationship because your life will make room for those who are supposed to be in it." A young man concluded his senior talk by explaining: "Now, I embrace my weirdness, and my teachers embrace me for who I am. Never feel as if there is not enough room for you to be yourself. There's always an open door waiting for you."

In her ninth-grade interview, Community Academy student Brandi explained that the senior talks "help me a lot. . . . Some of the seniors have the same problems that I have, and then to hear how they resolve it, I could use that, and like put it to work." Four years later as a graduating senior, Brandi explained of her own senior talk: "It was kind of like powerful because, afterwards, you notice how many people are affected by you, and you learn that your decisions—and what you've learned—when you can just pass it on, it saves everybody a lot of trouble from learning it on their own the hard way." In this example as well, Community Academy took advantage of the outsized influence of adolescents' peers by inviting graduating seniors to share their insights with the underclassmen on topics ranging from navigating the world as a young person of color to engaging in healthy relationships with parents and romantic partners.

As described in chapter 5, Community Academy's looser school culture often resulted in student behavior that posed a challenge to teaching and learning both in the classroom and in activities such as Community Circle.

A stark exception to this pattern was the senior talks to which the entire Community Academy student body listened in rapt, sometimes painful, silence. For better and for worse, Community Academy students treated the wisdom of their peers during these senior talks with a respect and a regard they sometimes withheld from the school's adults.

Opportunities to Effect School Change

A third theme evident across several schools was that youth character-ized opportunities for engaging in social action *within* their own school community as exerting a meaningful influence on their own critical con-sciousness development. Such characterizations were by no means a given. In their work on sociopolitical action, scholars Rod Watts and Carlos Hipolito-Delgado describe "external" actions aimed at the policies and practices of institutional targets as more impactful than "internal" actions aimed at one's colleagues, peers, and allies.[6]

Given these scholars' work, one might have expected adolescents in the participating schools to experience social action opportunities aimed at their own school community as too small in scope to be meaningful or consequential. But this was not the case. At Espiritu High School, for example, students in the eleventh-grade Civics course worked to challenge the school's blanket prohibition against headphones by researching the issues underlying the policy and then developing and delivering a presen-tation to the Espiritu community advocating for change. After ultimately succeeding in changing the school's headphone policy, Espiritu eleventh graders celebrated their hard-fought victory, and also characterized the experience as having deepened their feelings of political agency to effect change out in the "real world" as well.

Along similar lines, numerous students at Community Academy described themselves as having participated in efforts led by the school's Student Advocacy Club to change the uniform policy to allow students to wear shorts and colorful headbands. Similar to their peers at Espiritu High School, Community Academy students characterized their success in mak-ing these amendments to the school uniform policy as hard-won, mean-ingful, and likely to motivate their engagement in future activist efforts.

A final example from Harriet Tubman High School came in the form of an op-ed published by twelfth grader Maurice in the student newspaper, pushing back against the school's strict disciplinary policies. In the piece entitled "Rethinking Tubman's Disciplinary System," Maurice argued against the school's policy of removing students from class for "minor miscellaneous infractions: the color of socks, the size of earrings, headbands and hair wraps, as well as wearing more than two bracelets." In critiquing this disciplinary policy, Maurice drew an analogy to the "Broken Windows" approach to policing that, as Maurice wrote, has been found to perniciously hinder the trajectories of African American youth by creating an "unvirtuous cycle" of minor infractions, arrests, and punishments. Maurice asserted that a similar unvirtuous cycle existed at Harriet Tubman High School in that "[a] uniform infraction is a ticket to the dean's office, and being in the office causes students to miss class, which then causes them to miss work, and now their entire grade tumbles."

The student editors of the newspaper offered Tubman Principal Frank Pierce an opportunity to respond to this op-ed, and Principal Pierce took them up on their offer. In his own op-ed entitled "Maintaining the Margins," Principal Pierce began by explaining and defending Tubman High School's emphasis on addressing small infractions: "This environment of high standards and mutual respect requires maintenance, and maintenance always occurs on the margins. . . . The Broken Windows paradigm has gotten some bad press recently, but it does accurately describe some human tendencies." However, Principal Pierce also acknowledged:

> Maurice makes some excellent points about the dangers of In-School Suspension and Out-of-School Suspension. . . . I have taken Maurice's advice before, and I will do so again. In an effort to reduce the amount of time that some students spend in the Dean's office for uniform infractions, we will purchase additional socks and belts that can be worn on loan. We did this at the beginning of the year, but by mid-year we always run out. This can address the uniform problem while limiting the amount of time on In-School Suspension.

While Maurice's op-ed did not change Tubman High School's funda-mental approach to discipline, it did disrupt the "unvirtuous cycle" lead-ing to lost learning time for minor infractions. And, importantly, because this debate had played out publicly in the student newspaper, the entire Tubman student body had the opportunity to see one of their peers push back—and effect change—against a troubling school policy. Conse-quently, while Watts and Hipolito-Delgado are likely correct that "exter-nal" forms of sociopolitical action generally exert a greater influence on the world than "internal" actions aimed at one's colleagues or peers, it is also important to recognize that the school community represents a meaning-ful social world to young people. Successful activism in this social world serves as evidence for youth that larger political systems can be influenced by their activist efforts as well.[7]

Real-World Assignments

In addition to opportunities for youth to effect change within their own school communities, a fourth theme that emerged in several schools was assignments that pushed students to exert influence on the "real world" beyond the school walls. Perhaps the most substantial examples of such "real-world assignments" were the senior capstone projects at both Leader-ship High School and Espiritu High School that required students to research, design, and carry out their own small-scale social action projects in their respective communities. Participating seniors described these proj-ects as exerting a substantial effect on both their feelings of political agency and commitment to social action.

Additionally, teachers at Community Academy concluded units in courses ranging from science to foreign language to humanities by assign-ing their students to lobby elected representatives about the social or political issues about which they had learned. For example, students in Community Academy's physics class presented to a municipal transporta-tion board about a study they had conducted on insufficient signage on a busy street near their school. Students in several of the school's foreign language courses wrote a letter of protest and later met with the consul general of a European nation over a travel warning issued by that nation's foreign ministry to avoid the neighborhood in which Community Academy was located. Both in the letter of protest and subsequent meeting with the consul general, Community Academy students shared their perspective that racial and social class biases had motivated this travel warning. Finally, students in several of Community Academy's humanities courses wrote letters to elected officials at the conclusion of expeditions on Puerto Rico's relationship to the United States and the Syrian refugee crisis, expressing their own opinions about America's treatment of these groups. Multiple Community Academy students characterized these types of assignments as having deepened their understanding of the levers through which social and political change occurs.

Psychologist Lev Vygotsky and other learning theorists have argued that powerful learning entails individuals engaging in a particular role under the tutelage of a more senior community member and then gradually developing expertise in the "scripts" or skills of that role.[8] Assignments engaging youth at Leadership High School, Espiritu High School, and Community Academy in social action in the real world gave these youth opportunities to try on the role of political activist under the guidance and mentorship of their teachers.

Importantly, Make the Road Academy and Harriet Tubman High School featured many fewer real-world assignments. Perhaps as a result, at the end of their four years of high school, Make the Road Academy students demonstrated impressive abilities to engage in social analysis of racial injustice but simultaneously the weakest commitment to engaging in social action challenging such injustice. Likewise, youth attending Harriet Tubman High School concluded high school with the greatest confidence in their ability to navigate Whitestream settings and spaces but expressed uncertainty about how they might engage in collective social action challenging White supremacy or racism. Perhaps, then, both MtRA and Tubman students' weaker commitments to social action challenging racial injustice were attributable, in part, to the paucity of real-world assignments offered by their respective schools. Such real-world assignments seemed to offer youth at the three other featured schools opportunities for mentored practice in developing the scripts and skills of social activists.

Teachers Getting Personal

Finally, a fifth theme that was evident in two schools—Make the Road Academy and Community Academy—was teachers' willingness to share with students their own personal experiences with oppressive social forces such as racism and homophobia as well as their commitment to engaging in activism challenging these oppressive forces. At Make the Road Academy, for example, literature teacher Ms. Lyla Denette told her students about an experience during graduate school in which a White classmate had expressed doubt that she would actually graduate and how that judgment had affected her as the only Black student in her class. Likewise, MtRA Spanish teacher Ms. Bianca Castillo told her students about being (mis)treated by employees in an upscale clothing store as if she could not possibly afford to shop there. Ms. Denette and Ms. Castillo were just two of the many teachers at Make the Road Academy who shared with their students these types of encounters with racial injustice.

Teachers at Community Academy were also willing to share stories from their personal lives of contending with racism and other forms of oppression. For example, tenth-grade humanities teacher Mr. Jabari Dymon shared with his students during a lesson on racial profiling that he had recently been pulled over and questioned by police officers for seemingly no reason at all while picking up dinner one evening. Likewise, during a Community Circle presentation on LGBTQ rights, another Community Academy teacher, Ms. Jill Solomon, shared with the entire student body that, after she came out as gay, her mother didn't speak to her for several years. "But she changed," Jill explained, "and I want to say for those of you who are coming out or are thinking about coming out, it's not easy, but it's possible for people to change." Scholar bell hooks encourages teachers to share with students these types of confessional narratives in order to establish a school and classroom culture in which young people are likewise willing to share their reflections and experiences with oppression.

Perhaps the willingness of these and other teachers at Make the Road Academy and Community Academy to share such confessional narratives emanated from the leaders of these two schools being willing to do likewise. At Make the Road Academy, for example, Head of School Ms. Yvette Naylor underscored the importance of good attendance to the class of 2017 on their first day of ninth-grade orientation by revealing that, as a child, she and her family had experienced homelessness:

> I was homeless at one time as a child, and I still kept on going to school. Because I knew I needed to be in school. One time my family had to sleep in the airport, and I had to go into the bathroom to brush my teeth and then get up in the morning to go to school. And that's how important school is. Because you have the power to change anything. You can't let there be an excuse to keep you from being successful. And we are going to push you. Be prepared to be pushed. Be prepared to be aggravated. We do it because we love you, and we want you to be successful.

With these words, Ms. Naylor made clear to both her faculty and her newest cohort of students that Make the Road Academy was a school in which individuals could be candid about their challenges and that, in fact, overcoming those challenges was deeply connected to the broader mission of the school toward which faculty and students were jointly working.

Likewise, Community Academy principal Mr. Klarens Hill several times used his time at the school's weekly Community Circle to share his own feelings or reactions to racial injustice. In the wake of the killing of African American teenager Michael Brown in Ferguson, Missouri, and the subsequent protests in Ferguson, Klarens initiated a dialogue at Community Circle about the effectiveness of activism. Klarens began this discussion by sharing:

> There were lots of moments in my life where I felt like I didn't count. When I was in college there was a man, Mumia Abu-Jamal, in Philadelphia. There was an incident and he was put on death row for allegedly killing a cop. He is what is called a political prisoner. We protested. I remember the feeling. It was like I was making a change.

Following these remarks, Community Academy students engaged in a vigorous debate about whether or not activism can actually effect change. Such debate was made possible by Klarens's honesty about moments in his life when he had felt both very low and very high levels of political agency.

Two years later, Klarens spoke in a deeply personal way again at the Community Circle following the 2016 election of Donald Trump as president of the United States. "Bear with me," Klarens told the student body. "I've got a few words to share with you, and it comes with a heavy heart. I came to school yesterday feeling pretty down, and it was a direct result of the election that happened Tuesday night. . . . President-elect Trump said a lot of things that I think were intensely disrespectful. And he said them often and loudly." Klarens then went on to share his belief that "[t]he most revolutionary thing we can do to show who we are and how beautiful we are is to work hard every day to get the education we need to tear down the structures that are oppressing us." His words were by far the most personal of all the remarks we observed by school leaders in the wake of the 2016 election, and his remarks sent a strong message to Community Academy faculty and students that they too were allowed to bring their emotional responses to the election into their daily work as students and teachers.

Notably, the majority of these examples of educators sharing personal experiences of oppression came from educators of color. Students at Make the Road Academy and Community Academy picked up on this theme as well, and a number of these youth characterized their teachers of color as better equipped than their White teachers to "get personal" with students. In making this point, Leadership High School student Erik observed that his White teachers "didn't have to go through what a Black person has to go through, so . . . they try to understand, but like it's really hard 'cause like they didn't grow up around our situations." In short, then, teachers of color may be distinctively positioned to draw upon confessional narratives as a tool for fostering their students' critical consciousness of racial injustice.

That said, acknowledging the distinctive positioning of teachers of color does not exclude White teachers from drawing on their own confessional narratives around issues of race, identity, and their own positionality.

For example, a White teacher at Harriet Tubman High School, Mr. Dan Kamin, won enthusiastic praise from the students in his African American English elective for his openness to discussing how his own Whiteness influenced their learning. For example, midway through the course, a group of students met with Mr. Kamin to express some concerns about how his Whiteness was shaping the focus and nature of class discussions. Mr. Kamin described the meeting as "a great opportunity" to improve the course, and one of the students in the course, Melissa, said of Mr. Kamin's response to this meeting: "He was really receptive to their ideas, and I think he's gonna work on changing it, 'cause this is like the first year that the class was made, so I think the feedback was really helpful." In short, Mr. Kamin's openness and reflectiveness about his Whiteness also represented a form of "getting personal" that encouraged his students to be forthcoming about their own experiences with race and racism both inside and outside of his class.

SCHOOL SPACES FOR YOUTH CRITICAL CONSCIOUSNESS

Having identified a number of common teaching tools for fostering youth critical consciousness, we turn now to the spaces available in many secondary school settings for deploying these tools. Specifically, we focus on four such spaces: the core academic curriculum, elective courses, extracurriculars, and community meeting. We consider each of these spaces in turn, as well as the ways in which the teaching tools described in the first half of this chapter can be deployed most effectively within these spaces to support youth critical consciousness development.

Core Academic Curriculum

The core academic curriculum refers to the academic courses within a school that are required of all students and typically sit within traditional academic departments such as English, math, science, and history. Among the five schools featured in this book, Community Academy's humanities programming offered the strongest example of critical consciousness content embedded within the core academic curriculum. At all four grade levels, Community Academy's humanities curriculum featured in-depth case studies of racial injustice such as apartheid South Africa (ninth grade), the genocide of Native Americans (tenth grade), the civil rights movement (eleventh grade), and police violence against African Americans (twelfth grade). Importantly, all of these case studies gave equal attention to both the injustices perpetrated by oppressors and the ways in which oppressed individuals and groups challenged such injustice. As a result of this dual focus, Community Academy students emerged from their humanities coursework with a powerful understanding of how different groups throughout history and across the globe have challenged injustice.

In many cases, Community Academy educators then explicitly connected students' learning about challenging racial injustice with opportunities to engage in meaningful social action themselves. Namely, the final projects for many of these units engaged Community Academy students in *real-world assignments* such as lobbying elected officials for changes to the United States' relationship with Puerto Rico or producing viral video public service announcements illustrating racism within the criminal justice system. Assignments like these shifted Community Academy students from the role of passive learners about social change efforts to active participants themselves in social action work. Consequently, Community Academy students demonstrated steeper growth in their commitment to activism challenging racial injustice than their peers across the five schools featured in this book.

Community Academy went the furthest of the high schools featured in this book in infusing critical consciousness programming into its core academic curriculum. Two other schools, Make the Road Academy and Leadership High School, chose respectively to incorporate such programming onto the front end and back end of their students' high school years.

Make the Road Academy introduced youth to a powerful *theoretical framework* for recognizing and understanding oppression (the "Three I's") as part of the ninth-grade Social Engagement course. Because this course and its content were a required part of MtRA's ninth-grade curriculum, MtRA faculty across grade levels and subject levels could then utilize the Three I's framework as an entry point to literary texts, historical cases, and scientific topics within their own courses that raised issues of racial injustice as well. Accordingly, youth attending MtRA concluded high school with stronger social analysis skills than their peers across the five schools featured in this book.

Leadership High School took the opposite tack from Make the Road Academy by incorporating organizer Marshall Ganz's framework for successful social change movements into the Sociology of Change course that all students took in their final year of high school. Because Leadership twelfth graders were simultaneously designing and executing their Be the Change capstone projects, they were able to utilize Ganz's framework as a roadmap for their own fledgling social change efforts. Perhaps as a result, Leadership students concluded high school with a higher commitment to engaging in activism than their peers across the five high schools featured in this book.

In short, then, educators might consider two different roles for the core curriculum in fostering students' critical consciousness of racial injustice. The Community Academy approach entailed incorporating case studies relevant to racial injustice into all four years of students' humanities curriculum. Alternatively, educators might consider melding the approaches of Make the Road Academy and Leadership High School by book-ending students' high school years with core curriculum that strengthens their ability to analyze racial injustice (e.g., Social Engagement) and challenge racial injustice (e.g., Sociology of Change), respectively.

Elective Courses

Elective courses differ from the core academic curriculum in that students must proactively opt into such courses or select them from among a menu of options. One of the most powerful uses of elective coursework to foster youth critical consciousness came in the form of Espiritu High School's community improvement projects (CIPs). Espiritu ninth and tenth graders chose two semester-long CIPs from a menu of options that included the Poverty Project, Housing and Homelessness, Healthy Teens, Project Earth, Starting a Nonprofit, Diver-cities, Prisoner Pipeline, and Facing

History. These projects engaged Espiritu students in both academic learning about their respective social issues as well as volunteer work with local organizations such as Housing for All and Avanzar Latino seeking to address these issues. Moreover, these *real-world opportunities* for engaging in social action represented the first steps in a progression of learning experiences that contributed to Espiritu students concluding high school with both the highest levels and steepest growth in their feelings of political agency. Consequently, the community improvement projects represent another valuable and powerful lever for secondary schools committed to supporting the critical consciousness development of the youth they serve.

Leadership High School's theme-based English seminars illustrated another powerful approach to using elective coursework to foster youth critical consciousness. Leadership's eleventh and twelfth graders could choose four semester-long English seminars from a menu of offerings that included the Black Experience, Chicano Literature, Post-Colonial Literature, Multicultural Literature, Deconstructing Masculinity, and so on. These courses then allowed students to think deeply and engage in perspective taking about the experiences of a number of different identity groups to which they might or might not belong themselves. Several Leadership students noted that these seminars played an important role in shaping the focus of their Be the Change projects. Cumulatively, the theme-based seminars and Be the Change projects contributed to Leadership students concluding high school with a higher commitment to collective social action than their peers across the five high schools featured in this book. For this reason, adopting Leadership High School's menu of theme-based seminars for older high schoolers represents another powerful use of elective coursework for fostering youth critical consciousness.

Finally, a third approach to elective coursework was Tubman High School's use of Community Engaged Theater to strengthen students' ability to navigate Whitestream settings. Community Engaged Theater explicitly engaged Tubman students in practicing how to respond to oppressive events in their lives and communities, with the ultimate goal of strengthening their ability to navigate oppression in their real lives. Such opportunities for both students enrolled in the theater elective, as well as their peers who served as audience members and "spect-actors" for performances, contributed to Tubman High School students demonstrating both the steepest growth and highest confidence in their ability to navigate Whitestream settings. Accordingly, educators committed to fostering their own students' critical consciousness of racial injustice would do well to consider the use of elective coursework at all three of these schools.

Extracurriculars

Extracurricular activities—learning experiences that are school-sponsored but fall outside the academic curriculum—represent another key setting for fostering youth critical consciousness. At Community Academy, for example, youth participating in the Student Advocacy Club had opportunities to strengthen their burgeoning activist skills by campaigning successfully for changes to the school uniform policy. Even Community Academy students not directly involved with the Student Advocacy Club took notice of the club's successful activist efforts and cited such efforts to *effect school change* as having strengthened their belief in the power of social and political activism to effect meaningful change in the real world as well.

Along similar lines, at Tubman High School, youth participating in the school's extracurricular debate team developed the research, argumentation, and presentation skills that resulted in award-winning debate performances but also facilitated their ability to advocate for change within the Tubman High School community. For example, Tubman High School debaters successfully convinced Principal Frank Pierce to amend the school's uniform policy prohibiting headscarves. With support from their debate coach, the debaters also initiated a dialogue with Principal Pierce about increasing student involvement in school governance matters ranging from adjudicating student disciplinary issues to course reading lists. These efforts to effect school change also strengthened participating students' convictions about their ability to effect change in the world beyond Tubman High School as well.

Finally, Tubman High School worked to place students in extracurricular internships with local technology companies and university laboratories to increase their experience and comfortability in navigating such settings. These internships contributed to Tubman High School students reporting greater confidence than their peers in the other schools in their ability to successfully navigate Whitestream academic and professional spaces.[9] In sum, extracurricular activities ranging from the Student Advocacy Club to debate to corporate internships offered important opportunities for young people to develop and practice utilizing a number of the skills associated with the social action dimension of critical consciousness.[10]

Community Meeting

Finally, a fourth key space for fostering youth critical consciousness was the community meetings held on a weekly or monthly basis at several of the high schools featured in this book. At Espiritu High School, for example, the entire school community congregated one afternoon each month for an extended community meeting that was planned and led by rotating groups of students. Several Espiritu students cited the opportunities at these community meetings for *youth to teach youth* as having strengthened their belief in the ability of young people to engage in impactful social change. A similar dynamic marked the community circles held every Thursday morning at Community Academy, with Community Academy students citing, in particular, the powerful impact of the senior talks offered by the school's twelfth graders.

Because community meetings entail convening a school's entire faculty and student body, they represent a substantial investment of time—perhaps a school's most valuable resource. However, similar to core academic courses, community meetings also represent an opportunity to present critical consciousness programming to the entire school community, which faculty and students can then build upon in other spaces. As Espiritu teacher Agustín Montada observed: "It's a more equitable way of talking about issues because if everyone is taking part, it's more democratic, and I think that shapes the whole school culture." For this reason, community meetings represent another important space for cultivating youths' critical consciousness of racial injustice and other forms of oppression.

NO SINGLE APPROACH

The five schools featured in *Schooling for Critical Consciousness* came out of five different pedagogical traditions and took five different approaches to fostering youth critical consciousness. Consequently, the young men and women attending these five schools demonstrated outsized skills and growth on different dimensions of critical consciousness. From our perspective, reporting on such diverse schooling approaches and youth outcomes served our overarching goal in writing this book: to strengthen the capacity of schools and educators to support Black and Latinx youth in learning to analyze, navigate, and challenge racial injustice. Put another way, we believe our case studies of the work taking place at five very different high schools can broaden educators' understanding of the full range of practices available to them in supporting their own students' critical consciousness development.

We also discovered important differences in the pathways through which these five high schools came to embrace their role in fostering youth critical consciousness. Specifically, the focus on youth critical consciousness at Make the Road Academy, Espiritu High School, and Community Academy could be described as baked into these schools' DNA from their respective beginnings. In fact, these schools' founding documents outline their respective plans for implementing Freire Culture Circles, community improvement projects, and justice-oriented humanities curriculum. In other words, fostering youth critical consciousness at these three high schools was an explicit goal from day one.

On the other hand, Harriet Tubman High School and Leadership High School were both schools that adopted more critically conscious orientations several years after their founding. At Leadership High School, this shift occurred in a more top-down fashion when a new head of school deliberately chose to revise the school's curriculum and programming in ways that pointed the school in a more critically conscious direction. In contrast, the shift toward more critically conscious programming was more gradual and bottom-up at Harriet Tubman High School, where a handful of educators independently developed elective courses that sought to foster students' ability to *critically* navigate racial oppression. The presence of these elective courses—and their impact on students—then began nudging the entire Tubman community in a more critically conscious direction. In short, then, the five secondary schools featured in this book not only took different approaches to fostering their students' critical consciousness of racial injustice but also came to this work from different directions and orientations.

While we believe such diversity across the five featured schools to be valuable and important, we have also deliberately concluded *Schooling for Critical Consciousness* by identifying the many commonalities in these schools' tools and spaces for fostering youth critical consciousness. In so doing, we seek to encourage educators committed to fostering their own students' critical consciousness of racial injustice to draw on elements from *each* of the featured schools rather than adopt just one of the schooling models as a template for their own work.

Certainly, educators coming from a diverse range of schools and schooling models themselves will experience greater alignment with some of the featured schools and weaker alignment with others. Nonetheless, we believe there are important reasons for educators to give earnest consideration to the work of each of these schools and schooling models. Namely, the youth attending each of these schools demonstrated outsized skills or growth on a particular dimension of critical consciousness—social analysis, political agency, or social action—but meaningful growth in critical consciousness requires individuals to develop all three of these capacities. In fact, Paulo Freire warned that growth along just a single dimension of critical consciousness can hinder the ability of critical consciousness to lead to personal liberation and societal transformation.

According to Freire, individuals with strong social analysis skills but a weak commitment to social action are prone to engage in mere "verbalism" that does not advance the struggle for societal transformation.[11] Conversely, Freire argued that individuals who demonstrate a strong commitment to social action but weak ability to analyze oppressive social forces are prone to engage in "disastrous activism" that reifies oppression instead of challenging it.[12] Still other scholars have argued that political agency represents the crucial bridge for transforming an individual's analysis of oppression and injustice into consequential social action.[13] For these reasons, we believe that each of the schools featured in *Schooling for Critical Consciousness* has something important to offer educators committed to cultivating their own students' social analysis skills, political agency, and commitment to social action.

Bending Toward Justice

The young men and women in the class of 2017 featured in the preceding chapters came of age in an America in which racial injustice remains powerful, pernicious, and perhaps even more visible than in recent decades. These young people witnessed national media coverage of the extrajudicial killings of young people of color during each year of high school. They watched Donald Trump win the presidency of the United States via a campaign marked by xenophobic and racist rhetoric, and then they watched the actions of White supremacy movements emboldened by such rhetoric. Upon graduating from high school, many of these young people matriculated to college just as postsecondary institutions across the United States began reporting surges in the frequency of campus hate crimes and the dissemination of White supremacist propaganda.[14] That is all to say that, unfortunately, all evidence points to young people of color in the United States continuing to benefit from support in learning to analyze, navigate, and challenge racial injustice for the foreseeable future.

Nonetheless, we take heart in the words of Reverend Dr. Martin Luther King Jr. that "the arc of the moral universe is long, but it bends toward justice."[15] These words acknowledge the many challenges that lie ahead but also express a sense of agency and radical possibility to surmount them. In this way, Dr. King's words epitomize the spirit of critical consciousness in both their recognition *and* commitment to challenging racial injustice. With *Schooling for Critical Consciousness*, we have sought to equip educators and youth to carry out the work necessary to fulfill King's promise.

A Note on Research Methods

Schooling for Critical Consciousness reports on a longitudinal, mixed methods research study involving more than six hundred adolescents in the class of 2017 from nine different public high schools in four northeastern cities. In chapter 1, we described the key features of this research study. We do not reiterate those central points here but, instead, offer additional information about the study's sample, methods, analytic strategy, and results for interested readers.

RESEARCH QUESTIONS

The research questions guiding this research study were the following:

1. What differences, if any, emerge in the critical consciousness of racial and economic injustice of adolescents attending high schools featuring similar civic goals but different pedagogical approaches?
2. How do adolescents attending these schools describe and understand the schooling practices that contributed to their critical consciousness development?

As these questions reveal, the broader research study from which this book emerged considered adolescents' developing critical consciousness of *both* racial and economic injustice, and we have written a number of academic papers focused on youths' critical consciousness of both forms of injustice.[1] We chose to focus this book primarily on youth critical consciousness of racial injustice, though of course overlaps and intersections exist between the two forms of inequity.

PARTICIPATING YOUTH AND SCHOOLS

To consider these research questions, our research team recruited youth (n = 335) in the class of 2017 attending five public charter high schools located in four northeastern cities.[2] These five high schools were highly similar in their size, geography, governance, student demographics, admissions policies, and explicit goals for fostering students' academic *and* civic development (see table A1). Yet, these schools took five different pedagogical approaches to teaching and learning: problem-posing, expeditionary learning, habits of mind, no excuses, and action civics. Over four years, we collected five waves of survey data and four waves of interview data from youth attending these five schools.

In the final year of the study, we recruited youth in the class of 2017 attending four additional high schools in these same northeastern cities (n = 275) to join the study. Two of these schools were also charter high schools, and two were traditional district high schools. These four additional high schools were highly similar to the original five in their geography and student demographics, but their mission statements did not cite explicit goals for youth civic development or a singular pedagogical approach to teaching and learning. For this reason, they served as a useful comparison group to the youth attending the five featured high schools. More information about each of these participating schools is presented in table A1.

DATA COLLECTION

The youth in the class of 2017 attending the five high schools featured in this book completed critical consciousness surveys at five different time points over their four years of high school. These five time points included fall 2013 (Time 1), spring 2014 (Time 2), spring 2015 (Time 3), spring 2016 (Time 4), and spring 2017 (Time 5). Youth attending the four

TABLE A1

Descriptions and demographics of participating schools (j = 9)

SCHOOL	SCHOOLING MODEL	URBAN CONTEXT	BLACK & LATINX STUDENTS	FREE/ REDUCED LUNCH	MISSION, PHILOSOPHY, OR CORE VALUES
			Featured SCC Schools		
Community Academy	Expeditionary Learning	Large northeastern city	99%	75%	Philosophy: Develop in students the knowledge, skills, and commitment to envision a better world and work toward achieving it.
Make the Road Academy	Problem-Posing	Midsize northeastern city	100%	76%	Mission: To offer students an education that strengthens our community by equipping them to address educational and social inequities.
Espiritu High School	CES Habits of Mind	Small northeastern city	91%	78%	Mission: Community involvement and improvement are central goals at Espiritu Academy. . . . Students engage in deep learning and reflection about their own experiences and relationships to others in our community.
Leadership High School	Action Civics	Large northeastern city	100%	81%	Mission: To educate socially responsible students for a life of active and engaged citizenship.
Harriet Tubman High School	No-Excuses	Midsize northeastern city	100%	77%	Core Value: We work to improve our community, country, and world.
			Comparison Schools		
Hyde High School	District HS	Large northeastern city	97%	77%	Mission: Guiding all students to succeed academically and become powerful leaders.
Carruth High School	District HS	Large northeastern city	98%	76%	Mission: To prepare young people to succeed at the college or university of their choice.
Shine Academy	Charter HS	Small northeastern city	97%	77%	Mission: To prepare students to succeed in college and beyond.
Fortitude Prep	Charter HS	Large northeastern city	92%	83%	Mission: To prepare students to graduate from college and thrive in their careers and lives.

comparison high schools completed this same critical consciousness survey in the spring of 2017 (Time 5) as well.

The critical consciousness survey included eight previously validated measures associated with the three key dimensions of critical consciousness: social analysis, political agency, and social action. More information about these eight measures is presented in table A2. Youth responded to all of the items comprising these measures along 5-point Likert scales in which a "1" represented "No way!" or "Not like me at all," and a "5" represented "Definitely!" or "Very much like me." We analyzed participating youths' shifts on each of these eight individual measures rather than merging them together into a single composite measure of critical consciousness or composites of the three central dimensions of critical consciousness.

We also conducted qualitative interviews with 10–12 youth at each of the featured high schools (n = 60) at the end of each academic year for a total of 222 student interviews. Additionally, we conducted interviews with 32 faculty and staff members across these five schools, and carried out 334 days of observations (approximately 15 days per school per year). The protocol for these interviews and the focus of these observation days are described in greater detail in Chapter 1.

DATA ANALYSIS

This study utilized a sequential explanatory analytic strategy in which we first analyzed quantitative survey data to test relationships and then qualitative interview and field notes data to explain and interpret initial results.[3] In so doing, our quantitative findings motivated the themes we explored in our qualitative data; however, we also remained open to qualitative results that contradicted our quantitative findings.

Surveys

For each of the measures, we first compared the Time 5 scores of youth attending the five featured high schools to their peers attending the four comparison high schools using independent samples t-tests. Our goal with these initial analyses was to consider whether attending a high school with an explicit civic mission had contributed to youths' critical consciousness over and above normative development in this area.

Next, we conducted longitudinal hierarchical linear modeling (HLM) with effects coding to compare the critical consciousness levels and rates of change of students in each of the five featured high schools to their peers

TABLE A2
Critical consciousness measures

CATEGORY	MEASURE	ADAPTED FROM	# ITEMS	α	SAMPLE ITEM
Social Analysis	Awareness of Interpersonal Racism	D. Oyserman, L. Gant, and J. Ager. "A Socially Contextualized Model of African American Identity," *Journal of Personality and Social Psychology* 69, no. 6 (1995): 1216–32.	3	0.79	"Some people will treat me differently because I am (youth's racial-ethnic group)."
	Awareness of Systemic Racism	P. Gurin, B. Nagda, and X. Zuniga, *Dialogue Across Difference: Practice, Theory and Research on Intergroup Dialogue* (New York: Russell Sage, (2011).	4	0.67	"Racism in the educational system limits the success of Blacks, Latinos, and other racial minorities."
	Awareness of Systemic Causes of Poverty	NPR-Kaiser-Harvard, "National Survey on Poverty in America," *Kaiser Family Foundation,* 2001, http://www.kff.org/kaiserpolls.	5	0.75	"A shortage of jobs is a major cause of poverty."
Political Agency	Youth Sociopolitical Control	N. Peterson, C. Peterson, L. Agre, B. Christens, and C. Morton, "Measuring Youth Empowerment: Validation of a Sociopolitical Control Scale for Youth in an Urban Community Context," *Journal of Community Psychology* 39, no. 5 (2011): 592–605.	6	0.79	"There are plenty of ways for youth like me to have a say in what our community or school does."
	Youth Social Responsibility	S. M. Pancer, M. Pratt, B. Hunsberger, and S. Alisat, "Community and Political Involvement in Adolescence: What Distinguishes the Activists from the Uninvolved?," *Journal of Community Psychology* 35, no.6 (2007): 741–59.	8	0.82	"Young people have an important role to play in making the world a better place."
Social Action	Commitment to Activism	A. F. Corning and D. J. Myers, "Individual Orientation Toward Engagement in Social Action," *Political Psychology* 23, no. 4 (D. J. (2002): 703–29.	9	0.80	"How likely is it now or in the future that you will take part in a protest, march, or demonstration?"
	Achievement as Resistance	D. Oyserman, L. Gant, and J. Ager, "A Socially Contextualized Model of African American Identity," *Journal of Personality and Social Psychology* 69, no. 6 (J. (1995): 1216–32.	4	0.78	"If I am successful, it will help the (youth's racial-ethnic group) community."
	Social Intelligence	N. Park and C. Peterson, "Moral Competence and Character Strengths Among Adolescents: The Development and Validation of the Values in Action Inventory of Strengths for Youth," *Journal of Adolescence* 29 (2006): 891–905.	5	0.71	"I am good at getting along with all sorts of people."

across all five featured high schools. Youth attending the four comparison high schools were *not* included in these analyses.

The first step of our HLM entailed testing an unconditional, intercept-only model, which allowed us to assess the proportion of total variance in scores that was due to between-individual variation (i.e., ICC). For these analyses, the Level 1 outcome variables were the eight submeasures of critical consciousness. The second step involved building the Level 1 model by adding to the intercept-only model a time variable indicating the year in which the survey was administered and centered at the most recent measurement occasion (i.e., Time 5). Finally, the Level 2 model was built by adding student characteristics to the random slopes and intercepts model as predictors of intercept and slope variability. In these analyses, the Level 2 predictors were demographic variables (e.g., gender, racial-ethnic identity) as well as four effects code variables for the school attended by each participant.

Because each of the five schools in our sample used a different pedagogical approach, our inclusion of school attended as student-level effects code variables both fully accounted for the clustering of students within school and also allowed us to investigate differences in levels and rates of change on the various submeasures of critical consciousness for youth exposed to different pedagogical approaches in comparison to the overall sample (i.e., Research Question #1). All models were estimated in SAS 9.4 using the PROC MIXED procedure, and restricted maximum likelihood estimation was used. The final fitted model for analyzing these longitudinal data was the following:

$$Critical\ Consciousness\ Submeasure = B_0 + (B_1 + \mu_{1i})Year_{ij} +$$
$$B_2 Gender_i + B_3 Latinx_i + B_4 MultiRacial_i + B_5 Espiritu_i +$$
$$B_6 Community_i + B_7 Leadership_i + B_8 Tubman_i + B_9 Year_{ij}*Espiritu_i +$$
$$B_{10} Year_{ij}*Community_i + B_{11} Year_{ij}*Leadership_i + B_{12} Year_{ij}*Tubman_i$$
$$+ \varepsilon_{ij} + \mu_{0i}$$

where

- B_0 is the intercept parameter (representing the average critical consciousness score at the most recent measurement period).

- B_1 represents the time-varying Level 1 predictor, year, centered at the most recent measurement period.
- B_2–B_4 represent the effects of Level 2 demographic control predictors on the outcome.
- B_5–B_8 represent the time-invariant Level 2 predictors, school attended, on the outcome.
- B_9–B_{12} represent the interaction between the growth parameter at Level 1 and school predictors at Level 2.
- ε_{ij} represents the Level 1 residual error.
- μ_{0i} represents the residual random effects for each participant around the intercept.
- μ_{1i} represents the residual random effects for each participant around the Year slope.

In the final fitted model, a fifth school, Make the Road Academy, served as the referent school. However, all models were reestimated using a second set of effects codes (i.e., a different school set as the reference) to obtain estimates for all five schools in the study.

Interviews and Field Notes

All interviews with students and faculty were audio-recorded and transcribed verbatim. Our analysis of these interviews was a multistep process consistent with qualitative research methods that seek to balance etic/outsider and emic/insider perspectives.[4] Beginning with an etic structure, during the spring of 2014, our research team utilized our research questions, interview protocols, and conceptual framework to construct categories that represented key dimensions of our inquiry.[5]

Next, we worked collaboratively to populate these superordinate categories with code names drawn from both etic concepts from the extant research literature on critical pedagogy, racial socialization, and civic development as well as emic descriptions by study participants emerging from our qualitative interviews that added depth or texture to one or more of these superordinate categories.[6]

Each qualitative interview was then coded independently by two members of the research team using NVivo Research 10 software. After coding each interview independently, two members of the research team then compared their analyses of each interview transcript, recoded, and then compared again until all coding discrepancies were resolved. Our team then utilized NVivo's "cutting and sorting" capabilities to compile summary tables for each individual code, organized by the superordinate categories, so as to identify emergent patterns and themes in the coded data that offered insight into Research Question #2.[7] A similar process was then carried out with the 334 sets of field notes.

RESULTS

The results of the analyses are reported in detail in chapters 2–6. However, we include in table A3 the results of our longitudinal HLM analyses with effects coding for each of the eight submeasures of critical consciousness.

LOOKING AHEAD

Schooling for Critical Consciousness compares the critical consciousness development of youth attending five different schooling models over their four years of high school. Each of the case-study chapters concludes with these youths' high school graduations in the spring of 2017. However, as we were writing this book, we also collected a sixth wave of survey data and fifth wave of interview data from a portion of these youth when they were one year beyond high school. Through this final set of surveys and interviews, we sought to collect data that would offer insight into how these young people's critical consciousness development during the high school years had influenced their subsequent experiences in college and the workforce. With this book now complete, we plan in the coming months to turn our attention to that question. Consequently, we hope that this book represents an important inflection point—but not our final destination—in thinking, writing, and reporting on the development and effects of youth critical consciousness.

TABLE A3

Longitudinal HLM with effects coding for critical consciousness submeasures (n = 335)

	AWARENESS OF INTERPERSONAL RACISM					AWARENESS OF SYSTEMIC RACISM					AWARENESS OF SYSTEMIC CAUSES OF POVERTY				
	b	SE	t	p	% Red in Var	b	SE	t	p	% Red in Var	b	SE	t	p	% Red in Var
Intercept	4.10	0.07	61.46	<.001		3.99	0.06	77.69	<.001		3.82	0.05	76.06	<.001	
Year	0.18	0.02	11.00	<.001		0.14	0.01	10.39	<.001		0.14	0.01	11.74	<.001	
Gender	-0.20	0.07	-2.72	.006		-0.10	0.06	-1.88	.06		-0.09	0.05	-1.84	.07	
Latinx	-0.17	0.10	-1.59	.112		0.07	0.08	0.86	0.391		-0.12	0.08	-1.66	.09	
MultiRacial	-0.05	0.10	-0.53	.596		0.07	0.07	1.04	0.298		0.08	0.07	1.05	.29	
Predicting Intercepts (Means)					10.4%					2.6%					3.2%
Espiritu	-0.37	0.11	-3.11	.002		-0.09	0.09	-1.02	0.309		0.14	0.09	1.51	.13	
Community	-0.23	0.13	-1.83	.07		-0.02	0.10	-1.63	0.105		-0.24	0.10	-2.47	.01	
Leadership	-0.02	0.09	-0.16	.87		-0.04	0.07	-0.59	0.559		0.06	0.07	0.83	.41	
Tubman	0.47	0.09	5.14	<.001		0.08	0.07	1.09	0.277		0.13	0.07	1.92	.06	
Make the Road	0.15	0.09	1.46	.14		0.22	0.08	2.80	0.005		-0.09	0.08	-1.14	.26	
Predicting Slopes (Change)					7.0%					12.8%					7.9%
Espiritu	0.09	0.03	2.73	.006		0.09	0.03	3.18	0.002		0.03	0.02	1.35	.18	
Community	-0.03	0.04	-0.89	.375		-0.04	0.03	-1.36	0.176		0.01	0.03	0.15	.88	
Leadership	-0.01	0.03	-0.09	.92		-0.05	0.02	-2.36	0.019		0.02	0.02	1.12	.27	
Tubman	-0.02	0.03	-0.67	.51		-0.02	0.02	-1.07	0.283		-0.04	0.02	-2.06	.04	
Make the Road	-0.04	0.03	-1.21	.23		0.03	0.03	1.20	0.229		-0.02	0.02	-0.87	.38	

Note: Models for each of these measures were reestimated with a second set of effects codes to obtain estimates for all five participating schools.

(continued)

TABLE A3 *(continued)*
Longitudinal HLM with effects coding for critical consciousness submeasures cont. (n = 335)

	YOUTH SOCIOPOLITICAL CONTROL					YOUTH SOCIAL RESPONSIBILITY					COMMITMENT TO ACTIVISM				
	b	SE	t	p	% Red in Var	b	SE	t	p	% Red in Var	b	SE	t	p	% Red in Var
Intercept	3.95	0.04	93.56	<.001		4.44	0.04	122.71	<.001		3.34	0.05	64.67	<.001	
Year	0.07	0.01	7.31	<.001		0.08	0.01	10.48	<.001		0.07	0.01	6.20	<.001	
Gender	-0.12	0.05	-2.38	.02		-0.17	0.04	-4.03	<.001		-0.19	0.06	-3.48	.001	
Latinx	0.04	0.07	0.53	.59		0.07	0.06	1.15	.249		-0.02	0.08	-0.26	.80	
MultiRacial	-0.01	0.07	-0.20	.84		-0.04	0.06	-0.73	.47		0.03	0.08	0.38	.70	
Predicting Intercepts (Means)					0%					0%					4.3%
Espiritu	0.06	0.06	0.91	.36		0.06	0.05	1.15	.25		0.01	0.09	0.02	.99	
Community	0.04	0.06	0.58	.56		-0.15	0.05	-2.99	.003		-0.03	0.09	-0.30	.76	
Leadership	-0.05	0.04	-1.06	.29		0.01	0.04	0.23	.82		0.13	0.07	1.81	.07	
Tubman	0.01	0.05	0.24	.81		0.09	0.04	2.45	.01		0.12	0.07	1.62	.11	
Make the Road	-0.06	0.05	-1.13	.26		-0.01	0.04	-0.17	.86		-0.22	0.08	-2.76	.006	
Predicting Slopes (Change)															
Espiritu	—	—	—	—		—	—	—	—		0.01	0.03	0.14	.89	19.5%
Community	—	—	—	—		—	—	—	—		0.08	0.03	2.81	.005	
Leadership	—	—	—	—		—	—	—	—		0.02	0.02	1.08	.28	
Tubman	—	—	—	—		—	—	—	—		0.01	0.02	0.58	.56	
Make the Road	—	—	—	—		—	—	—	—		-0.12	0.02	-5.03	<.001	

(continued)

TABLE A3 (*continued*)

Longitudinal HLM with effects coding for critical consciousness submeasures cont. (n = 335)

	ACHIEVEMENT AS RESISTANCE					SOCIAL INTELLIGENCE				
	b	SE	t	p	% Red in Var	b	SE	t	p	% Red in Var
Intercept	4.11	0.06	73.79	<.001		3.83	0.06	68.28	<.001	
Year	0.04	0.01	2.87	.004		0.06	0.01	4.44	<.001	
Gender	-0.06	0.06	-0.96	.337		0.05	0.06	0.87	.39	
Latinx	-0.01	0.08	0.00	.99		0.14	0.08	1.64	.10	
MultiRacial	-0.07	0.08	-0.87	.38		-0.07	.08	-0.84	.40	
Predicting Intercepts (Means)					0%					3.7%
Espiritu	-0.02	0.10	-0.18	.86		0.15	0.10	1.50	.13	
Community	0.04	0.10	0.36	.71		-0.01	0.11	-0.06	.95	
Leadership	0.07	0.08	0.92	.36		-0.13	0.08	-1.67	.10	
Tubman	-0.02	0.08	-0.25	.81		0.18	0.08	2.32	.02	
Make the Road	-0.07	0.09	-0.85	.39		-0.20	0.09	-2.33	.02	
Predicting Slopes (Change)					8.8%					4.9%
Espiritu	0.05	0.03	2.00	.05		0.02	0.03	0.75	.45	
Community	-0.03	0.03	-1.14	.25		-0.01	0.03	-0.16	.87	
Leadership	0.02	0.02	0.70	.49		-0.05	0.02	-2.01	.05	
Tubman	-0.01	0.02	-0.59	.56		0.06	0.02	2.51	.01	
Make the Road	-0.02	0.03	-0.88	.38		-0.03	0.03	-1.01	.32	

NOTES

CHAPTER 1

We gratefully acknowledge Aaliyah El-Amin and Lauren Kelly for their significant contributions to the ideas presented in this chapter.

1. James Baldwin, "A Talk to Teachers," in *City Kids, City Teachers: Reports from the Front Row*, eds. William Ayers and Patricia Ford (New York: New Press, 1996), 219–27.

2. Nicole Mirra, *Educating for Empathy: Literacy Learning and Civic Engagement* (New York: Teachers College Press, 2018); Michelle Alexander, *The New Jim Crow: Mass Incarceration in the Age of Colorblindness* (New York: Free Press, 2010); Centers for Disease Control and Prevention, *CDC Health Disparities and Inequalities Report—United States* (Washington, DC: CDC, 2013); Matthew Desmond, *Evicted: Poverty and Profit in the American City* (Princeton, NJ: Princeton University Press, 2016).

3. Gary Orfield and Chungmei Lee, *Why Segregation Matters: Poverty and Educational Inequality* (Cambridge, MA: The Civil Rights Project, 2005).

4. Anne Gregory, Russell Skiba, and Pedro Noguera, "The Achievement Gap and the Discipline Gap: Two Sides of the Same Coin," *Educational Researcher* 39, no. 1 (2010): 59–68; Carolyn Jones, "Latino, African Americans Have Less Access to Math, Science Classes, New Data Show," *EdSource*, May 22, 2018.

5. US Department of Education, Office of Civil Rights, "2013–2014 Civil Rights Data Collection: A First Look," https://www2.ed.gov/about/offices/list/ocr/docs/2013-14-first-look.pdf.

6. Paulo Freire, *Pedagogy of the Oppressed* (New York: Continuum, 1970).

7. Jones Irwin, *Paulo Freire's Philosophy of Education: Origins, Developments, Impacts and Legacies* (New York: Continuum, 2002).

8. James Baldwin, "A Talk to Teachers." 20.

9. Freire, *Pedagogy of the Oppressed*.

10. Scott Seider, Shelby Clark, and Daren Graves, "The Development of Critical Consciousness and Its Relation to Academic Achievement in Adolescents of Color," *Child Development* (in press). Available online at https://onlinelibrary.wiley.com/doi/abs/10.1111/cdev.13262; Shawn Ginwright, *Black Youth Rising: Activism and Radical Healing in Urban America* (New York: Teachers College Press, 2010); Guerda Nicolas et al., "A Conceptual Framework for Understanding the Strengths

of Black Youth," *Journal of Black Psychology* 34, no. 3 (2008): 261–80; Anna O'Leary and Andrea Romero, "Chicana/o Students Respond to Arizona's Anti-Ethnic Studies Bill, SB1108: Civic Engagement, Ethnic Identity, and Well-Being," *Aztlan: A Journal of Chicano Studies* 36, no. 1 (2011): 9–36; Matthew Diemer and Chueh-An Hsieh, "Sociopolitical Development and Vocational Expectations Among Lower Socioeconomic Status Adolescents of Color," *Career Development Quarterly* 56, no. 3 (2008): 257–67; Matthew Diemer and Cheng-Hsien Li, "Critical Consciousness Development and Political Participation Among Marginalized Youth," *Child Development* 82, no. 6 (2011): 1815–33; Roderick Watts, Matthew Diemer, and Adam Voight, "Critical Consciousness: Current Status and Future Directions," *New Directions for Child and Adolescent Development* 134 (2011): 43–57; Marc Zimmerman, Jesus Ramirez-Valles, and Kenneth Maton, "Resilience Among Urban African American Male Adolescents: A Study of the Protective Effects of Sociopolitical Control on Their Mental Health," *American Journal of Community Psychology* 27, no. 6 (1999): 733–51; Matthew Diemer and David Blustein, "Critical Consciousness and Career Development Among Urban Youth," *Journal of Vocational Behavior* 68, no. 2 (2006): 220–32; Erin Godfrey, Carlos Santos, and Esther Burson, "For Better or Worse? System-Justifying Beliefs in Sixth-Grade Predict Trajectories of Self-Esteem and Behavior Across Early Adolescence," *Child Development* 90, no. 1 (2019): 180–95.

11. Shawn Ginwright, *Black Youth Rising*.

12. Beverly Daniel Tatum, *Why Are All the Black Kids Sitting Together in the Cafeteria? And Other Conversations About Race* (New York: Basic Books, 1997), 47.

13. Roderick Watts, Derek Griffith, and Jaleel Abdul-Adil, "Sociopolitical Development as an Antidote for Oppression—Theory and Action," *American Journal of Community Psychology* 27, no. 2 (1999): 255; Olivia Phan, "The Psychological Armor of Urban Adolescents: Exploring the Influence of Critical Consciousness and Racial Identity on Career Adaptability" (PhD diss., Boston College, 2010), 1.

14. Watts, Diemer, and Voight, "Critical Consciousness," 43–57; Roderick Watts and Constance Flanagan, "Pushing the Envelope on Youth Civic Engagement: A Developmental and Liberation Psychology Perspective," *Journal of Community Psychology* 35, no. 6 (2007): 779–92.

15. Roderick Watts and Carlos Hipolito-Delgado, "Thinking Ourselves to Liberation?: Advancing Sociopolitical Action in Critical Consciousness," *Urban Review* 47, no. 5 (2015): 849.

16. Elizabeth Beaumont, "Political Agency and Empowerment: Pathways for Developing a Sense of Political Efficacy in Young Adults," in *Handbook of Research on Civic Engagement in Youth*, eds. Lonnie Sherrod, Judith Torney-Purta, and Constance Flanagan (Hoboken, NJ: John Wiley & Sons, 2010), 525–58.

17. Scholars also use the terms *critical reflection*, *critical motivation*, and *critical agency* to refer to these three dimensions of critical consciousness.

18. Freire, *Pedagogy of the Oppressed*, 72.

19. Julio Cammarota and Michelle Fine, *Revolutionizing Education: Youth Participatory Action Research in Motion* (New York: Routledge, 2008); Jeffrey Duncan-Andrade and Ernest Morrell, *The Art of Critical Pedagogy: Possibilities for Moving from Theory to Practice in Urban Schools* (New York: Peter Lang, 2008); Ben Kirshner, *Youth Activism in the Era of Education Inequality* (New York: New York University Press, 2015).

20. Julio Cammarota, "A Social Justice Approach to Achievement: Guiding Latina/o Students Toward Educational Attainment with a Challenging, Socially Relevant Curriculum," *Equity & Excellence in Education* 40, no. 1 (2007): 87–96; Augustine Romero, Sean Arce, and Julio Cammarota, "A Barrio Pedagogy: Identity, Intellectualism, Activism, and Academic Achievement Through the Evolution of Critically Compassionate Intellectualism," *Race, Ethnicity, and Education* 12, no. 2 (2009): 217–33.

21. Scott Seider et al., "Fostering the Sociopolitical Development of African American and Latinx Adolescents to Analyze and Challenge Racial and Economic Inequality," *Youth & Society*, Available online https://journals.sagepub.com/doi/full/10.1177/0044118X18767783; Natalie Davis, "Hope in Those Places of Struggle: A Critical Exploration of Black Students' Agency in One Place-Based and One African-Centered Elementary School" (PhD diss., University of Michigan, 2018).

22. Scott Seider et al., "Preparing Adolescents Attending Progressive and No-Excuses Urban Charter High Schools to Analyze, Navigate, and Challenge Race and Class Inequality," *Teachers College Record* 118, no. 12 (2016): 1–54.

23. Daniel Perlstein, "Minds Stayed on Freedom: Politics and Pedagogy in the African American Freedom Struggle," *American Educational Research Journal* 39, no. 2 (2002): 269.

24. Erin Godfrey and Justina Grayman, "Teaching Citizens: The Role of Open Classroom Climate in Fostering Critical Consciousness Among Youth," *Journal of Youth & Adolescence* 43, no. 11 (2014): 1801–17; Duncan-Andrade and Morrell, *The Art of Critical Pedagogy*.

25. Gretchen Lopez, Patricia Gurin, and Biren Nagda, "Education and Understanding Structural Causes for Group Inequalities," *Political Psychology* 19, no. 2 (1998): 305–29.

26. N. Andrew Peterson et al., "Measuring Youth Empowerment: Validation of a Sociopolitical Control Scale for Youth in an Urban Community Context," *Journal of Community Psychology* 39, no. 5 (2011): 592–605.

27. Alexandra Corning and Daniel Myers, "Individual Orientation Toward Engagement in Social Action," *Political Psychology* 23, no. 4 (2002): 703–29.

28. Baldwin, "A Talk to Teachers," 219.

29. Dan Bauman, "After 2016 Election, Hate Crimes on Campus Seemed to Jump, Here's What the Data Tells Us," *Chronicle of Higher Education*, February 16, 2018; Megan Zahneis, "White Supremacist Propaganda on Campuses Rose 77% Last Year," *Chronicle of Higher Education*, June 28, 2018.

CHAPTER 2

We gratefully acknowledge Melanie Cabral, Jamie Johannsen, and Kathryn Sabath for their significant contributions to the analyses of interviews and field notes presented in this chapter.

1. Myles Horton and Paulo Freire, *We Make the Road by Walking* (Philadelphia, PA: Temple University Press, 1990).

2. Paulo Freire, *Education for Critical Consciousness* (New York: Continuum, 1973), 72.

3. Paulo Freire, *Pedagogy of Freedom: Ethics, Democracy, and Civic Courage* (Lanham, MD: Rowman & Littlefield, 1998).

4. Freire, *Education for Critical Consciousness.*

5. Nina Wallerstein, "Problem-Posing Education: Freire's Method for Transformation," in *Freire in the Classroom*, ed. Ira Shor (Portsmouth, NH: Boynton Cook, 1987), 33–44.

6. Freire, *Pedagogy of the Oppressed*, 87.

7. Freire, *Education for Critical Consciousness.*

8. Devah Pager and Hana Shepherd, "The Sociology of Discrimination: Racial Discrimination in Employment, Housing, Credit, and Consumer Markets," *Annual Review of Sociology* 34 (2008): 181–209.

9. Julie Hughes and Rebecca Bigler, "Predictors of African American and European American Adolescents' Endorsement of Race-Conscious Social Policies," *Developmental Psychology* 47, no. 2 (2011): 479–92; Stephen Quintana, "Racial Perspective-Taking Ability: Developmental, Theoretical, and Empirical Trends," in *Handbook of Race, Racism, and the Developing Child*, eds. Stephen Quintana and Clark McKown (New York: John Wiley & Sons, 2008), 16–36; Erin Seaton et al., "Developmental Characteristics of African American and Caribbean Black Adolescents' Attributions Regarding Discrimination," *Journal of Research on Adolescence* 20, no. 3 (2010): 774–88; Scott Seider et al., "Black and Latinx Adolescents' Developing Beliefs About Poverty and Associations with Their Awareness of Racism," *Developmental Psychology* 55, no. 3 (2019): 509–24.

10. Gretchen Lopez, Patricia Gurin, and Biren Nagda, "Education and Understanding Structural Causes for Group Inequalities," *Political Psychology* 19, no. 2 (1998): 305–29.

11. This comparison between the five featured high schools and four comparison high schools on the Awareness of Systemic Racism Scale at Time 5 was calculated using an independent samples t-test ($t(626) = 2.20$, $p < .02$).

12. This comparison between youth attending Make the Road Academy and the broader sample of youth from the five featured high schools was calculated using hierarchical linear modeling with effects coding. These analyses are included in the appendix, "A Note on Research Methods" (table A3).

13. Roderick Watts, Matthew Diemer, and Adam Voight, "Critical Consciousness: Current Status and Future Directions," *New Directions for Child and Adolescent*

Development 134 (2011): 43–57; Roderick Watts and Constance Flanagan, "Pushing the Envelope on Youth Civic Engagement: A Developmental and Liberation Psychology Perspective," *Journal of Community Psychology* 35, no. 6 (2007): 779–92.

14. We interviewed twelve MtRA ninth graders in the spring of 2014, but four of these students left the school between the spring of 2014 and spring of 2017 and did not complete four yearly interviews with our research team.

15. John Jost et al., "A Decade of System Justification Theory: Accumulated Evidence of Conscious and Unconscious Bolstering of the Status Quo," *Political Psychology* 25, no. 6 (2004): 881–919.

16. Rakesh Kocchar and Richard Fry, "Wealth Inequality Has Widened Along Racial-Ethnic Lines Since End of Great Depression," http://www.pewresearch .org/fact-tank/2014; Carmen DeNavas-Walt and Bernadette Proctor, *U.S. Census Bureau: Income and Poverty in the United States* (Washington, DC: US Government Printing Office, 2014).

17. Charmaine Wijeyesinghe and Bailey Jackson, *New Perspectives on Racial Identity Development: Integrating Emerging Frameworks* (New York: New York University Press, 2012).

18. Rebecca Bigler, Cara Averhart, and Lynn Liben, "Race and the Workforce: Occupational Status, Aspirations, and Stereotyping Among African American Children," *Developmental Psychology* 39, no. 3 (2003): 572–80; Clark McKown and Michael Strambler, "Developmental Antecedents and Social and Academic Consequences of Stereotype-Consciousness in Middle Childhood," *Child Development* 80, no. 6 (2009): 1643–59; Davido Dupree, Tirzah Spencer, and Margaret Beale Spencer, "Stigma, Stereotypes and Resilience Identities: The Relationship Between Identity Processes and Resilience Processes Among Black American Adolescents," in *Youth Resilience and Culture,* eds. Linda Theron, Linda Liebenberg, and Michael Ungar (Switzerland: Springer Dordrecht, 2015), 117–129; Patricia Gurin et al., "Intergroup Dialogues; Race Still Matters," in *Race and Social Problems,* eds. Ralph Bangs and Larry Davis (Switzerland: Springer, 2015), 39–60; Erin Seaton, "The Influence of Cognitive Development and Perceived Racial Discrimination on the Psychological Well-Being of African American Youth," *Journal of Youth & Adolescence* 39, no. 6 (2010): 694–703.

19. Brian Christens and Tom Dolan, "Interweaving Youth Development, Community Development, and Social Change Through Youth Organizing," *Youth & Society* 43, no. 2 (2011): 528–48; Jerusha Conner, "Lessons That Last: Former Youth Organizers' Reflections on What and How They Learned," *Journal of the Learning Sciences* 23, no. 3 (2014): 447–84; Julio Cammarota and Augustine Romero, "A Critically Compassionate Intellectualism for Latina/o Students: Raising Voices Above the Silencing in Our Schools," *Multicultural Education* 14, no. 2 (2006): 16–23; Jeffrey Duncan-Andrade and Ernest Morrell, *The Art of Critical Pedagogy: Possibilities for Moving from Theory to Practice in Urban Schools* (New York: Peter

Lang, 2008); Ben Kirshner, *Youth Activism in the Era of Education Inequality* (New York: New York University Press, 2015).

20. Freire, *Pedagogy of the Oppressed.*

21. Ron Ritchhart, *Intellectual Character: What It Is, Why It Matters, and How to Get It* (San Francisco, CA: Jossey-Bass, 2002).

22. Erik Erikson, *Identity: Youth and Crisis* (New York: W. W. Norton, 1968).

23. Theresa Perry, Claude Steele, and Asa Hilliard, *Young, Gifted, and Black* (Boston: Beacon Press, 2003), 106.

24. Wallerstein, "Problem-Posing Education."

25. Freire, *Pedagogy of the Oppressed.*

26. Freire, *Education for Critical Consciousness.*

27. Ron Ritchhart, *Intellectual Character: What It is, Why it Matters, and How to Get It*, 2002; Diana Hess, *Controversy in the Classroom: The Democratic Power of Discussion* (New York: Routledge, 2009).

28. Patricia Gurin, Biren Nagda, and Ximena Zuniga, *Dialogue Across Difference: Practice, Theory, and Research on Intergroup Dialogue* (New York: Russell Sage Foundation, 2013).

29. bell hooks, *Teaching to Transgress* (New York: Routledge, 1994).

30. Thomas Dee, "Teachers, Race, and Student Achievement in a Randomized Experiment," *Review of Economics and Statistics* 86, no. 1 (2004): 195–210; Donald Easton-Brooks, Chance Lewis, and Yubo Zhang, "Ethnic-Matching: The Influence of African American Teachers on the Reading Scores of African American Students," *National Journal of Urban Education & Practice* 3, no. 1 (2010): 230–43; Anna Egalite, Brian Kisida, and Marcus Winters, "Representation in the Classroom: The Effect of Own-Race Teachers on Student Achievement," *Economics of Education Review* 45 (2015): 44–52; Constance Lindsay and Cassandra Hart, "Teacher Race and School Discipline: Are Students Suspended Less Often When They Have a Teacher of the Same Race?," *Education Next* 17, no. 1 (2017): 72–79.

31. Horton and Freire, *We Make the Road by Walking*, 104.

32. Jelani Cobb, "Is Willie Lynch's Letter Real?," *Jim Crow Museum of Racist Memorabilia Question of the Month*, May 2004.

33. Cobb, "Is Willie Lynch's Letter Real?"

34. Elizabeth Beaumont, "Political Agency and Empowerment: Pathways for Developing a Sense of Political Efficacy in Young Adults," in *Handbook of Research on Civic Engagement in Youth*, eds. Lonnie Sherrod, Judith Torney-Purta, and Constance Flanagan (Hoboken, NJ: John Wiley & Sons, 2010), 525–58.

35. James Huguley et al., "Parent Ethnic-Racial Socialization Practices and Ethnic-Racial Identity: A Research Synthesis and Meta-Analysis," *Psychological Bulletin* 145, no. 5 (2019): 437–58.

36. Beverly Daniel Tatum, *Why Are All the Black Kids Sitting Together in the Cafeteria? And Other Conversations About Race* (New York: Basic Books, 2018), 128.

CHAPTER 3

We gratefully acknowledge Shelby Clark, Kristen Martin, Sherri Sklarwitz, and Madora Soutter for their significant contributions to the collection and analyses of field notes and interviews presented in this chapter.

1. Because all teachers and staff at Espiritu High School go by their first names, we likewise refer to them by their first names throughout this chapter.

2. *Horace: The Newsletter of the Coalition of Essential Schools* 1, no. 1 (1985): 4–5.

3. Theodore Sizer, *Horace's Compromise: The Dilemma of the American High School* (Boston, MA: Houghton Mifflin, 1984).

4. Coalition of Essential Schools, "Common Principles," http://essentialschools .org/common-principles.

5. Coalition of Essential Schools, "Common Principles."

6. Coalition of Essential Schools.

7. Matthew Diemer and Luke Rapa, "Unraveling the Complexity of Critical Consciousness, Political Efficacy, and Political Action Among Marginalized Adolescents," *Child Development* 87, no. 1 (2016): 221–38.

8. Dominic Abrams and Georgina Randsley de Moura, "The Psychology of Collective Political Protest," in *The Social Psychology of Politics*, eds. Victor Ottati et al. (Boston, MA: Springer, 2002), 193–214; Elizabeth Beaumont, "Political Agency and Empowerment: Pathways for Developing a Sense of Political Efficacy in Young Adults," in *Handbook of Research on Civic Engagement in Youth*, eds. Lonnie Sherrod, Judith Torney-Purta, and Constance Flanagan (Hoboken, NJ: John Wiley & Sons, 2010), 525–58; Michael McCluskey et al., "The Efficacy Gap and Political Participation: When Political Influence Fails to Meet Expectations," *International Journal of Public Opinion Research* 16, no. 4 (2004): 437–55; Brett Levy, "Fostering Cautious Political Efficacy Through Civic Advocacy Projects: A Mixed Methods Case Study of an Innovative High School Class," *Theory & Research in Social Education* 39, no. 2 (2011): 238–77.

9. Beaumont, "Political Agency and Empowerment."

10. Steven Finkel, "Reciprocal Effects of Participation and Political Efficacy: A Panel Analysis," *American Journal of Political Science* 29, no. 4 (1985): 891–913; Meira Levinson, *No Citizen Left Behind* (Cambridge, MA: Harvard University Press, 2012); Sydney Verba, Kay Schlozman, and Henry Brady, *Voice and Equality: Civic Voluntarism in American Politics* (Cambridge, MA: Harvard University Press, 1995).

11. Roderick Watts, Matthew Diemer, and Adam Voight, "Critical Consciousness: Current Status and Future Directions," *New Directions for Child and Adolescent Development* 134 (2011): 43–57.

12. N. Andrew Peterson et al., "Measuring Youth Empowerment: Validation of a Sociopolitical Control Scale for Youth in an Urban Community Context," *Journal of Community Psychology* 39, no. 5 (2011): 592–605.

13. This comparison between the five featured high schools and four comparison high schools on the Political Agency Scale at Time 5 was calculated using an independent samples t-test (t(551) = 2.75, p < .006).

14. As can be seen in figure 3.2, youth attending Espiritu High School demonstrated steeper growth, on average, in their political agency over four years of high school than their peers in the broader sample of five featured high schools. We sought to test the statistical significance of these differences in growth in political agency using hierarchical linear modeling with effects coding, and these analyses are included in the appendix, "A Note on Research Methods" (table A3). However, insufficient variance across the five featured high schools prevented HLM analyses from considering the statistical significance of differences in growth in political agency between students across these five schools.

15. Independent samples t-tests revealed Espiritu students' political agency at the conclusion of high school (Time 5) to be significantly higher than that of their peers in the comparison schools (t(317) = 2.69, p < .008) as well as higher than that of their peers in the other featured high schools at a level approaching statistical significance (t(274) = 1.61, p = .10).

16. Albert Bandura, *Self-Efficacy: The Exercise of Control* (New York: W. H. Freeman, 1997); Beaumont, "Political Agency and Empowerment."

17. Bandura, *Self-Efficacy.*

18. Beaumont, "Political Agency and Empowerment."

19. Dale Schunk and Frank Pajares, "Self-Efficacy Theory," in *Handbook of Motivation at School*, eds. Kathryn Wentzel and Allan Wigfield (New York: Routledge, 2009), 35–53.

20. Beaumont, "Political Agency and Empowerment," 543.

21. Bandura, *Self-Efficacy.*

22. Because "race" is a social construct rather than a biological one, it is often difficult to disentangle race from other identity markers such as ethnicity or religious affiliation. For this reason, although individuals who practice Islam constitute a religious group rather than an ethnic or racial group, these individuals' experiences with Islamophobia are often enmeshed with racism because (a) Muslims often are also people of color who experience traditional forms of racism and (b) stereotypical conceptions of Muslims in the United States serve to racialize this group.

23. Peter Levine, "Education for a Civil Society," in *Making Civics Count*, eds. David Campbell, Meira Levinson, and Frederick Hess (Cambridge, MA: Harvard Education Press, 2012), 37–56; Anna Saavedra, "Dry to Dynamic Civic Education Curricula," in *Making Civics Count*, eds. David Campbell, Meira Levinson, and Frederick Hess (Cambridge, MA: Harvard Education Press, 2012), 135–59.

24. Richard Niemi and Jane Junn, *Civic Education: What Makes Students Learn* (New Haven, CT: Yale University Press, 1998); David Sears and Sheri Levy, "Childhood and Adult Political Development," in *Oxford Handbook of Political Psychology*, eds. Leonie Huddy, David Sears, and Jack Levy (New York: Oxford University Press; 2003), 60–109.

25. Albert Bandura, "Adolescent Development from an Agentic Perspective," in *Self-Efficacy Beliefs of Adolescents*, eds. Tim Urdan and Frank Pajares (Greenwich, CT: Information Age Publishing, 2006), 30.

26. Beaumont, "Political Agency and Empowerment."

27. Beaumont.

28. Beaumont.

CHAPTER 4

We gratefully acknowledge Megan Kenslea, Saira Malhotra, and Jennifer Yung for their significant contributions to the analyses of field notes and interviews presented in this chapter.

1. In recent years, a number of the public charter networks most associated with a "no-excuses" approach to education (e.g., KIPP, Uncommon Schools, Achievement First) have shifted away from using the term itself to describe their schooling approach in favor of phrases such as a "high expectations, high support" approach to schooling. This shift seems to be primarily due to the recognition that opponents of the no-excuses approach were using the term to suggest such schools and networks took an inflexible and unsympathetic approach to working with students. Nonetheless, we believe the term *no excuses* remains a useful shorthand for describing the schooling approach guiding schools such as Harriet Tubman High School.

2. Samuel Carter, *No Excuses: Lessons from 21 High-Performing, High-Poverty Schools* (Washington, DC: Heritage Foundation, 2000).

3. Michael McShane and Jenn Hatfield, *Measuring Diversity in Charter School Offerings* (Washington, DC: American Enterprise Institute, 2015).

4. Albert Cheng et al., "No Excuses Charter Schools: A Meta-Analysis of the Experimental Evidence on Student Achievement," *Journal of School Choice* 11, no. 2 (2017): 209–38.

5. Alexandra Boyd, Robert Maranto, and Caleb Rose, "The Softer Side of No Excuses: A View of KIPP Schools in Action," *Education Next* 14, no. 1 (2014): 48–54; Philip Gleason et al., "Do KIPP Schools Boost Student Achievement?," *Education Finance and Policy* 9, no. 1 (2014): 36–58; Robert Pondiscio, "No Excuses Kids Go to College," *Education Next* 13, no. 2 (2013): 9–14.

6. Joan Goodman, "Charter Management Organizations and the Regulated Environment: Is It Worth the Price?," *Educational Researcher* 42, no. 2 (2013): 89–96; Brian Lack, "No Excuses: A Critique of the Knowledge Is Power Program (KIPP) Within Charter Schools in the USA," *Journal for Critical Education Policy Studies* 7, no. 2 (2009): 126–53; Sigal Ben-Porath, "Deferring Virtue: The New Management of Students and the Civic Role of Schools," *Theory and Research in Education* 11, no. 2 (2013): 111–28.

7. Joanne Golann, "The Paradox of Success at a No-Excuses School," *Sociology of Education* 88, no. 2 (2015): 104.

8. Beth Sondel, "Raising Citizens or Raising Test Scores? Teach For America, No Excuses Charters, and the Development of the Neoliberal Citizen," *Theory & Research in Social Education* 43, no. 3 (2015): 289–313.

9. Golann, "The Paradox of Success"; Sondel, "Raising Citizens or Raising Test Scores?"

10. Luis Urrieta, *Working from Within: Chicana and Chicano Activist Educators in Whitestream Schools* (Tucson, AZ: University of Arizona Press, 2010), 181.

11. Raygine DiAquoi, "Colorblind and Colorlined: African American Parents Talk to Their Adolescent Sons About Racism" (EdD diss., Harvard University, 2015), 129.

12. DiAquoi, "Colorblind and Colorlined," 135.

13. Roderick Watts and Carlos Hipolito-Delgado, "Thinking Ourselves to Liberation?: Advancing Sociopolitical Action in Critical Consciousness," *Urban Review* 47, no. 5 (2015): 847–67.

14. Urrieta, *Working from Within*.

15. Urrieta, *Working from Within*; Nansook Park and Christopher Peterson, "Moral Competence and Character Strengths Among Adolescents: The Development and Validation of the Values in Action Inventory of Strengths for Youth," *Journal of Adolescence* 29, no. 6 (2006): 891–909.

16. Mary Tenopyr, "Social Intelligence and Academic Success," *Educational and Psychological Measurement* 27, no. 4 (1967): 961–65; John Kihlstrom and Nancy Kantor, "Social Intelligence," in *Cambridge Handbook of Intelligence*, eds. Robert Sternberg and Scott Kaufman (Cambridge, UK: Cambridge University Press, 2011), 564–81.

17. Joseph Braga and R. Patrick Doyle, "Student Activism and Social Intelligence," *Youth & Society* 2, no. 4 (1971): 425–40.

18. This comparison between the five featured high schools and four comparison high schools on the Social Intelligence Scale at Time 5 was calculated using an independent samples t-test ($t(544) = 0.11$, $p = .91$).

19. These comparisons in levels and growth of social intelligence between youth attending Harriet Tubman High School and the broader sample of youth from the five featured high schools were calculated using hierarchical linear modeling with effects coding. These analyses are included in the appendix, "A Note on Research Methods" (table A3).

20. Lisa Delpit, "Other People's Children: Cultural Conflict in the Classroom," *Harvard Educational Review* 65 (1995): 510; Concha Delgado-Gaitan and Henry Trueba, *Crossing Cultural Borders: Education for Immigrant Families in America* (Bristol, PA: Falmer Press, 1991); Prudence Carter, "Straddling Boundaries: Identity, Culture, and School," *Sociology of Education* 79, no. 4 (2006): 304–28.

21. Daniel Solorzano and Dolores Delgado Bernal, "Examining Transformational Resistance Through a Critical Race and LatCrit Theory Framework: Chicana and Chicano Students in an Urban Context," *Urban Education* 36, no. 3 (2001): 308–42; Tara Yosso, "A Critical Race and LatCrit Approach to Media Literacy: Chicana/o Resistance to Visual Microaggressions" (PhD diss., University of California, Los Angeles, 2000).

22. Shawn Ginwright, *Black Youth Rising: Activism and Radical Healing in Urban America* (New York: Teachers College Press, 2010).

23. Solorzano and Delgado Bernal, "Examining Transformational Resistance Through a Critical Race and LatCrit Theory Framework"; Yosso, "A Critical Race and Lat-Crit Approach to Media Literacy."

24. Ginwright, *Black Youth Rising*; Matthew Diemer and Chueh-An Hsieh, "Sociopolitical Development and Vocational Expectations Among Lower Socioeconomic Status Adolescents of Color," *Career Development Quarterly* 56, no. 3 (2008): 257–67; Matthew Diemer and Cheng-Hsien Li, "Critical Consciousness Development and Political Participation Among Marginalized Youth," *Child Development* 82, no. 6 (2011): 1815–33; Marc Zimmerman, Jesus Ramirez-Valles, and Kenneth Maton, "Resilience Among Urban African American Male Adolescents: A Study of the Protective Effects of Sociopolitical Control on Their Mental Health," *American Journal of Community Psychology* 27, no. 6 (1999): 733–51; Matthew Diemer and David Blustein, "Critical Consciousness and Career Development Among Urban Youth," *Journal of Vocational Behavior* 68, no. 2 (2006): 220–32; Erin Godfrey, Carlos Santos, and Esther Burson, "For Better or Worse? System-Justifying Beliefs in Sixth-Grade Predict Trajectories of Self-Esteem and Behavior Across Early Adolescence," *Child Development* 90, no. 1 (2019): 180–95; Scott Seider, Shelby Clark, and Daren Graves, "The Development of Critical Consciousness in Youth of Color and Its Relation to Academic Achievement," *Child Development* Available online at https://onlinelibrary.wiley.com/doi/abs/10.1111/cdev.13262.

25. Yosso, "A Critical Race and LatCrit Approach to Media Literacy."

26. Mandy Savitz-Romer and Suzanne Bouffard, *Ready, Willing, and Able: A Developmental Approach to College Access and Success* (Cambridge, MA: Harvard Education Press, 2012).

27. David Miller et al., "The Development of Children's Gender Science Stereotypes," *Child Development* 89, no. 6 (2018): 1943–55.

28. Albert Bandura, *Self-Efficacy: The Exercise of Control* (New York: W. H. Freeman, 1997).

29. Perry, Steele, and Hilliard, *Young, Gifted, and Black*, 88.

30. Yosso, "A Critical Race and LatCrit Approach to Media Literacy."

31. Dani Snyder-Young, "Rehearsals for Revolution? Theatre of the Oppressed, Dominant Discourses, and Democratic Tensions," *Research in Drama Education: The Journal of Applied Theatre and Performance* 16, no. 1 (2011): 29.

32. Erik Erikson, *Identity: Youth and Crisis* (London, UK: W. W. Norton, 1968).

33. Sharon Daloz-Parks, *Big Questions, Worthy Dreams: Mentoring Emerging Adults in Their Search for Meaning, Purpose, and Faith* (San Francisco, CA: Jossey-Bass, 2001); William Damon, *The Path to Purpose: How Young People Find Their Calling in Life* (New York: Simon and Schuster, 2009).

34. Jeffrey Duncan-Andrade and Ernest Morrell, *The Art of Critical Pedagogy: Possibilities for Moving from Theory to Practice in Urban Schools* (New York: Peter Lang, 2008), 104.

3 5. Yosso, "A Critical Race and LatCrit Approach to Media Literacy"; Dorinda Carter, "Achievement as Resistance: The Development of a Critical Race Achievement Ideology Among Black Achievers," *Harvard Educational Review* 78, no. 3 (2008): 466–97.

CHAPTER 5

We gratefully acknowledge Aaliyah El-Amin, Lauren Kelly, and Jalene Tamerat for their significant contributions to the collection and analyses of interviews and field notes presented in this chapter.

1. Because all teachers and staff at Community Academy go by their first names within the school community, we refer to them by their first names as well throughout this chapter.

2. For full disclosure, one of this book's authors (Scott Seider) began serving on the research advisory board to EL (Expeditionary Learning) Education in 2016.

3. EL Education, "Design Principles: Core Values of EL Education," https://eleducation.org/resources/design-principles.

4. EL Education, "Design Principles."

5. EL Education, "Structure and Principles of a Learning Expedition," https://eleducation.org.

6. EL Education, "Design Principles."

7. Alexandra Corning and Daniel Myers, "Individual Orientation Toward Engagement in Social Action," *Political Psychology* 23, no. 4 (2002): 703–29.

8. Paulo Freire, *Pedagogy of the Oppressed* (New York: Continuum, 1970).

9. Corning and Myers, "Individual Orientation."

10. This comparison between the five featured high schools and four comparison high schools on the Commitment to Activism Scale at Time 5 was calculated using an independent samples t-test (t(555) = 3.47, p < .001).

11. This comparison between youth attending Community Academy and the broader sample of youth from the five featured high schools was calculated using hierarchical linear modeling with effects coding. These analyses are included in the appendix, "A Note on Research Methods" (table A3).

12. Erik Erikson, *Identity: Youth and Crisis* (London, UK: W. W. Norton, 1968).

13. William Damon, *The Path to Purpose: Helping Our Children Find Their Calling in Life* (New York: Simon and Schuster, 2008); Sharon Parks, *Big Questions, Worthy Dreams: Mentoring Young Adults in Their Search for Meaning, Purpose, and Faith* (San Francisco, CA: Jossey-Bass, 2000); James Youniss and Miranda Yates, *Community Service and Social Responsibility in Youth* (Chicago, IL: University of Chicago Press, 1997); Ben Kirshner, *Youth Activism in an Era of Education Inequality* (New York: New York University Press, 2002); Daniel McFarland and Reuben Thomas, "Bowling Young: How Youth Voluntary Associations Influence Adult Political Participation," *American Sociological Review* 71, no. 3 (2006): 401–25; Roderick Watts and Carlos Hipolito-Delgado, "Thinking Ourselves to Liberation?:

Advancing Sociopolitical Action in Critical Consciousness," *Urban Review* 47, no. 5 (2015): 847–67.

14. Outward Bound, "Educational Framework," https://www.outwardbound.org/about-outward-bound/philosophy/.

15. EL Education, "Design Principles."

16. Beverly Daniel Tatum, *Why Are All the Black Kids Sitting Together in the Cafeteria? And Other Conversations About Race* (New York: Basic Books, 2018), 128.

17. EL Education, "Design Principles."

18. Bettina Love, *We Want to Do More Than Survive: Abolitionist Teaching and the Pursuit of Educational Freedom* (Boston, MA: Beacon Press, 2019), 52.

19. None of the Community Academy students in the class of 2017 self-identified as either Native American or part Native American.

20. Nicole Mirra, *Educating for Empathy: Literacy Learning and Civic Engagement* (New York: Teachers College Press, 2018), 20.

21. Jane Howard, "Telling Talk from a Negro Writer," *Life* 54 (1963): 4.

22. Peter Singer, *The Life You Can Save: Acting Now to End World Poverty* (New York: Random House, 2009), 49.

23. Singer, *The Life You Can Save.*

24. Emily Hanford, "Kurt Hahn and the Roots of Expeditionary Learning," *American RadioWorks,* September 10, 2015, http://www.americanradioworks.org/segments/kurt-hahn-expeditionary-learning/.

25. Jean Lave and Etienne Wenger, *Situated Learning: Legitimate Peripheral Participation* (Cambridge, UK: Cambridge University Press, 1991); Barbara Rogoff, *The Cultural Nature of Human Development* (Oxford, UK: Oxford University Press, 2003).

26. Lave and Wenger, *Situated Learning*; Rogoff, *The Cultural Nature.*

27. Lave and Wenger, *Situated Learning*; Frank Margonis, "From Student Resistance to Educative Engagement: A Case Study in Building Powerful Student-Teacher Relationships," *Counterpoints* 259 (2004): 39–53.

28. Lave and Wenger, *Situated Learning*; Erikson, *Identity*; William Damon, *The Path to Purpose: Helping Our Children Find Their Calling in Life* (New York: Simon and Schuster, 2008.)

29. Erikson, *Identity*; John Gastil and Michael Xenos, "Of Attitudes and Engagement: Clarifying the Reciprocal Relationship Between Civic Attitudes and Political Participation," *Journal of Communication* 60, no. 2 (2010): 318–43; Parks, *Big Questions, Worthy Dreams*; Youniss and Yates, *Community Service and Social Responsibility.*

30. EL Education, "Design Principles."

31. This comparison between youth attending Community Academy and the broader sample of youth from the five featured high schools on the Awareness of Systemic Racism and Awareness of Systemic Poverty scales was calculated using hierarchical linear modeling with effects coding. These analyses are included in the appendix, "A Note on Research Methods" (table A3). As can be seen in these analyses,

Community Academy students demonstrated significantly weaker understandings of systemic causes of poverty than their peers across all five featured high schools, and a weaker understanding as well of systemic causes of racism that approached statistical significance.

3 2. Freire, *Pedagogy of the Oppressed.*

3 3. Myles Horton and Paulo Freire, *We Make the Road by Walking* (Philadelphia, PA: Temple University Press, 1990), 141.

CHAPTER 6

We gratefully acknowledge Shelby Clark, Pauline Jennett, Lauren Kelly, and Madora Soutter for their significant contributions to the collection and analyses of interviews and field notes presented in this chapter.

1. We have withheld this citation to maintain the anonymity of Leadership High School.

2. Carla O'Connor, "Dispositions Toward (Collective) Struggle and Educational Resilience in the Inner City: A Case Analysis of Six African-American High School Students," *American Educational Research Journal* 34, no. 4 (1997): 593–629; Ellen McWhirter and Benedict T. McWhirter, "Critical Consciousness and Vocational Development Among Latina/o High School Youth: Initial Development and Testing of a Measure," *Journal of Career Assessment* 24, no. 3 (2016): 543–58; Scott Seider, Shelby Clark, and Daren Graves, "The Development of Critical Consciousness in Adolescents of Color and Its Relation to Academic Achievement," *Child Development.* Available online at https://onlinelibrary.wiley.com/doi/abs/10.1111/cdev.13262.

3. Meira Levinson, *No Citizen Left Behind* (Cambridge, MA: Harvard University Press, 2012).

4. Ben Moscowitz, "Overhauling One High School Subject Is Our Best Hope for the Future of Democracy," *Quartz*, January 23, 2017.

5. Diana Hess and Paula McAvoy, *The Political Classroom: Evidence and Ethics in Democratic Education* (New York: Routledge, 2014); Peter Levine, "Education for a Civil Society," in *Making Civics Count: Citizenship Education for a New Generation*, eds. David Campbell, Meira Levinson, and Frederick Hess (Cambridge, MA: Harvard Education Press, 2012), 37–56.

6. Scott Seider, Madora Soutter, and Shelby Clark, "The Role of Character Development in Fostering Student Success at School," in *Handbook of Social Influences in School Contexts: Social-Emotional, Motivation, and Cognitive Outcomes*, eds. Kathryn Wentzel and Geetha B. Ramani (Hoboken, NJ: Wiley-Blackwell, 2016), 293–311.

7. Ann Colby, Elizabeth Beaumont, Thomas Ehrlich, and Jason Stephens, *Educating Citizens: Preparing America's Undergraduates for Lives of Moral and Civic Responsibility* (Hoboken, NJ: John Wiley & Sons, 2003); Lonnie Sherrod, Constance Flanagan, and James Youniss, "Dimensions of Citizenship and Opportunities for

Youth Development: The What, Why, When, Where, and Who of Citizenship Development," *Applied Developmental Science* 6, no. 4 (2002): 264–72.

8. National Action Civics Collaborative, "Action Civics Framework," http://action civicscollaborative.org/why-action-civics/framework.

9. David Campbell, "Civic Education in Traditional Public, Charter, and Private Schools: Moving from Comparison to Explanation," in *Making Civics Count: Citizenship for a New Generation*, eds. David Campbell, Meira Levinson, and Frederick Hess (Cambridge, MA: Harvard Education Press, 2012), 229–46; Constance Flanagan and Brian D. Christens, "Youth Civic Development: Historical Context and Emerging Issues," *New Directions for Child and Adolescent Development* 134 (2011): 1–9; Joseph Kahne, David Crow, and Nam-Jin Lee, "Different Pedagogy, Different Politics: High School Learning Opportunities and Youth Political Engagement," *Political Psychology* 34, no. 3 (2013): 419–41; Ben Kirshner, *Youth Activism in an Era of Educational Inequality* (New York: New York University Press, 2015); Laura Wray-Lake and Amy K. Syvertsen, "The Developmental Roots of Social Responsibility in Childhood and Adolescence," *New Directions for Child and Adolescent Development* 134 (2011): 11–25; James Youniss, "How to Enrich Civic Education and Sustain Democracy," *Making Civics Count: Citizenship Education for a New Generation* (Cambridge, MA: Harvard Education Press, 2012), 115–33.

10. Arielle Jennings, "Civics Law Provides Solid Foundation for Teachers, Students," *CommonWealth Magazine*, November 14, 2018.

11. Alexandra Corning and Daniel J. Myers, "Individual Orientation Toward Engagement in Social Action," *Political Psychology* 23, no. 4 (2002): 703–29.

12. Paulo Freire, *Pedagogy of the Oppressed* (New York: Continuum, 1970); Roderick Watts and Constance Flanagan, "Pushing the Envelope on Youth Civic Engagement: A Developmental and Liberation Psychology Perspective," *Journal of Community Psychology* 35, no. 6 (2007): 779–92.

13. Corning and Myers, "Individual Orientation Toward Engagement."

14. As noted in chapter 5, this comparison between the five high schools featured in this book and the four comparison high schools on the Commitment to Activism Scale at Time 5 was calculated using an independent samples t-test ($t(555) = 3.47, p < .001$).

15. This comparison between youth attending Leadership High School and the broader sample of youth from the five featured high schools was calculated using hierarchical linear modeling with effects codes. These analyses are included in the appendix, "A Note on Research Methods" (table A3).

16. Roderick Watts and Carlos Hipolito-Delgado, "Thinking Ourselves to Liberation?: Advancing Sociopolitical Action in Critical Consciousness," *Urban Review* 47, no. 5 (2015): 847–67.

17. Watts and Hipolito-Delgado.

18. James Youniss, Jeffrey A. McLellan, and Miranda Yates, "What We Know About Engendering Civic Identity," *American Behavioral Scientist* 40, no. 5 (1997): 620–31.

19. Watts and Hipolito-Delgado, "Thinking Ourselves to Liberation?"; James Youniss and Miranda Yates, *Community Service and Social Responsibility in Youth* (Chicago, IL: University of Chicago Press, 1997).

20. William Faulkner, *Light in August* (New York: Smith & Haas, 1932).

21. Nicole Mirra, *Educating for Empathy: Literacy Learning and Civic Engagement* (New York: Teachers College Press, 2018), 9.

22. Michelle Alexander, *The New Jim Crow: Mass Incarceration in the Age of Colorblindness* (New York: New Press, 2010).

23. Zadie Smith, *White Teeth* (New York: Vintage, 2001).

24. Salman Rushdie, "The Power of the Pen," PEN America, June 1, 2006, https://pen.org/the-power-of-the-pen-salman-rushdie.

25. Eric Hirsch, "Sacrifice for the Cause: Group Processes, Recruitment, and Commitment in a Student Social Movement," *American Sociological Review* 55, no. 2 (1990): 243–54.

26. Jesse Gainer, "21st-Century Mentor Texts: Developing Critical Literacies in the Information Age," *Journal of Adolescent & Adult Literacy* 57, no. 1 (2013): 16–19.

27. Diana Hess and Paula McAvoy, *The Political Classroom: Evidence and Ethics in Democratic Education* (New York: Routledge, 2014).

28. Sidney Verba, Kay Schlozman, and Henry Brady, *Voice and Equality: Civic Voluntarism in American Politics* (Cambridge, MA: Harvard University Press, 1995).

29. Verba, Schlozman, and Brady, *Voice and Equality.*

30. Jeni Warburton and Jennifer Smith, "Out of the Generosity of Your Heart: Are We Creating Active Citizens Through Compulsory Volunteer Programmes for Young People in Australia?," *Social Policy & Administration* 37, no. 7 (2003): 772–86.

31. Alisa Henderson et al., "Mandated Community Service in High School and Subsequent Civic Engagement: The Case of the 'Double Cohort' in Ontario, Canada," *Journal of Youth & Adolescence* 36, no. 7 (2007): 849–60.

32. Mica Pollock, *Colormute: Race Talk Dilemmas in an American School* (Princeton, NJ: Princeton University Press, 2009); Glenn Singleton and Cyndie Hays, "Beginning Courageous Conversations About Race," in *Everyday Antiracism: Getting Real About Race in School*, ed. Mica Pollock (New York: New Press, 2008), 18–23.

33. Pollock, *Colormute.*

CHAPTER 7

1. Erik Erikson, *Identity: Youth and Crisis* (London, UK: W. W. Norton, 1968).

2. William Damon, *The Path to Purpose: Helping Our Children Find Their Calling in Life* (New York: Simon & Schuster, 2008); Susan Parks, *Big Questions, Worthy Dreams: Mentoring Young Adults in Their Search for Meaning, Purpose, and Faith* (San Francisco, CA: Jossey-Bass, 2000).

3. Bettina Love, *We Want to Do More Than Survive: Abolitionist Teaching and the Pursuit of Educational Freedom* (Boston, MA: Beacon Press, 2019), 132.

4. Erikson, *Identity*.

5. Susan Harter, "Self and Identity Development," in *At the Threshold: The Developing Adolescent*, eds. Shirley Feldman and Glen Elliott (Cambridge, MA: Harvard University Press, 1990), 352–87; Parks, *Big Questions, Worthy Dreams*.

6. Roderick Watts and Carlos Hipolito-Delgado, "Thinking Ourselves to Liberation?: Advancing Sociopolitical Action in Critical Consciousness," *Urban Review* 47, no. 5 (2015): 847–67.

7. Watts and Hipolito-Delgado, "Thinking Ourselves to Liberation?"; Albert Bandura, "Adolescent Development from an Agentic Perspective," in *Self-Efficacy Beliefs of Adolescents*, eds. Tim Urdan and Frank Pajares (Greenwich, CT: Information Age Publishing, 2006), 1–43.

8. Lev Vygotsky, *Mind in Society: The Development of Higher Psychological Processes* (Cambridge, MA: Harvard University Press, 1980); Jean Lave and Etienne Wenger, *Situated Learning: Legitimate Peripheral Participation* (Cambridge, UK: Cambridge University Press, 1991); Barbara Rogoff, *The Cultural Nature of Human Development* (Oxford, UK: Oxford University Press, 2003).

9. Luis Urrieta, *Working from Within: Chicana and Chicano Activist Educators in Whitestream Schools* (Tucson, AZ: University of Arizona Press, 2009).

10. Such findings align with prior work that has found extracurricular activities to play an important role in strengthening young people's civic engagement. See, for example, Joseph Kahne and Susan Sporte, "Developing Citizens: The Impact of Civic Learning Opportunities on Students' Commitment to Civic Participation," *American Educational Research Journal* 45, no. 3 (2008): 738–66.

11. Paulo Freire, *Education for Critical Consciousness* (New York: Continuum, 1973), 66.

12. Freire, *Education for Critical Consciousness*, ix.

13. Roderick Watts and Constance Flanagan, "Pushing the Envelope on Youth Civic Engagement: A Developmental and Liberation Psychology Perspective," *Journal of Community Psychology* 35 (2007): 779–92.

14. Dan Bauman, "After 2016 Election, Hate Crimes on Campus Seemed to Jump, Here's What the Data Tells Us," *Chronicle of Higher Education*, February 16, 2018; Megan Zahneis, "White Supremacist Propaganda on Campuses Rose 77% Last Year," *Chronicle of Higher Education*, June 28, 2018.

15. Brandon Terry and Tommie Shelby, *To Shape a New World: The Political Philosophy of Martin Luther King Jr.* (Cambridge, MA: Harvard University Press, 2018).

APPENDIX

1. Scott Seider et al., "Preparing Adolescents Attending Progressive and No Excuses Urban Charter High Schools to Analyze, Navigate, and Challenge Race and Class Inequality," *Teachers College Record* 118, no. 12 (2016): 1–54; Scott Seider et al., "Developing Sociopolitical Consciousness of Race and Class Inequality in

Adolescents Attending Progressive and No Excuses Urban High Schools," *Applied Developmental Science* 22, no. 3 (2018): 169–87; Scott Seider et al., "Fostering the Sociopolitical Development of African American and Latinx Adolescents to Analyze and Challenge Racial and Economic Inequality," *Youth & Society*, 2018, Online First; Scott Seider et al., "Investigating Adolescents' Critical Consciousness Development Through a Character Framework," *Journal of Youth & Adolescence* 46, no. 6 (2017): 1162–68.

2. We initially recruited a sixth school to participate in the study but ultimately chose not to include the school in this book when it became clear that the school featured relatively little curriculum or programming focused on supporting youth critical consciousness development.

3. John Creswell and Vicki Clark, *Designing and Conducting Mixed Methods Research* (Thousand Oaks, CA: Sage, 2011).

4. Paul Erickson and Liam Murphy, *A History of Anthropological Theory* (Toronto, ON: University of Toronto Press, 2008).

5. Kathleen MacQueen et al., "Codebook Development for Team-Based Qualitative Analysis," *Field Methods* 10, no. 2 (1998): 31–36.

6. Gery Ryan and H. Russell Bernard, "Techniques to Identify Themes," *Field Methods* 15, no. 1 (2003): 85–109.

7. Yvonne Lincoln and Egon Guba, *Naturalistic Inquiry* (Thousand Oaks, CA: Sage, 1985); Matthew Miles and Michael Huberman, *Qualitative Data Analysis: An Expanded Sourcebook* (Thousand Oaks, CA: Sage, 1994).

ACKNOWLEDGMENTS

First and foremost, we are grateful to the students, faculty, and administrators at the high schools featured in this book for so graciously inviting us into their respective communities. More than six hundred young people in these schools completed our critical consciousness survey, and sixty of these young people (and thirty-two of their teachers) sat down with us year after year to share their thoughts about their own developing critical consciousness. These same students and teachers also welcomed us as observers into their classrooms, community meetings, and extracurricular activities on more than three hundred days over four years. We are deeply grateful to all of these young people and educators, and wish that we could publicly thank them all by name.

We also owe an enormous debt of gratitude to the members of our research team without whom this book simply would not exist. Shelby Clark, Aaliyah El-Amin, and Lauren Kelly served as postdoctoral collaborators on this project and made incalculable contributions to the quality of the data collected as well as its analyses and interpretations. Likewise, Pauline Jennett, Sherri Sklarwitz, Madora Soutter, and Jalene Tamerat made tremendous contributions to this project during their work as doctoral students at Boston University, during which time they forged relationships with students and faculty at the participating schools that enriched the entire project. Their coauthorship of numerous academic papers and conference presentations also powerfully informed the ideas presented within these pages. Our undergraduate and graduate research assistants—Melanie Cabral, Jamie Johannsen, Megan Kenslea, Saira Malhotra, Kristen Martin, Kathryn Sabath, and Jennifer Yung—worked incredibly hard to complete the thousands of hours of data entry, transcription, and coding that paved the way for all of the analyses and writing that followed. Moreover, these young people then offered valuable insights and ideas about these data (that they knew better than anyone!) that unquestionably informed our team's papers, conference presentations, and this book as well. We are also sincerely grateful to the family members of all these members of our research team who so graciously accommodated the scores of trips to visit schools in four different states that this project required.

This project also would not have been possible without generous funding support from the National Academy of Education, John Templeton Foundation, Spencer Foundation, and Boston University Undergraduate Research Opportunities Program. At the National Academy of Education, we are grateful for the leadership and support of Abigail Bell, Amy Berman, and Gregory White. At the John Templeton Foundation, we thank Richard Bollinger, Sarah Clement, Heather Templeton Dill, Michael Murray, and Caitlin Pollock for their support of this project, in particular, and also for their longstanding interest and enthusiasm about our work and their efforts to include us in a network of like-minded scholars. Finally, at the Spencer Foundation, we are grateful for the support of Annie Brinkman, Doris Fischer, Maricelle Garcia, Diana Hess, Michael McPherson, and Na'ilah Suad Nasir. To Diana Hess, in particular, we are deeply appreciative of her support for helping us to expand the project to include the comparison schools, more fine-grained ethnographic work, and a fifth year of data collection (still to be written about!). Finally, we are grateful to Tom Gilmore and Melissa Johnson for their leadership of Boston University's Undergraduate Research Opportunities Program, which provided generous funding support for many of this project's undergraduate research assistants.

At Harvard Education Press, we had the very good fortune to work with editor-in-chief Caroline Chauncey, who has been an enthusiastic supporter of this project from the very beginning and whose editorial suggestions significantly improved this book. We are also grateful to Charles Hutchinson for his careful and skillful copyediting and to Sumita Mukherji for guiding us through the editorial and production process.

A number of colleagues and mentors also generously offered their time, support, and insights in various ways that strengthened and improved this project. Those colleagues include Josefina Boñales, Lavada Berger, Erin Borthwick, Jenne Colasacco, Hardin Coleman, Matthew Diemer, Christina Dobbs, Amanda Gardner, Howard Gardner, Ben Kirshner, Carol Lee, Peter Levine, Meira Levinson, Jesse Margolis, Sara Rimer, Onnie Rogers, Ben Shuldiner, Scott Solberg, Marianne Taylor, and Doannie Tran. We are particularly grateful to Carol Barry for her work and support on the survey analyses at every phase of this project.

Finally, we are each grateful above all for the love and support of our families.

I (Scott) am grateful to my wife, Amanda, for all of the ways big and small in which she made this project possible over the past six years. From the very first day I met her, Amanda has been the person in my life most fiercely and authentically dedicated to improving the educational experiences and outcomes of youth in communities across Massachusetts, so her belief from day one that this was a project worth pursuing provided invaluable motivation and reassurance on days where uncertainty crept in. The first roots of this project are also inextricably connected to the birth of our daughter, Naomi, and my desire to think and learn more about the knowledge, skills, and commitments that youth of color need to survive, thrive, and transform the world. For this reason, I have told Naomi over the past several years that this book is really *for* her, even if it will be many years before she can read it. And the next one will be for my son, Isaac. Together, the two of them have brought so much joy, meaning, and fun to my life. Finally, I am grateful for the love and support of a large and wonderful extended family that includes my parents (Bonnie and Ross), sister (Wendy), parents-in-law (Fletcher and Trayce), grandmother-in-law (Barbara), sisters-in-law (Beth, Brittany, Chaniah, Domonique, Elizabeth, Gloria), brothers-in-law (Brad, Drian, Fletcher), niece (Victoria), and nephews (Damon, Fletcher, Jabari, Jeremy, Nathan, Theo). Both my life and this book have also unquestionably been shaped and improved by family members who are no longer with us, including Carolyn, Charlotte, David, Selma, and Seymour.

I (Daren) am standing on the shoulders of family and ancestors, who sacrificed their livelihoods and their lives for me to be in this position. I am especially grateful to my parents, Sherryl and Michael, and, by extension (may they rest in peace), Hattie Browne (my maternal grandmother), Sylvia Polanco Rogers (my paternal grandmother), and Eva Bullock (my paternal great-grandmother), who instilled in me a sense of the importance of education and whose hard work I am materially benefitting from. Standing right next to me is my brother, Camar, whose wisdom and creativity have inspired me to work smarter and to speak truth to power. I could not be more grateful to my wife, Autumn, and my daughters, Sakeenah, Jannah, and Yusra. They have held me accountable in all the best ways, and I look up to each of them because of their unique and respective senses of courage, intelligence, strength, and compassion. With Autumn taking the lead, they have been patient, supportive, and enlightening in ways that have made me a better brother in humanity to all of us. Not all family is kin, and I would be remiss not to mention other sets of family who are here with me and have held me to such high standards. My undergrad family: Steve, Melissa, Halimah, Jemina, Rashida, and Imani. My grad school familia: Louie, Dorinda, Frank, Vajra, Lionel, Tara, Heather, Eddie, and Rich. My brothers in faith, jokes, and sports fanaticism: Kojo, Ayyub, and Linwood. My Sports Profs family: Steve and Leanne. My Union School family: Joy, Anne, Betsy, Lindsay, and Patricia. Thanks to all of you for helping me fight the beautiful struggle.

ABOUT THE AUTHORS

SCOTT SEIDER is an associate professor of applied developmental psychology at the Boston College Lynch School of Education & Human Development. Dr. Seider's research focuses on the civic development of adolescents, and he has reported on this work in more than seventy academic publications. He is also the author of two previous books, *Shelter: Where Harvard Meets the Homeless* (Continuum, 2010) and *Character Compass: How Powerful School Culture Can Point Students Toward Success* (Harvard Education Press, 2012), both of which won the American Educational Research Association's outstanding book award in moral development and education. Prior to joining the Boston College faculty, Dr. Seider worked as a teacher-educator at Boston University and as a secondary English teacher in the Boston Public Schools.

DAREN GRAVES is an associate professor of education at Simmons University, where his research lies at the intersection of critical race theory, racial identity development, and teacher education. His work has been published in numerous academic journals including *Developmental Psychology, Applied Developmental Science,* and *Youth & Society.* He also coteaches Critical Race Theory in Education at Harvard Graduate School of Education. Dr. Graves currently serves as cochair of the AERA Hip Hop Theories, Praxis & Pedagogies Special Interest Group and as the liaison between Simmons University and the Boston Teachers Union Pilot School, a public K–8 school where he works closely with teachers and students.

INDEX